KYOTO CSEAS SERIES ON ASIAN STUDIES 20
Center for Southeast Asian Studies, Kyoto University

NETWORKED

KYOTO CSEAS SERIES ON ASIAN STUDIES 20
Center for Southeast Asian Studies, Kyoto University

NETWORKED
Business and Politics in Decentralizing Indonesia, 1998–2004

Wahyu Prasetyawan

NUS PRESS
Singapore

in association with

KYOTO UNIVERSITY PRESS
Japan

The publication of this book is financially supported by the National Graduate Institute for Policy Studies (GRIPS) through the Global COE Program "The Transferability of East Asian Development Strategies and State Building" and the publication funds of the "International Program of Southeast Asian Collaborative Research" (IPCR) at the Center for Southeast Asian Studies, Kyoto University.

© 2018 Wahyu Prasetyawan

All rights reserved. No part of this publication may be reproduced or transmitted in any form or by any means, electronic or mechanical, including photocopy, recording, or any information storage or retrieval system, without permission in writing from the publisher.

NUS Press
National University of Singapore
AS3-01-02, 3 Arts Link
Singapore 117569
http://nuspress.nus.edu.sg

ISBN 978-981-4722-97-1 (Paper)

Kyoto University Press
Yoshida-South Campus, Kyoto University
69 Yoshida-Konoe-Cho, Sakyo-ku
Kyoto 606-8315
Japan
www.kyoto-up.or.jp

ISBN 978-4-8140-0163-7

National Library Board, Singapore Cataloguing in Publication Data

Name(s): Prasetyawan, Wahyu.
Title: Networked: business and politics in decentralizing Indonesia, 1998–2004 / Wahyu Prasetyawan.
Other titles: Kyoto-CSEAS series on Asian studies.
Description: Singapore: NUS Press in association with Kyoto University Press, [2018] | Includes bibliographic references and index.
Identifiers: OCN 1022286402 | 978-981-47-2297-1 (paperback)
Subjects: LCSH: Decentralization in government--Economic aspects--Indonesia | Indonesia--Politics and government--Economic aspects.
Classification: DDC 320.8509598--dc23

Cover design: Irvan Wicaksono

Printed by: Markono Print Media Pte Ltd

For
Lani, Irvan and Azkia

CONTENTS

List of Illustrations	ix
List of Abbreviations	xi
Preface	xiii
Introduction	1
1. Institutions and Political Networks	22
2. Decentralization and Changes in Political Economy	34
3. Indonesia in a Time of Transition	54
4. Your Mine or Mine: The Divestment Process in East Kalimantan	78
5. The Conflict over the Privatization of Semen Padang	112
6. Resources Conflict in Riau: An Oil Block's Tale	140
Conclusion: Political Networks and Political Economy	169
Appendices	183
Bibliography	185
Index	197

LIST OF ILLUSTRATIONS

Maps

1. East Kalimantan   82
2. West Sumatra   114
3. Riau Province and Riau Archipelago Province   141

Figures

1. Export of KPC in million tons   88
2. Comparison of net-profit margin between KPC and mining   95
3. Dividends for province's 2.49-percent share   96

Tables

1. Number of military members who occupied non-military posts   59
2. Pillars of the New Order government and their impact on   59
   central-regional relations
3. Indonesian parliamentary election, 7 June 1999   67
4. Semen Padang's production over the years   121

LIST OF ABBREVIATIONS

BAKIN	Badan Koordinasi Intelijen Nasional National Intelligence Coordinating Body
Bappenas	Badan Perencanaan Nasional National Development Planning Board
BKPM	Badan Koordinasi Penanaman Modal Indonesian Capital Coordinating Board
BPIS	Badan Pengelola Industri Strategis Strategic Industry Management Body
BUMN	Badan Usaha Milik Negara State Owned Enterprise (*see also* SOE)
BSP	Bumi Siak Pusako (a regional government-owned company in Siak)
Cemex	Cementos of Mexico (a Brazilian company, owns a 25-percent share of Cement Gresik)
CoW	Contract of work
CPI	Caltex Pasific Indonesia (a US-based oil company operating in Riau Province)
CPS	Contract production sharing
CPP	Coastal Plain of Pekanbaru (previously owned by CPI)
DPR	Dewan Perwakilan Rakyat National Parliament
DPR-GR	Dewan Perwakilan Rakyat Gotong Royong National Parliament Mutual Cooperation
DPRD	Dewan Perwakilan Rakyat Daerah Regional Parliament
GDRP	Gross Domestic Regional Product
Golkar	Golongan Karya Functional Group
ICMI	Ikatan Cendekiawan Muslim Indonesia Association of Indonesian Muslim Intellectuals

KPC	Kaltim Prima Coal (a group of foreign investors from Britain and Australia)
MIBS	PT Melati Intan Bhakti Satya
MPR	Majelis Permusyawaratan Rakyat People's Consultative Assembly
PAN	Partai Amanat Nasional National Mandate Party
PDI	Partai Demokrasi Indonesia The Democratic Party of Indonesia
PDI-P	Partai Demokrasi Indonesia-Perjuangan Indonesian Democratic Party of Struggle
PKB	Partai Kebangkitan Bangsa National Awakening Party
PPP	Partai Persatuan Pembangunan United Development Party
PSDM	Pertambangan dan Sumber Daya Mineral Mining and Mineral Resources (refers to the Ministry of Mining and Mineral Resources)
RM	Riau Merdeka Riau Freedom Movement
Semen Gresik	A state-owned enterprise in the cement industry, located in East Java, the parent company to Cement Padang
Semen Padang	A state-owned enterprise in the cement industry, located in West Sumatra Province, a subsidiary of Cement Gresik
SOE	State Owned Enterprises (*see also* BUMN)
SOKSI	the All Indonesian Organization of Socialist Functionaries

PREFACE

There are turning points in history which reverberate throughout the period that follows. The transitional years of 1998 to 2004 were one such turning point for Indonesia. These years of dramatic transformation marked the beginning of a new era that continues to today, particularly in matters of political economy.

Newmont Nusa Tenggara, a mining contractor owned by American and Japanese interests, was required under the terms of its operating agreement to divest some of its shares—3 percent in 2006, 7 percent in 2007—to Indonesian interests. Three years later, in 2010, it was to divest its remaining 51 percent share in the mining operation. Its divestiture of shares was the fulfilment of an obligation written into the contract that foreign companies like Newmont made with the Indonesian government. The governor of West Nusa Tenggara, the province where the Newmont mines are located, took the opportunity to demand a portion of these shares. This action was repeated by local elites from Sumbawa and West Sumbawa, two regencies or *kebupaten* in the same province with similar mining operations. These elites then established political networks with a powerful businessperson and Golkar politician who controlled Bumi Resources, one of Indonesia's largest mining companies.

The Indonesian government made history at the end of 2013 by successfully acquiring majority control of Indonesian Asahan Aluminium (Inalum), increasing its share from 41.13 percent to 58.9 percent, in a transaction worth US$556.7 million. Inalum, established in 1975 and located in North Sumatra province, is the only aluminium smelter in Indonesia and the biggest in Southeast Asia. Before the government's acquisition, Inalum was controlled by the Japanese investors in the Nippon Asahan Aluminium consortium, which included the Japan International Corporation Agency, Itochu Corporation, Sojitz Corporation, Mitsubishi Corporation, Sumitomo Corporation and others. Even before Indonesia's central government took control of Inalum's shares, the governor of North Sumatra and its surrounding municipalities filed a demand to obtain 60 percent shares for their local governments.

The biggest copper producer in the country, Freeport Indonesia, a subsidiary of NYSE-listed Freeport McMoran, has been under an obligation to divest its shares since 1991. This is stipulated in the contract of work (CoW) negotiated between Freeport McMoran and the Indonesian government in that year. The American company was compelled to sell up to 51 percent of its shares in the Indonesian operation to an Indonesian interest by 2011. However, as of 2017 the company's divestiture was not yet completed. The divestment process had become a serious dispute between the American company and the Indonesian government as they sought to convert the CoW into a new agreement. In 2019 the contract will expire. This dispute grew more complicated when local elites from Mimika proposed that they should assume 10 percent to 20 percent of Freeport's shares. Indeed, local elites from West Papua had already filed a request in 2015 to obtain 10 percent of the company's shares.

All these cases describe resource-driven conflicts; they have received a large amount of news coverage in both television and printed media. Local elites, from the regency or province, stand at center stage in these conflicts. They constitute important elements of the stories about these conflicts because they have voiced regional concerns. The centrality of these elites resulted from their bravery in advancing a demand to manage or even own a portion of their region's natural resources. The story of this local-elite challenge to the central government and foreign investors made the stories even more interesting. The centrality of locally-based elites in the conflict reveals that Indonesia's political landscape has changed. Their actions betrayed an awareness of the wealth and power that could be generated by the natural resources if they could manage or own them. They labelled their fights as correctives to the improper distribution practices of the past. In their eyes, the central government and foreign investors had failed to distribute the benefits from extracted natural resources.

Are these three cases a development of the last five years? The answer is no. These cases are not the first such natural resource disputes to take place in the country. On the contrary, they resemble disagreements of the past. In particular, the claim by local elites for shares in natural resource operations controlled by the central government and foreign investors began to take shape between 1998 to 2004. These years are crucial to understanding the profound change that altered the power relations of these three parties.

This book tells the story of this transformation, one that defined new relationships between the central government, foreign investors, and local elites. It also offers a narrative that ends up with a new equilibrium among these players. In order to provide a new narrative, it evaluates

Preface

three disputes over natural resources in the provinces of East Kalimantan, Riau and West Sumatra. In these regions, local elites opposed the central government's policies on natural resource management. The foreign investors in East Kalimantan had to divest their shares, while those in Riau had to release an entire oil block. The case in West Sumatra is slightly different; in this province, the central government faced opposition by local elites who wanted management control of a large cement factory.

By analyzing these three regional cases, this book is able to reveal the interplay between political networks, the emergence of local elites, and conflicts over natural resources. These cases unpack stories of prolonged quarrels between the central government and local governments—and, to a certain degree, foreign investors—over the ownership and management of natural resources.

The emergence of local elites was born out of the initial democratization and decentralization of the Indonesian government that began in 2000. For more than three decades, local politicians and power-brokers had difficulty voicing their concerns to the central government; indeed, voicing demands to manage and own natural resources proved close to impossible. The Suharto government perceived any move to dispute the management and ownership structure of natural resource extraction operations as an expression of resistance, to which it therefore responded with repression. However, after Suharto was gone and both decentralization and democratization began to develop, local elites began to emerge as important political players.

Conflict over natural resources constitutes the main element of the stories told in this book. A more crucial component of its narrative, however, is the ability of local elites to form political networks. The new institutions of decentralization and democratization did not place local elites automatically at center stage. These elites seized opportunities provided by these institutions by establishing political links with those in power in Jakarta. In short, local elites had the initiative to create political links. As a result, they have more room to maneuver and take the initiative to create political connections with power holders in Jakarta.

The stories in this book differ much from standard narratives. The standard accounts tell stories about local elites who are in a central position because decentralization policy put them there. It was the new policy that shifted the center of gravity in politics from the national to the regional level. It should be no surprise that some of these accounts describe the process of local power-brokers becoming important political figures as almost an automatic process. These narratives are partially correct. Other narratives focus on the links between the central and local governments.

This book offers an alternative narrative, one that suggests the primacy of political networks in understanding current Indonesian political economy. This book tells stories in which local elites advance to the center of politics because they are capable of creating wide-ranging political networks. Accordingly, this account aims to supplement existing interpretations rather than replace or supplant them.

To tell this story of conflict, this book borrows its understanding from two bodies of literature, one on networks and another on institutions. The applicability of institutions to this discussion of conflict lies in the way they provide the foundations upon which political actors can operate in order to pursue their interests. Institutions render incentives to different political actors. This is evident in the rapidity with which the local elites surveyed here quickly grasped the opportunity, once it arose, to bolster their position vis-à-vis the central government and foreign investors. Imagine a local elite, already empowered, seeing an opportunity to benefit from a divestment share by a foreign contractor; surely, such a person will seek a loophole in existing regulations to claim the right of her/his local government to manage or own the firm in question.

The political networks described in this book assist local elites to not only challenge central government policies but also support their interests politically. A local elite who can tap into a significant number of political networks can sustain disputes for quite a long time. On the contrary, a local power-broker without wider political networks is very weak. A local politician who can create political networks has many friends who hold power at both the national and local level. The stories told in this book reveal that having friends in national-level politics proves decisive in determining conflict outcomes.

Disagreements over natural resources often bring in the question of the role of foreign investors who have long been involved in Indonesian natural resource extraction. They are key players in the country's mining industry, where their presence has a long history. Some of the firms surveyed have existed since colonial times. Many of them were already mining minerals when Indonesia proclaimed its independence in 1945. In essence, the behavior of foreign investors in the mineral sector is inspired by the search for profits. More importantly, they also pursue political protection because of the nature of their investment. Foreign interests are, in a way, "trapped" in their host country because their often huge investments cannot easily move to another country, or even to another locality. This book reveals the various endeavors of foreign investors to adapt to the new political landscape. Some are willing to side with

Preface xvii

the new power holders at the center of politics, while abandoning local elites. Others want to cooperate with local elites.

This book offers an analytical narrative as a contribution to the current debates over political economy in Indonesia. While this book is trying to marry the two bodies of scholarships on institutions and networks, its method of analysis is highly attentive to the details of the interaction between the central government and local elites. Even though this book uses phrases like "institutions" and "political networks", it tries to avoid unnecessary misunderstanding by giving concrete examples.

How the local elites perceived and understood written regulations is important, and this book makes an effort to reveal it. It explains how and why the elites surveyed here understood regulations in a very different way than did members of the central government or foreign investors. Local elites and the central government certainly interpreted various regulations differently; in many cases, their interpretations contradicted each other.

To reach this understanding, data was gathered from published and unpublished works, from internal government documents and studies (some of them classified), and from scores of interviews conducted with local elites and people in the central government. For foreign investors, this book makes extensive use of business advisory publications, annual reports to investors, interviews with staff in Jakarta and in localities, and their unpublished reports.

The results of the aforementioned approach reveal narratives that marry current appraoches to Indonesia's political economy and are quite microscopic in their focus—with careful attention to the details and texture of policymaking and the investment decision-making process during a time of transition. The picture that emerges depicts real actors operating within a political and economic "space" as a result of the creation and functioning of new institutions.

Since the intended readership extends beyond the research communities of politics and economics, this book tries to avoid the difficult jargon inherent in the scholarship on both networks and institutional economics. However, chapter 1 briefly outlines some technical terminology in an effort to formalize certain ideas, and partly because the use of some of these terms could not be avoided.

The initial research for this book took place from 2000 to 2006. Research and writing took place from 2010 to 2017, with reference to more recent developments, and the way scholarly debates on Indonesian political economy have evolved.

The ideas and information contained here reflect the efforts, contributions, criticisms and support of many people in Japan and Indonesia. First, I am deeply indebted to Shiraishi Takashi of the National Graduate Institute for Policy Studies (GRIPS) for his constant encouragement during my studies, research and book writing. I owe special thanks to him for his generous willingness to share his intellectual understanding of Indonesian politics and economy from various perspectives. I thank him for his patience and challenging questions during the process of writing this book. Sincere thanks are due to Caroline Hau of the Center for Southeast Asian Studies (CSEAS), Kyoto University, for her help in posing difficult questions about the arguments I was developing. She also encouraged me to seek a much higher standard of scholarship. Deep thanks are offered to Hamashita Takeshi, who encouraged me during the writing process with his perspective of economic history and networks. Thanks are also extended to Patricio Abinales of the University of Hawai'i, who generously offered his time to discuss my material with me from a political-science perspective. Thanks are given to Mizuno Kosuke for sharing his knowledge of institutional economics. I also would like to extend my gratitude to Alexander Irwan, who introduced me to Shiraishi Takashi in Jakarta in 1997, which led to my fruitful academic journey in Kyoto.

I would like to thank my colleagues in Kyoto, who have been very generous with their time, comments and criticisms in both seminars and informal meetings. Among these are Morishita Akiko, Aizawa Nobuhiro, the late Mizutani Yasuhiro, Onimaru Takeshi, the late Murakami Saki, Okamoto Masaaki, Uchida Haruko, Nissim Otmazgin, Jun Honna and Nathan Badenoch.

I would like to express my sincere thanks to the late Benedict Anderson, Pasuk Pongphaichit, Chris Baker and Peter Katzenstein, who generously answered my questions regarding the general picture of political economy in Southeast Asia when they visited Kyoto and Tokyo. I also thank Indonesian scholars for sharing information with me: Among these are Yasmin Sungkar, Ikrar Nusa Bakti, Mochtar Pabottingi and Thung Ju Lan of LIPI. I would also like to express my gratitude to Azyumardi Azra, for supporting my effort to continue my education at Kyoto University as well as his continuing intellectual support. I appreciate the continued intellectual support from the late Nurcholish Madjid. Finally, I would like to express my gratitude to Ginandjar Kartasasmita, who shared his vast knowledge of mineral industry and technocracy.

Preface

I also thank those who helped me with collecting data, arranging interviews and addressing editorial matters. In Jakarta, I would like to thank Achmad Djauhar, Arief Budisusilo and I Wayan Maryasa of the daily *Bisnis Indonesia* for the access they provided to the business world in Indonesia. I also benefited from help offered by Abdullah Khusairi, Saldi Isra, Oktavianus Rizwa, Elwi Daniel, Nanda Utama and Tularji during my stay in Padang, the capital of West Sumatra. In Riau, I would like to thank Sanul, who accompanied me during my research in Pekanbaru. Thanks extends to Levna Ervan and Al Azhar, who shared precious information with me regarding local politics in Riau. In East Kalimantan, I would like to thank Rusman for his generosity in accompanying me during data collection. No words can express my thanks to the government officials in Jakarta and in the provinces, not to mention the officers of the companies I researched, for their unfailing politeness and patience in answering detailed questions and explaining their position regarding the disputes they had to face.

I would like to extend my thanks to my Indonesian friends who at various point of time were studying in the Graduate School of Asian and African Area Studies at Kyoto University, and the members of the Indonesian study club in Kyoto who provided me with an Indonesian intellectual atmosphere. Among these are Dave Lumenta, Jafar Suryomenggolo, Arie Damayanti and Agus Trihartono.

I gratefully acknowledge the financial assistance of the Monbukagakusho, which funded my study in Kyoto University's Graduate School of Asian and African Area Studies from 2000 to 2006. I would like to acknowledge the support of the COE 21 Century Project for partially funding my research in Indonesia. Intermittently between 2010 and 2016, I collected additional data from government officials and the officers of foreign investors; I also thank them for sharing their information with me.

I am very grateful for financial support from GRIPS, through the Global COE Program entitled "The Transferability of East Asian Development Strategies and State Building"—MEXT—which enabled me to stay on this nice campus to write my book. For this, my thanks go to Shiraishi Takashi, who made this fund available to me. I would like to express my gratitude to Hara Yonosuke, Onimaru Takeshi and Kawano Motoko for their valuable help during my stay in Tokyo. I received another fund from GRIPS in 2016. This book manuscript was completed while I was Visiting Scholar at GRIPS through the support of the Emerging State Project. My gratitude again goes to Shiraishi Takashi, who made this fund accessible to me. I also thank Takagi Yusuke for his help and generosity in discussing the book's ideas with me.

I gratefully acknowledge that the publication of this book was made possible with the financial support of the International Program of Collaborative Research at CSEAS, Kyoto University. I am indebted to Yoko Hayami and Narumi Shitara, who assisted me at every step of preparing the manuscript. I offer my thanks to the three anonymous referees who offered their useful critical questions and suggestions for improvement. I am also indebted to Paul Kratoska of NUS Press for accepting the manuscript for publication, to managing editor Lena Qua for overseeing the book's production, and to Danielle McClellan for carefully editing it.

I thank the journal *Indonesia* of the Southeast Asia Program at Cornell University for their permission to use my article, entitled "The Unfinished Privatization of Semen Padang", published in issue number 81 in April 2006. In addition, I also would like to express my gratitude to the *Journal of Southeast Asian Studies* at the Center for Southeast Asian Studies of Kyoto University for permitting me to use my articles "Government and Multinational: Conflict over Economic Resources in East Kalimantan, 1998–2003" (volume 43, number 2, September 2006) and "The Political Economy of Post Soeharto Indonesia: Intergovernmental Conflict in Riau, 1998–2004" (volume 45, number 1, June 2007). I have added new data to reflect new developments in academic discussions on political economy and political networks. These improvements are intended to keep discussions of this book relevant to recent developments in Indonesian political economy.

I thank my father Abdul Hadi and my late mother Mudjiatun, who allowed me to pursue higher education overseas, first in the UK and then in Japan. I also thank them for their blessing and emotional support during this difficult time in my life. I wish my mother could have seen this work. Finally, I would like to thank my wife Lani Evayani, my son Irvan Wicaksono and my daughter Azkia Nastiti for their enduring emotional and psychological support with their presence in Kyoto, Jakarta and Tokyo. Their support was indispensible while finishing this book in these three cities. To these special persons, I dedicate this book.

INTRODUCTION

Political Networks

The fall of Suharto marked the end of a long episode in Indonesia's political economic history and the beginning of a new one. It began with the economic crisis in 1997 and 1998, and was quickly followed by a political crisis. The economic and political crises have provided fertile ground for different interpretations of the country's political-economic situation. There have been two main analytical frameworks deployed to interpret Indonesia's current political economy: pluralist and oligarchic. There is an additional populist analytical framework; however, this book treats it as part of an oligarchical analytical framework. Anderson (2009) mentions that political economy in Southeast Asia, which includes Indonesia, has been defined by oligarchies of wealth and power, which populism has been used as a label to challenge. For Anderson (2009: 218), the region's dominating factor has been "closed national oligarchies", where "power is shared among a small circle" whose members queue "for a turn at a lucrative post". In a slightly different fashion, Hadiz (2016: 63) tends to see populist politics as an effort to oppose oligarchies.

This section does not intend to delve into these two competing analytical frameworks. Instead, this evaluation is intended to create a necessary foundation for efforts to understand current debates about political economy.

Both pluralist and oligarchic approaches have deep academic traditions in political economy. In the Indonesian context, the pluralist approach has been represented by Pepinsky (2009, 2013). Of course, there are other scholars who use and develop this approach;[1] however,

---

[1] Donald K. Emmerson, "Understanding the New Order: Bureaucratic Pluralism in Indonesia", *Asian Survey* 23, 11 (1983): 1220–41; Dwight Y. King, "Bureaucracy and Implementation of Complex Tasks in Rapidly Developing States", *Studies in Comparative and International Development* 30, 4 (1995–96): 78–92; R. William Liddle, "The Politics of Shared Growth: Some Indonesian Cases", *Comparative Politics* 19, 2 (1987): 127–46; M. Hadi Soesastro, "The Political Economy of Deregulation in Indonesia",

this section addresses only Pepinsky's work, for the purpose of opening a way to discussion of the book's analytical framework. On the other hand, the oligarchic approach has been represented by scholars such as Robison and Hadiz (2004), Hadiz and Robison (2013) and Winters (2011, 2013).

Pepinsky considers Lukes' critique of power as one- and two-dimensional and reductive (Lukes 2005: 16–21). To understand power, Pepinsky (2013: 82) proposes that we take history and social structure seriously. Having proposed a much broader conception of power, he then can explain the interests of individuals or groups as ascribed to them by external actors, social structures or state institutions.

In essence, Pepinsky regards politics as competition among pressure groups that represent various interests in society. In his own words (2013: 85):

> My understanding of pluralism as applied to contemporary Indonesian politics begins from the perspective that political actors engage in politics to produce policies that they favor. Political conflict results from differences in the interests of various actors, both individuals and groups. Political outcomes are shaped by the resources available to conflicting groups and the institutions that aggregate or channel individual or collective preferences.

Pepinsky sees policy as the central point of political contestation in Indonesia. Therefore, he unsurprisingly considers that conflict about political institutions reflects a more fundamental contest for distribution, redistribution and recognition among various political actors.

In the context of Indonesia, he evaluates two dramatic conflicts over financial crisis and local economic governance in an era of decentralization.

In analyzing the impact of the institution of decentralization, Pepinsky (2013: 95) discusses mobilization. He considers the work of Tans (2012), who argues that it is possible to identify different types of political coalitions in various local contexts—mafias, machines and

---

Asian Survey 29, 9 (1989): 853–69; Andrew MacIntyre, "Institutions and the Political Economy of Corruption in Developing Countries", paper presented at "Workshop on Corruption", Stanford University, 31 Jan.–1 Feb. 2003; Ross H. Mcleod, "Soeharto's Indonesia: A Better Class of Corruption", *Agenda* 7, 2 (2000): 99–112. Pepinsky (2013: 86) explains how pluralism is understood differently by citing examples of King and Emmerson's "bureaucratic pluralism" (1983); Bresnan's "managed pluralism" (1993); and Soesastro and Drysdale's "constrained pluralism" (1990). In his paper, Pepinsky provides long lists of books and articles on pluralism. This book looks only at the works that provide an entry into a discussion of Indonesian political economy.

Introduction 3

mobilizing coalitions—despite the presence of money politics in Indonesian local elections. Pepinsky observes that mobilizing coalitions become most conducive to interest group representation in the pluralist mode and that machines are more likely to provide public goods than mafias. Pepinsky considers work by von Lübke (2012) on local elite competition, which allow some private interests to seek representation, as in accord with the pluralist approach. To some extent, the evaluation carried out by Tomsa (2015) on local corruption in an electoral democracy could be categorized under the pluralist tradition, because he sees competition among elites over policy. He highlights a crucial consequence of competitiveness in local politics, namely, the increased risk among local elites for involvement in corruption scandals. He believes that corrupt officials—at both national and local levels—face a much greater risk of detection and prosecution than they did during the time when decentralization began more than a decade ago.

From the discussion above, it should be clear that the pluralist approach takes political conflict as its core unit of analysis. While the oligarchic approach centers more on the shared interests of oligarchs, it does also consider conflict among various political actors, or different oligarchs. Winters (2011: 7) defines oligarchs as "actors who command and control massive concentrations of material resources that can be employed to defend or enhance their personal wealth and exclusive social position". Winters sees wealth as supremely versatile, in that it easily converts into other manifestations of power.

In a slightly different fashion, Robison and Hadiz (2004: 16–17n6) define oligarchy as follows:

> Any system of government in which virtually all political power is held by a very small number of wealthy ... people who shape public policy primarily to benefit themselves financially through direct subsidies to their agricultural estates or business firms, lucrative government contracts, and protectionist measures aimed at damaging their economic competitors—while displaying little or no concern for the broader interests of the rest of the citizenry. "Oligarchy" is also used as a collective term to denote all the individual members of the small corrupt ruling group in such a system.[2]

Hadiz and Robison (2013: 46) argue that the Suharto regime can be seen as resting upon a broad system of oligarchic relations that had become the

---

[2] Pepinsky (2013: 88) cites this understanding of oligarchy. However, he criticizes this definition, as there are interest groups and actors that do not possess wealth but do exercise power. This book emphasizes the general characteristics of oligarchy.

central glue for a social order, and that had determined the way in which power and wealth were accumulated and allocated from Jakarta to the regions. Robison and Hadiz (2004: 86) add that conflict can erupt from time to time among the oligarchs.

By contrast, Winters (2011: 7) looks at oligarchy as a system that refers to "the politics of wealth defense by materially endowed actors". In essence, the politics of oligarchs, for Winters, consists of defending wealth. All of these scholars agree that wealth serves as the basis of power for the oligarchs. They also agree that these oligarchs were nurtured under Suharto's authoritarian regime. It is obvious for these scholars that Suharto's long reign, which lasted for more than three decades, provided a fertile ground from which oligarchs could emerge. Scholars furthermore agree that in 1998, during the period following Suharto's fall, the oligarchs were able to sustain their prominence in Indonesian politics by using their wealth. They argued that decentralization policies gave oligarchs opportunities to expand their power down to the regional level. Electoral contestation has allowed the wealthy and powerful to expand their influence. Hadiz (2010) has argued that the country's decentralization policies have given opportunities to power holders previously at the heart of Suharto's New Order to assert their power down to the local level. Hadiz and Robison (2013: 54) continue to see that the vast majority of local political actors looking for positions as district heads (*bupati*) and mayors have been drawn from a pool of local bureaucrats, party members and businesspersons, many of whom had helped to exercise power at the local level on behalf of the old authoritarian regime.

Furthermore, Winters (2013: 25) argues that these oligarchs are not only sustaining their wealth but also expanding the investment of their wealth into other business and political interests. In fact, he lists some of the wealthy who have ventured into media and political parties. He states that 96 percent of the country's national television stations belong to oligarchs—who, according to Winters, also control five of the country's six major Indonesian-language newspapers. Winters adds that some of these oligarchs have even established political parties, including Aburizal Bakrie and Surya Paloh, who own their own television networks.

In sum, scholars who employ the oligarchic approach consider three characteristics of Indonesian political economy. First, they—especially Robison and Hadiz—observe that the current political actors who dominate Indonesia's political economy are the same as those who served under Suharto's New Order. Many of them do not operate at the national level, but they are those who operated at the local level on behalf of

Suharto. These powerful and wealthy political actors built their power base and were incubated during Suharto's long reign in Indonesia. Second, the dominance of these players is based on the wealth they control. Even though the scholars who study them do not reject the relevance of institutions and other societal forces, they place emphasis on the primacy of wealth. Winters (2011: 73) argues that the politics of oligarchs focus on defending wealth; he contends (2013: 12) that wealth is the most potent and flexible of all power resources. Third, these scholars tend to see local politics as a microcosm of national-level politics.

These two approaches used to interpret Indonesian political economy, pluralist and oligarchic, have both strengths and weaknesses. It is not the intention in this book to detail the merits and demerits of each form of analysis. Rather, any consideration here is regarded as a springboard to a better understanding of Indonesia's current political economy. Both oligarchic and pluralist approaches tend to view local politics as able to stand alone without any crucial connection to the national level of politics. Or, at least, they tend to encourage an evaluation of political economy from the perspective of the power holders residing at the center of their political economy, which in this case is either Jakarta or Java. Indeed, they mention political alliances but tend to see them as sets of relations established by national-level power holders.

In order to engage with the above-mentioned discussion of the country's political economy, this book employs a form of analysis based on the scholarship of political networks. While the oligarchic approach considers wealth as the key feature of Indonesian political economy, and pluralist analysis tends to see conflict among interest groups as its main feature, this book instead seriously considers relations among political actors. Its approach adopts an understanding of power as proposed by Lazer (2011: 66–7) who considers power intrinsically relational: that is, it derives from its capacity to affect other actors. Lazer believes that the relationships of a political actor to others is more than an attribute; it actually represents the power that a political actor possesses.

The relevance of political networks can be found in various works by scholars who have emphasized political relationships. Halberstam and Knight (2016) investigate the role of homophily—a tendency to interact with similar individuals—in the diffusion of political information in social networks. They develop a model that predicts disproportionate exposure to like-minded information and more connections for larger groups. Fowler et al. (2011) argue for the primacy of political networks and the vital role they play in politics. Networks shape the way in which citizens appropriate and decode political information (Huckfeldt and Sprague 1987 and 1995; McClurg 2006; Mutz 2006). Nickerson (2008) explains how social network ties may rouse voters to vote. Fowler (2006) explains how political networks sway legislatures to cooperate on bill sponsorship. Both Grossman and Dominguez (2009) and Koger, Masket and Noel (2010) mention political networks in facilitating party cooperation over contesting factions. Heaney and Rojas (2007, 2008) explain cooperation in social movements through intersecting networks. Connection among political actors both inside and outside the formal process could be seen to be important enough to define the legislative process (Carpenter, Esterling and Lazer 2004; Heinz, Laumann, Nelson and Salisbury 1993; Laumann and Knoke 1987).

Furthermore, this book analyses the newly emerged local political elite and their engagement in conflicts. It considers concepts of networks as proposed by various scholars, but specifically the one developed by Barabási (2002, 2016). In this connection, the general understanding of networks serves as the foundation of the story about the disputes between political actors at the center and in the regions. Moreover, this book expands and modifies the concept of networks into one of political networks. A network is a repeated connection between at least two actors who have mutual trust and shared goals. This understanding refers to any network without specifying the context in which a network is established. Therefore, it could be a social network, a network of friends, or any other kind of social connection. A political network is an enlargement and revision from Barabási's concept of preferential attachment (2002: 285) in which actors prefer to be attached to those who have more influence. In a political context, it should be that actors with more political power tend to be approached by those who have less capacity to influence other actors. In addition to that, political networks can be characterized as possessing the capability to change and grow (Newman, Barabási and Watts 2006). In other words, political networks are very fluid and have no formal structure.

Assimilating various works, this study explores two kinds of networks, personal and communal, to understand the necessity of political networks. Personal linkages can emerge in the context of a ethnic or religious community groups, or an organization such as a political party (to be discussed in the following chapter).

Other than using a theoretical framework developed from scholarship on political networks, this book discusses the relevance of institutions, which serve as a foundation for any political actor, both at the center and in the regions, to carry out her/his activities. It does not assess causal relationships between institutions and political actors; that is beyond the scope of this study. As discussed in the ensuing chapter, institutions are relevant because they create incentives for political players who usually operate within the framework created by these institutions. However, this study shows that institutions have also been challenged and contested by various political actors.

To discuss institutions, this book evaluates the new institutional scholarship originally proposed by North (1990), who hardly pays attention to the importance of political process over the making of institutions. To supplement previous works that lack a political dimension, this book adopts an approach that seriously takes into consideration politics and political process in making institutions. Therefore, it is relevant to take into account Acemoglu and Robinson (2012: 68), who infuse politics and political process into the discussion of institutions.

To summarize, the conceptual foundation of this book is developed from a combination of two scholarly subjects, networks and institutions. The combination of these two forms of scholarship serves as a lens through which to evaluate the political dynamics that connect a center and its regions. Thus, the theoretical groundwork of this book differs markedly from most other works on Indonesian political economy.

This book's narrative describes a novel pattern of political economy, in its initial stage of formation during the period 1998 to 2004, which grew in relevance to politics at the provincial level, especially in relation to powers in Jakarta. To understand this phenomenon, the book analyzes the emergence of provincial politicians by examining their capacity to develop networks within new institutional arrangements. Furthermore, it reveals how these politicians have come to develop political capability as well as political networks, eventually emerging as new forces that shape politics in the regions. It focuses on provincial politicians and their cohesiveness and fluidity. Since political networks, local and national, define the strength or bargaining leverage of a person, then it can be said that provincial politicians who were connected on a permanent basis with those who were powerful and influential in Jakarta had more political power. Otherwise, these provincial politicians would be considered politically weak. The provincial politicians' chances of winning disputes with the central government were defined by these networks. Two case studies will show that provincial politicians were able to change the direction of national economic policies. Another case study shows the failure of provincial politicians to oppose the central government policy on revenue sharing.

Although it discusses the oligarchic and pluralist approaches to analysing the general pattern of the Indonesian political economy, this book does not claim to challenge them. Rather, it presents a different interpretation by looking at political-economic dynamics at the local level through the lens of political networks and institutions. It also develops a much more specific narrative to explain the development of political economy. The narrative developed in this book, therefore, stands opposite the existing explanations in scholarship of decentralization and political economy in Indonesia. Works on decentralization policy can be categorized into two main groups. The first addresses the political and economic background of policy issuance (Smith 2008; Hofman and Kaiser 2004; Crouch 2010). The second body of literature looks generally at the impact of decentralization policy on local political dynamics.[3] The scholarship on current Indonesian political economy has a tendency to view post-Suharto Indonesia as a continuation of the New Order oligarchy (Hadiz 2004, 2010). These works will be discussed in chapter 2.

The new phenomena of the rising importance of local political actors cannot be dissociated from the ability of those actors to establish political networks further afield. In the context of decentralized Indonesia, political networks connected local political actors in two general sites—those at the center of power in Jakarta, the capital of Indonesia, and those in the regions. The book emphasizes the political dynamics at work on both the local and national levels of politics and illustrates how local and central relations have to be viewed across very fluid boundaries. Both local and national actors are able to move these boundaries.

More importantly, these political networks were initially established by local rather than central politicians. Thus, this study narrates one of the most important political economic developments in post-Suharto Indonesia, where competition to manage and control natural resources is no longer limited only to national-level political players and interests, and at the same time, cannot be restricted solely to the local level. Importantly, it also mentions changes in the structure of political economy as the result of deep engagement by local actors in disputes with the central government over natural resources. In the end, these disputes have provided a way for changes to be made in the rent distributions of natural resources among different political players.

---

[3] See Kingsbury and Aveling 2003; Ray and Goodpaster 2003; Morishita 2008; Okamoto and Hamid 2008; Erb and Sulistiyanto 2009; Mietzner 2007; Buehler and Tan 2007; Choi 2009; Choi 2011; Tyson 2010; and Kimura 2007, 2013.

Introduction

Having mentioned that local politicians were on the rise as a result of changes in political structure and were thus starting to advance their interests, it is important to add that the political relations of central and local governments also progressed along a new trajectory, especially by comparison to the New Order. As a consequence, any discussion of decentralization requires a much wider perspective that considers broader social, political and economic factors. The essential issue here is that local politicians were using new regulations on decentralization to pursue their political and economic interests in the regions. The local politicians from the Suharto regime shared with new players an ability to create political linkages and maneuver within the newly established political institutions. If the ability of local politicians to use violence or coercion can be referred to as hard skills, then the skill to create political links and to bargain can be described as soft skills.

While it is true that local political actors could establish political links with whomever they trusted, their efforts to set up such linkages differed from Suharto's efforts because they did not control Golkar (Golongan Karya or the Functional Group)—the political party machine used by Suharto—or equally hierarchical structures like the bureaucracy or the military. Local political actors might have controlled one of these political machines, however, their ability to use them was limited. They could only operate under existing institutions. Therefore, when they began to set up connections with trusted friends, they carefully selected incentives that could be offered to their partner politicians on the national level. As a consequence, political maneuvers adopted by local political actors very greatly depending on the newly established political networks. These political networks served as the foundation on which they built their political strength to face the national politicians who opposed them. When local political actors defied central government policies, they were quite aware that their political survival depended on political support on both the local and national levels. Local political actors who were capable of establishing political networks on two fronts—the regional and national levels—had greater chances of engaging in conflict with the central government than those unable to set up such links.

In the beginning, these local political actors brought local concerns to the attention of the central government through the formal structure of government available to them. However, as the three cases demonstrate, they were hardly successful in their initial efforts. Therefore, these local elites changed their strategies by engaging in political disputes with the central government. They moved in such a way that they operated outside formal channels by questioning the authority of the central government over certain properties in their regions. The combined change in political regulations also altered the constellation of the political economy, because it created room for local politicians to maneuver and to question economic policy on natural resources.

This book examines the political efforts of local political actors to take advantage of the transition from a centralized to a decentralized system of government. As mentioned earlier, another consequence of their political strategies is that they created room to maneuver within these new institutions. This study carefully analyzes how these political actors tried to maximize benefits provided by changes in political institutions. At the beginning of their efforts, local political players questioned property rights over certain natural resources in their regions. In essence, the three cases illustrate that parties engaged in the political disputes were diverted from exercising power to achieve a fair allocation of resources and instead became preoccupied with determining the limits of power itself.

This leads to the claim that under the decentralization policies, local and national political players came to be connected with each other. Commonsensical notions of "networking" assume that various levels of government or political players are closely related or connected, and that they often ignore the possible political struggles and conflicts that arise from such connections. This study sheds light on political disputes that would not have been possible under Suharto's New Order with its highly centralized political structure and top-down decision-making process. It maintains that this competition stemmed from the very nature of institutional changes in the political arena, which transformed the country from a highly centralized political system to a decentralized one and adopted a democratic form of government over an authoritarian one.

The Three Cases

The first case under study is the takeover of Semen Padang in West Sumatra by local politicians. Semen Padang, a state-owned company that produces cement in West Sumatra, is a subsidiary of Semen Gresik located in East Java. At that time, Semen Gresik was in the process of privatization; as its subsidiary, Semen Padang was therefore a part of this process. A group of local politicians in Padang, the capital of West Sumatra, rejected privatization, and consequently assumed ownership of Semen Padang unilaterally from the central government. The takeover of Semen Padang was only possible because the country had moved from a centralized to a decentralized type of government. The privatization of Semen Padang took place exactly when local governments received more authority than they had had under Suharto. In short, the privatization process happened at the very moment the relationship between central and local governments experienced dramatic change.

The Semen Padang case reveals a riddle in the Indonesian political economy. Shortly after Suharto lost power, local politicians in West Sumatra—in the government broadly but including the parliament—exercised their power to hold negotiations over economic resources and refused the central government's policy of privatization for the cement factory. These local politicians were able to organize power, as indicated by their ability to gain the seemingly unanimous political support of the population. Having received political support, these local politicians challenged the central government's policy, which they thought did not provide any benefits to the region. The takeover of Semen Padang exhibits deep changes in the structure of the political economy operating in a more democratic and decentralized Indonesia.

A second striking example of opposition to central government economic policies comes from Riau province, a region endowed with oil resources. This oil-producing province was under the particularly tight control of the central government under Suharto. Suharto's reason for controlling Riau was to provide the political stability required for the operation of oil exploration and production. Foreign investors required this political stability in order to operate their businesses. Investors had no political capability to create political stability on their own, and therefore they expected the government to offer this service.

However, after the fall of Suharto, local politicians in Riau refused the central government's policy on the transfer of shares in Coastal Pekanbaru Plains, an oil block already in production. When the permit for the oil block operated by a foreign investor expired, officially the contract had to return to the central government. It was supposed to be a very smooth transfer between the foreign investor and the central government. However, local politicians saw an opportunity to challenge the central government by demanding a fair share of the equity in production from this oil block. Local politicians relied on their argument that, in the past, Suharto had treated the province badly, because it had never received a fair share of revenue from oil exploration. Moreover, they saw an opportunity to demand more revenue by optimizing opportunities created by the decentralization policy. They opposed the central government approach to transferring the oil block, and moved further by proposing that the oil block ownership should be transferred to the local government.

Political opposition also came from the resource-rich province of East Kalimantan. Local politicians there fought the central government's proposed sale of equity in Kaltim Prima Coal (KPC), a well-established coal mine operation. The process of selling shares from the foreign-owned contractors to the government was recognized as a divestment process. The relevant regulation stated that the foreign investors must sell 51 percent of their shares to Indonesian participants. The central government intended to sell the shares to Indonesian participants who had adequate capital to purchase them and had sound experience in managing coal mines. However, the provincial government of East Kalimantan expressed its interest in purchasing the shares, as they argued was provided for by law, despite their lack of experience. The problem rested in the way in which provincial government promoted its interest. Having interpreted the contract based on its own interests, the provincial government unsurprisingly maintained the opinion that it must be given first priority in making such a purchase.

How did these local politicians in West Sumatra, Riau and East Kalimantan rise to prominence and gain the capability to challenge the central government's policies? What constituted their political capital? The answers relate to the decentralization policy that dramatically changed the political institutions governing central and local relations. Such a policy is reflected in Law No. 22/1999 and Law No. 25/1999. For example, Law No. 22/1999 was designed to devolve some central government authority to the local government, in this case the regency/municipal or *kebupaten* level of government. The law retained the central government's authority over five areas: foreign affairs, defence and security, justice, monetary and fiscal affairs, and religion. It also maintains the central government's authority over macro-level planning, fiscal equalization, public administration, economic institutions, human resource development, natural resources utilization, strategic technologies, conservation and national standardization. Local governments were given authority over public works, health, education and culture, agriculture, transport, industry and trade, investment, environment, land matters, cooperatives and manpower.

With respect to the increasing importance of local politicians, the question is: In what ways were local politicians capable of challenging central government policies? What kinds of political and economic opportunities did decentralization provide local politicians, and how did

Introduction   13

local politicians use these opportunities to oppose policies of the central government?

This study contends that the marriage of personal networks and institutions under both the Suharto and the post-Suharto governments facilitated relatively different directions in policymaking. To test the utility of this contention, this study considers three cases to understand the formation of new national politics in post-Suharto Indonesia: the privatization of state-owned cement maker, Cement Padang, in West Sumatra; conflict over a the Coastal Pekanbaru Plains oil block in Riau; and the divestment process of Kaltim Prima Coal (KPC) in East Kalimantan.

The examination of these three cases is especially interesting for several reasons. First, as mentioned above, this book evaluates conflicts between political actors over ownership, management and rent distribution at both national and regional levels. Trapped in the middle of these conflicts, or sometimes involved as a party to these conflicts, sat the foreign investors. Many such studies of a decentralized Indonesia focus on political dynamics at the local level, even though there are some attempts to examine a kind of coalition that links central and regional political actors. The weight of analyses always rested in the regions and records detailing political processes and dynamics at the local level. This is not say that these analyses are unimportant. On the contrary, this book aims to provide a different narrative by emphasizing political networks and institutions. The conflicts illustrated in the three cases provide opportunities to closely look at the political dynamics that facilitate connections between political actors at the center of power and those in the regions. To understand this situation, it is better to mention here that many of Indonesia's natural resources are located in Indonesia's many regions, some very far indeed from the political center of Jakarta. The Indonesian constitution mentions that these resources belong to the state—meaning the central government. In the past, even provincial and much lower-level regional governments were parts of the central government. With the change in political arrangements that allow for a decentralized structure, the provincial, regency and municipal governments now compete to claim the natural resources located in their regions.

Second, these three cases offer a way to understand the relationships between the central and regional governments in the new political environment. Semen Padang, Coastal Pekanbaru Plains oil block, and Kaltim Prima Coal have been chosen because these companies linked three players at the same time: the central government, the provincial governments, and foreign investors. These cases offer an opportunity to develop arguments by employing the framework of institutions and networks, which will be discussed in chapter 2. These cases allow a discussion of the emergence of regional politicians and their capability to create networks under different institutional arrangements. Furthermore, these cases offer precious material for understanding the political economy of Indonesia after the fall of Suharto.

Relevance of Transition Period 1998–2004

The three cases under study—Semen Padang, Kaltim Prima Coal and the Coastal Pekanbaru Plain oil block—can only be understood in the wider context of institutional changes that transformed Indonesia from a centralized to a decentralized structure of government. Institutional changes clearly offered political opportunities and incentives to local governments pursuing their political and economic interests. Local governments, along with local prominent politicians, tapped the opportunities available to them by relying on their newly received authority and power. At the same time, they were also aware that the central government was not as strong as it was during Suharto's regime.

This book limits its study to a period of time that lasted from 1998 to 2004. There are reasons for considering only a six-year time span. First, during this time, Indonesia experienced a dramatic transformation from an authoritarian to a more democratic government, with contested elections and much the introduction of more activist political parties. One of the most crucial issues faced inside the political realm was the relaxation of restrictions on establishing political parties. Under Suharto's administration, political parties were limited to only three parties: the United Development Party (Partai Persatuan Pembangunan, a fusion of Islam-based political parties); the Indonesian Democratic Party (Partai Demokrasi Indonesia, a fusion of secular-nationalist parties); and Golkar. Suharto's New Order sought to simplify political parties, because it was unsympathetic to the idea of political parties based on ethnic, regional or religious affiliation. The strategy to simplify political parties is in line with the New Order's strategy of "depoliticizing" or "de-ideologizing" mass politics. The concept of the "floating mass"—that the masses were detached from political parties—was designed to ensure that party-based links to communal, religious and ideological agendas did not resurface (Ramage 1995; Kartasasmita and Stern 2015: 53). After Suharto's fall, the government of Bacharuddin Jusuf Habibie loosened the requirements for establishing political parties, resulting in an increase in the number of political parties. However, many of them were not eligible to participate in elections because they failed to meet certain mandatory conditions, such as fielding branches in all provinces. Within this framework of political changes in the democratic process, this period saw the emergence of new political parties such as the National Awakening Party (Partai Kebangkitan Bangsa, a traditional Islamic-based party); the National Mandate Party (Partai Amanat Nasional, a modernist Islamic-based party); the Democrat Party (Partai Democrat); the Justice Party (Partai Keadilan, a modernist-Islam party, but changed to Partai Keadilan Sejahtera or the Prosperous Justice Party, PKS); and the Gerindra Party (Movement of Great Indonesia Party, a secular party). This period also saw Golkar's transformation into the Golkar Party, and that of the PDI to PDI-P (Indonesian Democratic Party-Struggle).

Beginning in 2000, decentralization policies were implemented along with democratization processes. A crucial feature of political change included the elimination of hierarchical links that existed under Suharto's regime. Suharto controlled important political, military and bureaucratic channels. He had relatively full control over the decision to elect governors, even if the election process was carried out by the provincial parliaments. In the process, provincial-level parliaments submitted two or three candidates. Suharto usually revealed his preference among these candidates. The candidate of his choice was elected governor. To make this happen, Suharto relied on Golkar, which in many provinces dominated the entire parliament. He also used his military networks and, in many cases, appointed military personnel to serve as governors. In the resources-rich provinces of East Kalimantan and Riau, Suharto relied heavily on the military network and appointed military persons close to him. When Riau province was under Suharto, almost all of its governors originated from Java. Suharto demanded their loyalty. Native persons (*putra daerah*) had little to no chance of being elected governor. However, between 1998 and 2004 those political features faded from existence along with the New Order. Since this time, regents or mayors have become responsible to voters only through the system of local-level parliaments. Local political actors, as they are responsible to parliament at the provincial level, have more room to express local demands in a manner that had never existed before in Indonesian politics. This book reveals the capability of local political actors to openly oppose central government policies on natural resource ownership, management and rent distribution.

Second, the period from 1998 to 2004 is paradigmatic for understanding the formation of a new political pattern in which the new structure of institutions was in place and new personal political networks were in the making. Research that combines network and institutional frameworks challenges the premises of the once-dominant and conventional view of center-periphery relations. The story of state building in Indonesia always locates political processes at the center of political life in Jakarta. In this kind of political universe, local politicians were less important or have only a limited role in the decision-making process even for their own regions. In the past, many of these local politicians were either political protégés of politicians in Jakarta or local politicians who were likely to administer the policies of Jakarta. Politicians in Jakarta were the agents that created institutions and established political networks. With the fall of the New Order state, the process of state building began to follow different routes, with local politicians having much more power compared to what they had possessed in the past.

In contrast with the previous trend, the period 1998 to 2004 saw the making of the first political networks initiated by local political actors in the regions. This phenomenon of building political networks from the region extending out is relatively new, as in the past such links established by political actors operated from Indonesia's center of power, Jakarta. The emergence of local political actors able to create deep connections was facilitated by conflicts over management of natural resources, which prompted questions about ownership, management, and rent distribution. These conflicts constituted a relatively new phenomenon, as local political actors saw the possibility to exploit opportunities provided by political transformations in the period under study. Between 1998 and 2004, these local political actors were able to accrue benefit from a very fluid political situation marked by a split in the central government that allowed them to forge political networks with those in power in Jakarta. The conflicts over natural resources in a decentralized Indonesia were characterized by a new emerging trend in which local political actors became deeply involved wherever they could lift local voices up to the national level of politics. These local political actors seemed to be able to manage support from both those in power in the central government and in their home regions by manipulating either ethnicity or community bond. The conflicts, mentioned in this book, lasted quite a long time, and they provide examples of how political actors in both the center and the regions have negotiated with each other in pursuit of their interests. This is why this period saw a very deep engagement by local political actors in conflicts over the management of natural resources.

Introduction 17

Analysis of the period between 1998 and 2004 reveals an emerging trend in which just the opposite happens in conflicts over management and rent distribution from natural resources. In the past, any divestment process of a natural resource firm was fully controlled by Suharto in ways that benefited those close to him (Leith 2003; Kartasasmita 2013). Under Suharto's rule, almost none of the local political actors who were engaged in and benefited from selling shares of the mining company located in Papua tended to circle around the president.

It seems that local political actors were beginning to become aware that they could extend their own authority (or power) beyond the limits set by Indonesia's decentralization policies. With the ability of local political actors to set up political networks through new institutions, the relationships between the central and local governments had changed and even entered a new phase. National political actors were aware that their power and authority significantly decreased. In the past, by contrast, orders from the center's power holders could be implemented without facing serious opposition from local elites. This rule no longer existed. The period 1998–2004 saw open conflicts over different interests become the new rule.

Third, the events after 2004 actually resonate with the politics of the preceding era and run along the course already set by the three cases investigated in this book. It is more than likely that today's local political actors refer to the earlier cases evaluated in this book. They may learn to set up political networks, even though it would not be an easy political move, and go against the will of the central government over ownership, management and rent distribution of natural resources. If these local elites could not establish political networks that associate them with the power holders at the center of national politics, then they could create them at the local level. To be sure, after 2004 the relationships among the three different parties were never again the same as in the past. Needless to say, local political actors who came to hold power after 2004 period would imitate the political opposition molded in 1998–2004. To understand this claim, one should consider that Indonesian is rich with mineral resources located across its regions.

To anticipate other rounds of conflict over natural resources between 1998 and 2004, the central government issued a regulation that accommodated the interests of regions through Minister of Energy and Mineral Resources Regulation No. 35/2004, which was renewed by Regulation No. 37/2016. It rules that regions where natural resources are located have a participating interest right of 10 percent.

However, there is no guarantee that the relationships between the central and local governments, or between national- and local-level political actors, are smooth when disputing interests in natural resources. In addition to the cases discussed in this book, there are several divestment processes that have not been completed at the time of writing of this book. The most high profile is probably the divestment process of Freeport Indonesia, a mining firm operated by American interests and located in Papua. Equally, transfer of the ownership of Mahakam block, located in East Kalimantan and operated by Japan's Inpex and a French interest, was not completed until 2017.

Two conflicts that involved the central government, the local government and foreign investors are relevant to explaining why the period 1998–2004 can provide insight into the development of the Indonesian political economy. The conflict over Newmont Nusa Tenggara (NTT), a copper mine operated by American and Japanese interests and located in West Nusa Tenggara, created some difficulty for the central government (Prasetyawan 2017). The transfer of the Rokan oil block located in Riau Province is another difficult process. These conflicts exactly mimic the cases discussed in this book, at least in the efforts of local political networks vis-à-vis power holders in Jakarta.

Divestment of NTT shares should have been a closed case in the post-2004 period. Based on the contract of work, signed between the Indonesian government and operators in 1986, the operators had to divest their shares to an Indonesian interest. Between 2006 and 2010, NNT had to sell its 30-percent share. In fact, only 24 percent of its shares were successfully sold to Indonesian interests. The local elites in West Nusa Tenggara were able to establish political networks with power holders who had the capital to buy NTT's shares. However, the remaining 7 percent posed a difficulty, as the central government opposed the local government's plan to buy back those shares. The central government, under the minister of finance, preferred to sell the shares in question to Aneka Tambang, a mining state-owned enterprise (SOE). This case was resolved when a consortium led by an Indonesian conglomerate bought the shares in 2016.

The case of the Rokan oil block in Riau may follow the political pattern of the previous era. For sure, this case exhibits a potential conflict among three parties: the central government, the local government and foreign investors. This case may soon explode, as it involves the biggest oil block in the country. The contractor, PT Chevron Pacific Indonesia (CPI), an American interest, must release its rights in 2021 when they expire. CPI has operated this block since 1971, and in 2017 it contributed a whopping 28 percent of Indonesia's total oil production. After learning that CPI had to discharge its rights in 2021, local political elites in both the provincial and regency governments started to express an interest in owning or managing this oil block. The government of Riau had started to establish a provincial company, PT Riau Petroleum. Similarly, regency governments followed suit and also set up companies.

The future of this potential conflict is uncertain. If local political actors are able to form political networks with power holders in Jakarta, the conflict would be long-lasting without a clue about the likely winner.

In the cases of Freeport Indonesia and the Rokan oil blocks, local political actors had already proposed that their interests total more than 10 percent of all shares. These political elites had started to communicate in order to set up political networks, so that they could face the central government's policies. The case of Rokan oil block is much more visible, because the political elites at provincial and district levels are working together. I am sure that they look back to the example of the case of the Coastal Pekanbaru Plain oil block, which this book investigates.

There are many possible disputes across Indonesia that could follow the pattern of the 1998–2004 period. Such disputes would focus on ownership, management and the distribution of rents from natural resource exploitation. One need only look at the list of natural resource exploration projects across the country. Indonesian law requires the foreign companies that operate these natural resource enterprises to divest shares, in the case of mining, and transfer ownership and operational control in the case of oil exploration and production—in both cases to Indonesian interests. The process of divestment and ownership transfer would open possible conflicts. Appendix 1 presents a list of possible conflicts, referring to 33 oil operators, mostly foreign companies, whose contracts will expire by 2022. Appendix 2 looks at coal companies which will be required to divest their shares. There are ten companies that will have to comply with the new regulation demanding a 10-percent participating interest for the region in which they operate (appendix 3). Data from the Ministry of Energy and Mineral Resources (MEMR) shows that, until 2011, there were seven companies holding work contracts, 46 companies holding mineral concessions, 35 companies holding coal contracts, and 105 companies holding coal concessions. In 2017 the minister of energy and mineral resources signed with 27 companies that hold work contracts and coal contracts. The point is that, in the future, Indonesia will likely face many conflicts over natural resources involving three players: national political actors, local political actors and foreign investors. These conflicts will likely proceed along a path similar to the one taken during the 1998–2004 period. In the future, such struggles will provide an avenue to understanding both political networks and political economy. The three conflicts discussed in this book provide various insights into how conflict would take form, how the local political elite would work to establish political networks, and how political actors would use their power and authority. Most importantly, these conflicts helped to mold Indonesia's political economy. This book opens a wide research area that has received little attention in the past.

Methodological Issues

This study mainly depends on interviews and written material. The interviews were conducted with various actors who were directly involved in the dispute and those who were not involved in the conflict. They were conducted with politicians in the provincial governments of West Sumatra, Riau and East Kalimantan. Interviewees included the secretary of a provincial government and members of a provincial parliament. On the national level, interviews were conducted with higher officials in the Ministry of State-Owned Enterprises and the Ministry of Energy and Mineral Resources. In addition, chief executives and officers of companies involved in the disputes analyzed agreed to interviews, which were conducted in order to get an insider's view of cases discussed. The interviews were carried out in two different time frames, first in 2000 to 2006 and second between 2010 and 2017. A second set of interviews focused mainly those who drafted decentralization policy and were carried out in Jakarta. In Riau, intensive interviews were conducted with the advocates of the Riau Freedom Movement regarding their position on sharing revenue derived from oil resources. There were also interviews with those who were not directly involved in the disputes, such as NGO workers, especially those who kept materials related to this study.

Written materials were collected from various sources such as government publications. Various official contracts between the central government and foreign investors fall under this category. These materials offer insights into the nature of the relationship between the central government and the foreign investors, and the types of regulations governing such relations. Unpublished materials were also collected. Various letters exchanged between central and provincial governments between the central government and foreign investors, were also analyzed to figure out the disputes and their respective positions. Finally, this book also depended on news items published by national and regional media for an overall picture of the disputes. These news items were mainly published during the period under study. News items are important because disputing parties use the media to inform Indonesians of their positions regarding the disputes. In East Kalimantan, for example, the governor was willing to purchase advertising space to announce his opposition to the central government.

Outline of the Book

The task of chapter 1 is to discuss existing explanations of political changes in Indonesia and to pose the key questions of this study. Chapter 1 also discusses the conceptual foundations of the book. Chapter 2 discusses the different views of scholarship on decentralization policies and political economy. Chapter 3 establishes the context of the study by looking at changes in the government's political form from centralized to decentralized. Chapter 4 analyzes the conflict over the divestment process of Kaltim Prima Coal in East Kalimantan. Chapter 5 explains the conflict surrounding the process of privatizing Semen Padang in West Sumatra. Chapter 6 discusses the dispute that erupted over an oil block in Riau by the name Coastal Pekanbaru Plains. The book closes with a discussion of the emergence of a new pattern of political economy in Indonesia due to the rising power of local politicians.

CHAPTER 1

Institutions and Political Networks

This chapter discusses, in a proper manner, the concepts of institutions and political networks. The discussion is derived from the existing scholarly works on these two subjects. It will serve as a framework to understand the emergence of political networks during a time of transition in Indonesia.

Institutions

The study of institutions has a long tradition. This study refers to the definition of institutions developed by Douglass North. North defines institutions as the rules of society's games, or formally speaking, as the humanly devised constraints that shape human interactions (1990: 3). This underlines the relevance of institutions to the study of both economy and polity. Recent research on institutions sprang from the work of economists. A key component of this work should be the theoretical work in which the institutional approach to the economy is a modification of neoclassical theory (North 1994: 359). North retains the neoclassical notions of scarcity and competition while at the same time adding the dimension of learning through time (1994: 360). He argues that neoclassical (standard) economic theory does not seriously take institutions into consideration, disregarding them as exogenous variables in its analyses.

How does this study of economy and politics relate to the existing debate on institutions? There are two answers located in the key elements of debate within the new institutional economics regarding property rights, contracts and government structure. In addition, some of the studies on institutions discuss the necessity of implementing the rule of law and of legal enforcement in doing business (Milgrom, North and Weingast 1990; Greif 1992; and North 1990).

22

North and Thomas (1973) argue for the importance of the development of a stable and secure property rights regime for economic development. Much of these literatures see politics and economic activity as interrelated. The business transaction can only take place if there are secure property rights protected by the government. In this sense, the government acts as the third party that should protect business contracts between two private parties. Following this logic, the government must protect contracts in order to ensure the function of the economy.

According to institutional economics research, it is the role of the government in an economy to make relationships between business and politics possible. In fact, the discussion between business and politics may be expanded, to look at how members of a society formulate political and economic institutions able to protect their rights whenever the market cannot operate in a proper manner.

Other scholars also illustrate the inseparability of economy and politics in any discussion of society. This relationship between politics and the economy in terms of institutions is also described by Kenneth Arrow (1963: 947), who states: "When the market fails to arrive at an optimum state, society will, to some extent at least, recognize the gap, and non-market social institutions will arise attempting to bridge it". The notion of market failure in this study refers to a situation in which an attempt to allocate resources by way of market mechanisms does not work properly. In a situation of market failure, individuals, including politicians, look for social or political institutions that will enable them to operate in order to achieve their goals. In their search, individuals can either redefine existing institutions or create new ones, even if the creation of institutions is not an easy venture. Efforts to redefine or create institutions are mainly aimed at changing incentives and existing governance structures. The political actors are aware of the notion of institutions as "resources that actors use to attain their ends" (Hall and Thelen 2006). Since there are individuals with different goals depending on their position in society, the incentives for them also likely differ. This reasoning implies that there will be conflicting goals among individuals; thus a conflict situation cannot be discounted when either creating or redefining institutions.

The relations between business and politics are also located in the discussion of property rights. Before this study discusses these relationships, it is necessary to clarify the concept of property rights. The concept of property rights can be understood as individuals having control over their assets for consumption, exchange or profit generation. Individuals can only benefit from their assets because an agency protects their rights from other parties. This is the task performed by the state. Here, the state is the agency that protects citizens' property rights against attempts by other parties to take their property away from them (Barzel 2002). The state acts as the third party that protects the property of all citizens under its jurisdiction. Any disputes regarding property rights have to go to the state for settlement. In order to perform the task of protecting property rights, the state is allowed to use its power. The inability of the state to protect the property rights of citizens will allow non-state actors to take part in the business of citizen assets (Varese 2004: 24).

From the explanations above, the idea of the state as a third party assumes that conflict can only emerge from among citizens, owners of rights, or non-state actors. Since a state will have different layers or levels of government, it is possible to think that conflict can emerge within a state.

Another definition of institution includes the notion of power. North (1990) offers a general understanding of institutions without any effort to relate them to other factors in social and political life. Only when North points out those institutions are likely to work on overtly political matters does he take politics into account. North states that an institution operates within a particular polity that honors and protects property rights, yet he gives little attention to its emergence as a product of negotiation and contestation of power. He rightly clarifies that an institution consists of "the formal rules [that] are created to serve the interest of those with bargaining power to create new rules" (North 1990: 16; 1995: 20). However, North does not argue that institutions are an outcome of political negotiations and settlement among different sets of players. He hardly considers an institution as a mechanism for the allocation and consolidation of power.

North's theoretical lacunae is filled by a group of scholars who strongly argue that the creation or maintenance of an institution "takes place not on a 'level playing field' of the market but rather within the political arena, in which some are endowed with greater power than others" (Bates 1995: 42). Since power cannot be ignored, the creation of an institution for a particular society depends on its political settlement. In order to understand an institution, it "requires an analysis of the inherited balance of power or 'political settlement'" (Khan 1995: 71). In relation to power and politics, institutions are "working rules that are used to determine who is eligible to make decisions in some arena, and what actions are allowed or constrained" (Ostrom 1990: 51).

The current development of work on institutional economics has recognized the relevance of politics and political process to understanding the dynamics of societies. The scholars who work in this line of scholarship not only advance politics but also accept the significance of interdependency among the various institutions, formal or informal, that serve as a stage on which members of a society can interact with one another. Ostrom (2005: 827), for example, mentions that institutional analysis cannot be separated from other institutions because "the impact on incentives and behavior of one type of rule is not independent of other rules". In an almost similar line of argument, Aoki (2001: 3) contends that institutions and the complexity of economics are better evaluated by "looking into the nature of interdependencies of institutions across economics, political, organizational, and social domains, as well as that of institutions' linkage to these domains". This development has led to the recognition that institutions not only support each other but also form incentives for various actors. Menard and Shirley (2005: 2) illustrate "how electoral procedures, political party norms and constitutional law and structure interact with one another to shape the incentive of politicians and voters, and, ultimately, to influence policy decisions". At the current stage, it appears that the relevance of politics and political process to the scholarship on institutional economics has been greatly appreciated. Furthermore, this development has recently received a new infusion of scholarship, as the new institutional economists have developed a deep interest in the political process as a way to understand the performance of an economy. Acemoglu and Robinson (2012: 68) propose: "to understand this [society], you have to go beyond economics and expert advice on the best [things] to do and, instead, study how decisions actually get made, who gets to make them, and why those people decide to do what they do. This is the study of politics and political processes". With this development, the scholarship on institutional economics has moved beyond its initial boundaries and added to the equation both politics and its process.

Considering all these ideas of institutions, it is clear that power and politics cannot be dissociated from any discussion of institutions, because institutions define those who are eligible to make decisions.

It is now necessary to mention why the concepts of institutions are relevant in this study of the political economy of Indonesia. There are several reasons. First, the changes that took place in Indonesia were mostly institutional changes, in a broad sense, because many new regulations were introduced after the fall of the New Order regime. Second, these

26   *Networked*

institutional changes offered incentives (and also disincentives) to local
politicians in the regions. Third, it is clear from the analysis in this study
that institutions can also be created through conflicts that involve several
political or economic players with different interests. Fourth, institutions
limit the behavior of various players in different ways, but these limita-
tions are also sometimes violated by the players themselves in order to
pursue their own gains—something that is quite obvious in the cases here
under study.

Political Networks

Networks

In social life, an individual's behavior is located within the wider context
of reciprocal interactions and relations. To pursue her/his political and
economic goals, an actor cannot work alone. This is simply because she/he
is embedded in a series of relationships with other actors who may support or deny her/his cause. In this case, a series of relations pave an
important path of development toward a more coherent set of interactions
that may result in a network. To consider that an actor cannot work
alone and in fact is embedded in a number of connections, this book
proposes the definition of a network given by Swedberg and Granovetter
(1992: 9), who define a network as a "regular set of contacts or similar
social connections among individuals or groups". They further emphasize:
"an action by a member of a network is embedded, because it is expressed
in intention with other people" (1992: 9). Almost a decade later, their
definition of a network was pushed further by Joel Podolny and Karen
Page (1998: 59), who define it as "any collection of actors (N≥2) that
pursue repeated, enduring exchange relations with one another and, at
the same time lack legitimate organizational authority to arbitrate and
resolve disputes that may arise during the exchange". Therefore, as long
as there is a collection of actors that share repeated exchange relations,
something can be categorized as a network, according to the definitions
of both Swedberg and Granovetter and Podolny and Page. This understanding seems to accord with the one developed by Rosenau, who
does not suggest any definition of a network but does characterize it.
Rosenau (2008: 102) contends that if people's actions are contextualized
in relationships, then those people are already embedded in a number
of networks. He suggests that networks vary in size, purpose, scope,
coherence, intensity, location and duration, but nonetheless share at least

one common feature. He claims, "all networks contribute in the way in which the individuals who participate in them spend their time and conduct their affairs" (Rosenau 2008: 102). Their understanding is relevant to this study because a network has several characteristics, especially: that more than two persons pursue shared goal(s); and that the nature of relations is informal without having any formal hierarchy or structure.

Having mentioned that relations of at least two people can create a network without any structural form, it is therefore safe to claim that networks are everywhere (Newman, Barabási and Watts 2006: 1). They also claim that networks exist in other phenomena, such as the internet, economics, networks of disease transmission and even terrorist networks. Contrasting with past works on networks, which had the tendency to treat networks as static structures, these scholars point out recent works that have recognized the ability of networks to evolve over time (Newman, Barabási and Watts 2006: 7). They prefer to evaluate networks as a product "of dynamical processes that add or remove vertices or edges" (Newman, Barabási and Watts 2006: 7). For them, social-structure network changes historically depend on the role of participants and the behavioral patterns of these participants. They provide examples of a social network of friendships that changes as individuals make and break ties with each other. Thus, they claim that the ties people experience affect the ties people make.

In contrast to the scholarship discussed above, there are works that characterize networks as having an image of an organization with hierarchies and structures. Gunaratna (2002: 95), in a discussion of Al Qaeda, suggests that its global networks were created in Khartoum, and that as it strives to "coordinate its overt and covert military operations ... it develops a decentralized, regional structure". In a similar line of argument, Kahler (2009: 5) contends that networks in the international relations domain tend to have structure and hierarchy.

Having addressed this scholarly understanding of networks, this book adopts a definition of network that falls very close to those posited by Barabási, Podolny and Karen, by Newman, Barabási and Watts, and by Rosenau. This book suggests that a network is a group of actors that may be closely or loosely connected through various means such as education, work experience and political parties, and that this connection may not have a formal structure or hierarchy like an organization. A network may have a limited number of core members whose connections are close—for example, as small as five or six people (Watts 2001). Nevertheless, a network does not merely refer to the relations or connections of individuals. As argued by Barabási, a network has many nodes that are connected to hubs. His important contributions to the study of networks are (1) his concept of preferential attachment (Barabási 2002: 85) and (2) his recognition of a network's evolving nature (Newman, Barabási and Watts 2006). In this sense, networks possess an advantage because of "their general virtues of speed, flexibility, inclusiveness, ability to cut across different jurisdictions, and sustained focus on a specific set of problems" (Slaughter 2004: 167).

Political Economy

The implication of Barabási's concept of preferential attachment for the study of political economy is that an individual actor in a particular network tends to relate to or connect with other actors (creating hubs) who have more influence and connections than he does. In the real world, a politician tends to relate to or connect with a better-connected politician. The actor who is connected to a more influential politician may calculate the degree to which such a link will influence her/his political future. These kinds of connections can be transformed into political networks, in that "the basic unit of any complex political system is not individual, but the position or roles occupied by social actors and the relations or connections between these positions" (Knoke 1990: 7). He furthermore argues that members of a cohesive group or clique are linked directly to one another by way of intense communication (1990: 11–12). In addition, this book also modifies Barabási's (2016) concept of social network, which is the sum of all professional, friendship and family ties. However, Barabási's definition apparently does not stress the role of trust. Any definition related to social life that includes personal relations and repeated contacts by the same people for a length of time may require trust among them. Granovetter (1992: 60) advanced the relevance of trust to personal relations and networks, in addition to emotional intensity, intimacy (mutual confiding) and reciprocal services (Granovetter 1973: 1361). Therefore, a political network is a series of relations formed specifically in a political context and aiming at shared goals. The characteristics of a political network are similar to any other network, in that it is very fluid and flexible; is able to move beyond religion, ethnicity and geographical boundaries in the pursuit of shared targets; enjoys trust among the actors involved; and has no structure or hierarchy. Political actors can seamlessly interact with each other as long as they share, at least to some extent, similar goals without worrying about their social position and backgrounds. In this book, political networks are used to underscore the fact that the relations of an individual actor or group of political actors are important. The influence of an individual political actor, therefore, depends on his connections or relations.

Understanding the notion of networks is important to the making of political networks. This is an expansion of an argument developed by Barabási (2002) that a network can develop and grow, and the work of Barabási (2016) on social networks. This study enlarges and modifies the explanation offered by Barabási (2002 and 2016) and analyzes it in the context of political economy. Why are Barabási's concepts relevant to this study? The answer lies in the capacity of Barabási's concept of networks to allow for the idea that a network is dynamic, which means it can grow and evolve. In the ensuing chapters and case studies, this book describes political networks as formed at individual, communal and structural levels. Each case presented in this book exhibits a different degree of influence over the foundations of political networks.

The making of political networks in this study had different stories from personal to communal linkages. As mentioned earlier, social networks can be formed on the basis of one or more modes of friendship, religion or professional background. The cases under study reveal that friendship serves as a key foundation for making linkages. But friendship may take place after actors come to know each other in the workplace, in educational institutions—schools or any other place of high-level training for bureaucrats—and in various local organizations at the community level. The pattern found in this study fits the proposition that friendships may serve as a key component of social networks, generating a series of direct, frequent, voluntary and purposeful interactions (Huckfeldt and Sprague 1993: 290). Therefore, it would be safe to claim that personal networks are built on the basis of friendships. Working in a slightly different manner are community networks, which could be based on religion, language or place of origin (Herziq 2010). These community networks are very useful to members who are living in places distant from their place of origin. The incorporation of religious and cultural activities strengthens ties among members. The close evaluation to the three cases presented in this book reveal that Minangkabau people from West Sumatra and Malays from Riau enjoyed advantages, because members from both communities worked as high-level politicians in the central government. At this point, it is necessary to note that the political networks evaluated in this book mostly started with the forging of either personal or communal ties among actors, and that these actors may or may not have had an association with political parties. For example, local actors of the Minangkabau ethnic group in West Sumatra who had relationships with Minangkabau power holders in Jakarta formed both personal and communal networks at the same time. At the other extreme, local actors from East Kalimantan formed relationships that are based not on communal ties but rather on personal relationships and connections to political parties. In short, personal linkages can develop in the context of a community or an organization such as a political party. However, it is necessary to note that even though political actors have links through political parties, the links they maintain possess the network characteristics mentioned above.

This study looks at the hubs of political networks that link regional actors and central government actors. The main point to studying networks is that it makes it possible to identify the hubs that were crucial to mediating the links between center and regions. The cases under study focus on the local politicians who connect politicians in the center and the regions. Most of these politicians occupy political offices in the regions and develop relationships with politicians in the center through various connections mediated through military, educational or ethnic ties.

Shiraishi (2002) has done empirical-level studies on networks in the Indonesian context in the process of policymaking in the economic domain. He aptly describes the networks of policymakers that took form under the Suharto government from the 1960s into the 1990s. He mainly argues that nodes in a policymaking network were preferentially attached to a hub in the form of the highly respected Widjojo Nitisastro, who worked with Suharto from the start of the New Order. Furthermore, Shiraishi mentions the places where the members of these networks met and spent time together: universities (mainly the faculty of economics of the University of Indonesia) and the offices of economic ministries. Shiraishi also further argues that Widjojo Nitisastro can speak the same language—that is, economics—as the other members of this network, who were mostly his juniors. Other than a network of technocrats, there existed other networks in Indonesia under Suharto's administration.

An empirical study done by Smith (2008) offers something that could be interpreted as a kind of political network, or rather a policy network. Smith (2008: 221) explains that several policymakers centered on Ryaas Rasyid worked to promote the formulation and implementation of decentralization policy. The members of these policy networks were mostly political scientists, including Andi Mallarangeng, Hamid Awaludin, Djohermansyah Djohan, Ramlan Surbakti and Anas Urbaningrum. In a Bourdieuan sense, Sidel (2007) discusses religious networks when he explains religious violence in Indonesia. Sidel (2007: 156–7) contends that Central Sulawesi Protestant Church (Gereja Kristen Sulawesi Tengah, GKST), established in 1947, with its hundred congregations and number of schools, hospitals, clinics and others services, served as the main network for its members. GKST served as a major network for its school graduates to enter the police, the military, the civil service and Golkar. He claims that mobilizing Protestant voters, as a direct result of democratization and decentralization, provides an environment for religious violence supported by the religious networks mentioned above. Sidel (2007: 202) reveals that the various bombings that occurred between 2000 and 2004 were attributed to another Central Java-based Islamic school network based around the Pesantren Al-Mukmin in Ngruki in Solo. He further explains that among those who were detained or arrested and convicted for the bombing include a number of alumni of the Ngruki *pesantren* and other *pesantren* and *halaqah* (discussion groups) founded by Ngruki graduates. It will be difficult to deny that these networks were formed by a kind of bond among their members.

Kartasasmita (2013: 59–60, 96–7) describes the existence of an inner circle that operated under the protection of Sudharmono. This inner circle had only a few members who held repeated meetings and discussions on various issues. Some of the members were Kartasasmita, Murdiono, Ismail Saleh and Sukarton. This inner circle fulfills the qualifications of a political network as described in the previous chapter. In addition, Kartasasmita (2013: 65, 97) reveals the existence of a network composed of *pribumi* or native Indonesian businesspersons, which at that time included Arifin Panigoro, Aburizal Bakrie, Wiwoho Basuki, Fadel Muhammad, Ponco Sutowo, Hartoto Hardikusumo, Omar Abdalla and Widarsa. These businesspersons were tied together by their intention to own a greater share of the Indonesian economy vis-à-vis Chinese Indonesians.

In comparison, McCargo (2005) contends that Thailand's political order is best characterized by network-based politics. He claims: "Thailand's 'network monarchy' is centred on Privy Council President Prem Tinsulanond. Network monarchy is a form of semi-monarchical rule: the Thai King and his allies have forged a modern form of monarchy as a para-political institution" (2005: 501). He describes the main feature of Thailand's network monarchy from 1980 to 2001 as the function of the monarch as the decisive arbitrator of political decisions in times of crisis; as the prime source of national legality, the king acts as an instructive commentator on national questions in order to help to fix the national agenda and intervenes actively in political developments by working through proxies such as privy councilors and trusted military figures. McCargo claims that from 1980 onwards, the main hub of Thailand's network monarchy was Prem Tinsulanond, handpicked by the king as the army's commander and later the government's prime minister. For the next 21 years, he continues, Prem Tinsulanond served as Thailand's director of human resources, masterminding appointments, transfers and promotions. McCargo's work easily fits into the conceptual framework of political networks used in this book. One important qualification, however, should be mutual trust between the actors engaged in a network.

Hutchcroft's (1998) work on booty capitalism in the Philippines to some extent discusses the relevance of political networks. In his words, "it is also common for families to diversify their political networks to guard against changes in political leadership" (1998: 39). He explains that the bankers use their power of loan allocation to strengthen their political networks and bolster their ties to powerful politicians who could reciprocate in some way at a later time (1998: 10). According to Hutchcroft (1998: 102–4), the story of the Far East Bank and Trust Company is instructive: its early years could not be dissociated from its founder, Jose B. Fernandez, and his ability to forge political networks with those who wielded power in the banking sector as well as with politicians. In fact, he was very close to Miguel Cuaderno, the first governor of the Philippines Central Bank. He also enjoyed close ties with Don Jose Cojuangco, head of a prominent powerful family (and father of future president Corazon Cojuangco Aquino). It should be quite clear that the political networks forged by Fernandez were based on trust and friendship as well as the pragmatic goal of protecting his business.

By combining the studies of institutional economics and networks, this book adds alternatives to interpreting Indonesian political economy both in the New Order period under Suharto and the post-Suharto period. Why is it so important to study Indonesian political economy by employing analytical tools from the scholarship on both institutional economics and networks? Because a perspective that combines institutional economics and networks could make it possible to evaluate fundamental issues from a distinctive angle, such as changes in the structure of a country's political economy during a transitional period from an authoritarian to a more democratic regime. In Indonesia, transition provided an impetus for dramatic changes in political architecture that served as a foundation for changes in connections between the local and central government. The changes in the political landscape in turn formed new incentives for political actors. This book argues that the political economy should be understood in a holistic perspective by using available intellectual tools, while at the same time still focusing on the issues at hand.

Furthermore, this study emphasizes the relevance of political networks that operate in a new set of institutional arrangements. This is not to say that a political network could operate only in a new situation. In fact, it can operate in any kind of situation. Relevant to this discussion is the observation that a set of institutions provides incentives and, at the same time, forms the parameters within which actors can operate. As the three case studies point out, political networks established by local actors have flexibility. Here, flexibility means the ability to move or operate beyond the boundaries established by existing institutions; it also means moving beyond geography, race, religion or even political ideology. Due to this flexibility, a political network can easily operate in very difficult situations, such as disputes.

The characteristics of political networks under Suharto, however, were relatively different from those that developed during post-Suharto times. The membership of political networks during Suharto's time was very limited. It centered on nearly similar educational backgrounds or professional associations. On the contrary, political networks in post-Suharto times have tended to involve many members with different backgrounds in geography, ethnicity or professional association.

CHAPTER 2

Decentralization and Changes in Political Economy

This chapter explains debates over political changes that occurred after the fall of Suharto. The passage of decentralization policies altered the political foundation of the central-local government relationship as well as Indonesia's political economy. The purpose of presenting these debates is to elaborate the ways in which decentralization policies drastically reshaped the political landscape and political-economic structure of the country. Fortunately, this political reordering was recorded in the literatures that emerged out of efforts to evaluate decentralization policies. Even though these works hardly discuss the relevance of the new institutions to the goal of providing paths toward establishing new incentives, this scholarship provides a good account of the political transformation that put local political actors at the center of the discussion. The debates are grouped into two different categories: the impact of decentralization policies on local politics and the change in political-economic structure.

Introduction

The claims in this chapter are threefold. First, it is relevant to take into account the incentives that directly result from the introduction of the new institutions of decentralization. In individual case studies, one has to assess the ability of local political players to derive benefit from the incentives created by the introduction of decentralization policies. Local political actors were able to maneuver within the boundaries set up by these institutions. Second, decision-making policymakers seemed unaware or had no relevant information regarding the future political behavior of local political actors who were the subjects of their policies. They appeared to have no clear perception of the manner in which local actors would unfairly employ decentralization policies as a means to disapprove

34

of the central government. Or, at least, policymakers seem to have been unable to calculate whether decentralization regulations would be used to dispute central government policies. Third, decentralization policies had refashioned the structure of the country's political economy, which provided an impetus for local political players to provoke altercations over natural resources located in their localities. In the past, disputes over natural resources rarely involved local political actors as key players. In the past, their involvement in feuds was merely as an extension of what political actors were doing at the national level.

The policies on decentralization, along with the regulations on political parties introduced in 1999, not only changed the political map of Indonesia but also the incentives that motivated local politicians in terms of politics and the economy. The changes in incentives provided opportunities for other political players who were not involved in the formulation or creation of institutions. In short, with these changes in incentives, outsiders who were not involved in any of the steps involved in creating and sustaining institutions had opportunities to gain benefits. The changes in incentives provided an impetus for local politicians to become important players at the local level. This tendency can be clearly observed in the three cases under study. Local governments began to assume areas of authority outside education, religion, defense and finance. Those authorities served as the political foundation for local actors to negotiate with the central government over such things as property rights. However, in the three regions under study, the local government, supported by local politicians, tended to extend the scope of their authority to various arenas, most of which were not incorporated into the regulation of decentralization.

In the New Order government, local politicians were marginal political players at the national level of politics. However, after decentralization and the regulations on political parties took effect, local politicians slowly began to emerge as key players at the local and to some extent the national level of politics. This does not mean, however, that local politicians became players at the national level of politics. Essentially, decentralization policies provided local players with access to the national political scene. They could bring, to a certain degree, local aspirations to political debates at the national level. Local actors who belonged to networks were able to do this. Political networks mediated the communication of local actors with their political counterparts at the national level. Some of them might contact politicians of the same party in Jakarta. Some of them used the educational institutions in which they were schooled.

In the post-Suharto order, the nature of political networks, created mainly by Suharto, changed because the relationships between the central government and the regional governments had reconfigured. But this shift was not extreme, and it did not occur because of the increasing importance of local politicians who were part of both national and local political networks. It happened because any change to political institutions always creates incentives that were unavailable in the past. Even though local politicians had less control over the three political machines that Suharto had used—Golkar (which later became the Golkar Party), the bureaucracy and the military—they slowly managed to establish different political networks by using one of these three machines.

Nevertheless, local politicians were more pragmatic, because they ignored ideological differences and seriously calculated political and economic gains. They were aware that they could not fight cases at the regional level because of the national importance of the issues. Therefore, they had to fight in the national political arena, and they had to seek political support from politicians operating at the epicenter of politics in Jakarta. In some cases, those local politicians offered nothing to their counterparts, because political players or businesspersons working on the national level had little choice except to work with local players. In other cases, local politicians offered national politicians political and economic incentives. For example, by networking with local politicians, a national politician might receive recognition in the form of high regional social status. Or such a politician could at least be involved in local issues important to her/him, which was beneficial considering that direct elections were being implemented throughout the country.

The local politicians in this book's case studies paint a picture of Indonesian local politics that differs from John Sidel's description of bossism in the Philippines (1999) and from Davidson's portrait of political elites in West Kalimantan (2005). In an almost similar fashion, they argue that local bossism has long been a characteristic of competition for power and economic resources. Also, they argue that these competitions in such places involved the extensive practice of money politics and, more importantly, the use of violence. In the past, for example, local elites in West Kalimantan were supported by political power in Jakarta. Since the fall of Suharto, they tended to operate only in the region without substantial political networks to connect them to powerful allies in Jakarta. Political contests in West Kalimantan after the introduction of decentralization have tended to be limited to the region. Those authors tended to downplay links between local and central government officials. Both writers focus instead on the "strong man's" capacity for violence rather than bargaining and negotiation skills as the main foundation for local politics and the pursuit of their own political and economic gains.

Decentralization and Its Incentives

This subsection accounts for institutional changes that occurred after the introduction of decentralization policies in 2000. In discussing decentralization, it would be better to evaluate the centralization trend adopted by both presidents Sukarno and Suharto. After exploring decentralization policies, this subsection evaluates the literatures that address the impact of the new regulations on central and local governmental relationships. The general scholarship on regional autonomy (or decentralization) can be divided into several categories: interpretations surrounding the birth of these policies, the possibility of Indonesia's breakup, the proliferation of regions, local elections, the emergence of local political oligarchies, ethnic conflicts, and natural resource battles. This scholarship obviously argues that the introduction of new institutions provided not only an impetus for structural changes but also local political-economic dynamics that were unimaginable in the past.

In the beginning of the post-revolutionary years under President Sukarno, there were regional rebellions triggered by various factors such as proper power distribution between the central and local government and the distribution of economic resources. Indeed, there were regional exceptions like Maluku, which wished to separate from Indonesia. The army helped Sukarno to quell these rebellions, and their coalition "led the way to the reintroduction of the presidential 1945 Constitution, which provided the institutional framework for Guided Democracy" (Crouch 1978: 33). It could be said that this event constituted the first step taken by the central government in its effort to recentralize power. By the early 1960s, the army had demonstrated its ability to impose the rule of the central government in most regions (Booth 2014: 32). Sukarno's effort to centralize his power became apparent when he and Mohammad Hatta ruled as president and vice president (Kimura 2013: 47).

When Suharto began his rule in 1967, he was most "concerned with curbing the power of regional army commanders" (Booth 2014: 33). Furthermore, he filled the country's posts of provincial governors with military men loyal to him in an attempt to ensure his political power and political stability. It would be safe to argue that the Suharto years were characterized by "an inexorable trend toward re-centralization of power" (Mackie 1980: 676). In 1974, seven years after his reign in politics stabilized, Suharto proposed to parliament Law No. 5/1974 on the Basic Principle on Administration in the Regions. This law offered a guideline for the implementation of decentralization, and it gave few concessions to the local government. Even though this law was directed at decentralization, in practice it established a hierarchical structure under which the country's regional heads were controlled by the central government. In addition, regional parliaments had little power, while many governors and district heads (*bupati*) came from the military (Booth 2014: 33). Given the nature of Suharto's authoritarian regime, "this law did not take into effect as the national government showed little, if any, political will to devolve its authority" (Baswedan 2007: 55). Practically, Suharto was in control of the regional government through the appointment of military men loyal to him in the political sphere. Other than that, the central government was also in control of budgetary resources (Mackie 1980: 677). Taking into account Suharto's ability to control regional heads and budgetary resources from the center of government, it would be difficult to argue that his government was in favor of decentralization, even though he proposed Law No. 5/1974. One of the characteristics that mark Suharto's highly centralized government can be found in the structure of the Ministry of Home Affairs, which held the power to coordinate and supervise the work of other departments. By using this powerful Ministry of Home Affairs, Suharto was able to strengthen his ability to exercise social and political control over the regions (Mackie and MacIntyre 1994: 22). The passing of Law No. 5/1974 finally concluded the unfinished centralization project begun under the Dutch by imposing a uniform vertical administrative system across the country (Vu 2010: 66). Local elections were now formally substituted by personnel arrangements made by the Ministry of Home Affairs and ultimately by Suharto.

Following the fall of Suharto's New Order on 21 May 1998, Habibie assumed the presidency of Indonesia in the midst of a deep economic crisis that provided an impetus for anti-government movements across the country. The central government under the Habibie administration introduced Law No. 22/1999 on Local Government and Law No. 25/1999 on Fiscal Balance Between the Central Government and the Regions, which offered more power to the regions to run their daily operations of government. Legally, Habibie had every right to continue his presidency until his term ended in 2003 as he fulfilled Suharto's term. However, he was forced by political elites outside the government to prepare for a political reformation, and one of them would be to change the part of the country's political foundation that regulates the relationship between the central government and local governments. Habibie adopted the policy of decentralization by enacting the two laws. This was possible only because the central government was much weaker than it had been under Suharto. The government was now committed to going forward with changing the political structure regulating the relationship between local and central government.

There were interpretations that surrounded the birth of regional autonomy: one technocratic and the other political. Authors from the World Bank presented a technocratic perspective. Hofman and Kaiser (2004) come to a conclusion that decentralization in Indonesia was "radical" in its speed and breadth. They begin their story by explaining the resentment some of the resource-rich regions harbored toward the central government, which they believed had stolen their natural resources. In addition to that, they also explain that the heavy-handed manner of the New Order regime triggered long-lasting armed conflicts in the regions, for example, in Aceh and East Timor. With the fall of centralized government under Suharto, political actors in the regions demanded power redistribution. It seems that Habibie had very little room to maneuver. He was fully aware that the MPR (Majelis Permusyawaratan Rakyat, the "people's consultative assembly", the country's highest political organization) still held the power to elect Indonesia's president—and it seems that he was—he should have approached regional political players and listened to their demands. For Habibie, "regional autonomy seemed the instrument of choice" (Hofman and Kaiser 2004: 17). The World Bank held a similar view, saying that "regional autonomy seemed the right price for obtaining their support" (World Bank 2003: 3). These scholars portray Habibie as the key player who instructed a team of bureaucrats and academics to write a new law that would accommodate the demands of the regions. Habibie's decision to adopt regional autonomy is seen as "the natural complement to the emerging democracy at the central level" (Hofman and Kaiser 2004: 17).

Smith (2008) offers a different interpretation that is more political in nature. He mentions that the main driving force behind the new administration's adoption of a decentralization policy seems to have been Habibie's willingness to listen to the advice of his team of experts. Smith (2008: 213) underscores his view:

> [Regional autonomy] became viable because the member of Team 7 took advantage of the conflicting short- and long-term interest between Habibie and the ruling party (Golkar) in (1) presenting democratic bona fides to the voters and (2) retaining the advantages that political centralization provided them, respectively.

Smith maintains that Team 7 managed to convince Habibie and the ruling party's elite of the benefit gained by supporting regional autonomy. Here, Smith claims that Habibie's support for decentralization would give him strong reformist credentials. For Habibie, it became very important political capital that he could use to compete in the upcoming election. Smith begins his story by emphasizing the importance of Reformasi (Reform), adopting the view that no consensus on the definition and meaning of Reformasi existed. Therefore, he continues, Habibie tried to define Reformasi with help from a team of experts soon to be known as Team 7. Originally, Smith continues, this team was charged with reforming Indonesia's electoral system in anticipation of the upcoming election of June 1999, but it was also tasked with drafting a comprehensive reform of the unitary system in which power would devolve to the regions.

Hofman and Kaiser, like Smith, appear to have paid little attention to the relevance of Habibie's personal motivation to remain longer as president and gain credit as a reformist during Indonesia's transitional period. It would be clear that Habibie's political efforts to promote decentralization could not be separated from his intention to accumulate credit as a strong reformist. It seems that Habibie thought his reformist image would earn him a positive image that very much reflected his efforts to make a break with the New Order. At a time of political uncertainty, any legacies from the New Order government were seen as liabilities; therefore, it is understandable that Habibie would make any effort to dissociate with the regime, even though he rose to power through Golkar, the very political machine that enabled it.

In the beginning of the decentralization period, several works argued for the possibility of the breakup of Indonesia's unitary state because of the various ongoing conflicts in many parts of the country. A collection of essays edited by Kingsbury and Aveling (2003: 4) argues:

> It did not appear, in the new millennium, that Indonesia is in imminent danger of disintegration. But, it was possible that, if Indonesia could not pull itself back from the brink very soon, it would slip into that category known as "failed state". Indonesia would exist in name and in territorial claim, but not in a functional sense.

In a similar tone, scholars in another edited book discuss various issues related to the complexity of the Indonesian nation-building process as discussed by Ruth McVey, Paul James and Ann Kumar. They assess four case studies—Aceh, Timor Leste, Papua, and South Sumatra—that they believe demonstrate the experience of long-standing friction with the central government. These cases express pessimism in terms of politics, suggesting exactly the kind of potential for political conflict that might occur in a decentralized Indonesia. Other studies share a similar pessimism in the economic domain. For example, Ray and Goodpaster (2003: 75) argue that the defects of decentralization "allowed or encouraged local government to create trade and citizenship barriers damaging to Indonesia's national interests". They explore how some regions created tax barriers to inter-regional trade, which they called a "third party contribution". They say, "this facility requires local business to provide 'voluntarily' payments to local government" (2003: 79). However, decentralization has yielded mixed results with regard to putting the country on the right track; at the same time, the country saw increased violence, decentralized corruption and vested interests at the local level (Bünte 2009: 119). Furthermore, the pessimism mentioned above did not materialize after 15 years of policy implementation. On the contrary, Mieztner (2014: 46) finds that "the Indonesian nation-state not only has survived, but is probably stronger today than at any other points in its history" because of the decentralization process. He sees the execution of the decentralization process as having a kind of taming effect on separatist movements in some regions.

There is also a literature on local elections that assesses political dynamics in various regions. At the core of decentralization policy has been direct local elections, which started in 2005. In general, scholars evaluate the democratic process at the local level by assessing direct local elections in many parts of the country. This form of direct local election is known as *pilkada* (*pemilihan kepala daerah langsung*). The legal basis for direct election is the Law on Local Government No. 34/2004 enacted by the national parliament—the Dewan Perwakilan Rakyat (DPR)—in late 2004. After local direct elections were implemented in various localities throughout the country, which happened between 2005 and 2007, scholars described the democratic consolidation that followed (Erb and Sulistiyanto 2009). The papers presented in one book offer various perspectives regarding the local elections: Mieztner on the relevance of local-level elections to keep separatist movements down; Buehler on the irrelevance of political parties; Choi, similar to Buehler, on weakened political parties in Batam city; and Subianto on the manipulation of ethnicity in West Kalimantan. Scholarship on local elections is also discussed by other scholars with reference to different regions, and draws various conclusions based on regional contexts. Numerous other studies of pilkada have been produced. For example, Mieztner (2007) argues that the gubernatorial election in West Papua and elections in Aceh demonstrated a better chance of reducing separatist demands than did special autonomy in 2001. Buehler and Tan (2007) conclude that the independence of candidates and political parties continue to attract little allegiance from voters. Choi (2009) argues that formal democratic institutions are still vulnerable to patrimonial manipulation. Choi (2011) was more cautious in her analysis of local elections in Indonesia. She claims that some post-Suharto local elections were marred by "money politics" and political intimidation, and finds that the democratization process at the local level was not an easy trajectory to follow given a very complex political process. Assessing the persistence of local democratization at the provincial level of politics, van Klinken (2009: 155) argues: "local elites are at home in their surroundings because they are patrons to many poor clients". According to him, these local elites exercise hegemony through numerous religious, political, regional and occupational organizations. Furthermore, he contends that local elites manage patronage because of the rents available in a provincial town. To some extent, van Klinken (2009) and Choi (2011) reach an almost similar conclusion, that local politics has been very important to the practice of democracy in Indonesia but at the same time has its defects.

The rising importance of local elections provides a political path for local political players to benefit from political openness. The introduction of decentralization has generated a growing body of work on the rise of local political elites in Indonesia (Sakai 2003; Aspinall and Fealy 2003; Kingsbury and Aveling 2003) and the functioning of the local government (Turner and Podger 2003). Michael Malley argues that the old political elites have reconsolidated their power despite the introduction of new political rules. He locates the reason for this phenomenon in the weakness of newly created institutions and the strength of old social forces (Malley 2003: 103). The old politico-administrative elite, he continues, managed to adapt to the new rules and consolidate their control, and the bureaucrats' political success drew attention to the weakness of political parties at the provincial level. To him, the parties appeared to lack strong candidates. In general, this body of scholarship mainly argues that Indonesia's local elites gained power due to a division of power between the central and local governments. Because those studies were done in the early years of decentralization—at that time still an understudied phenomenon —the scholars behind this literature took regional-level politics as their basic unit of analysis. As a result, they offer important accounts of the political dynamics at the regional level only; not surprisingly, they are reluctant to take into account the connection between the political center and the regions.

In a similar fashion, Hidayat (2007) argues that the rise of one regional oligarch relied on income from government contracts. He calls this oligarch Tuan Besar. His ability to tap money from government contracts in the form of project racketeering ensured his control of provincial parliament, which in turn appointed the governor and vice governor. The case of Tuan Besar in the province of Banten demonstrates that an oligarch may establish his power base by controlling economic activity. Okamoto and Hamid (2008) illustrate how a local oligarch by the name of Chasan Sochib benefited from the downfall of Suharto in deepening his political base in a newly established province. Chasan's power base initially rested on his role as *jawara* (local strongman). Democratization and decentralization provided opportunities for him to exercise his power by means of violence in order to accumulate benefit in terms of both politics and economy.

Regional proliferation or the formation of new regions is also discussed as a consequence of Indonesia's decentralization policies. The literatures on regional proliferation started to emerge as the result of the policies. Under the Suharto administration, the number of municipalities (*kota*) and districts (*kabupaten*) numbered only 292, and almost all of them remained static in structure for nearly three decades. After the decentralization policies were implemented, the number of those municipalities and districts dramatically increased, rising to 434 in 2003. Many of these increases occurred outside Java. Fitrani, Hofman and Kaiser (2005) argue that geographic dispersion, political and ethnic diversity, natural resource wealth, and the scope of bureaucratic rent-seeking influence the likelihood of regional splits. Kimura (2007) argues for the promotion of the new province of Gorontalo, whose creation in 2000 was triggered by the marginalization of the Gorontalo ethnic group. Before its creation, Gorontalo was a part of North Sulawesi province, which had a multiethnic society with a Christian majority. The formation of Gorontalo Province, according to Kimura, was relatively quick and took less than a year. The creation of Gorontalo was possible because the political transition had weakened the state and changed previous institutions, which provided a situation in which political players at both the national and local levels seek their own interests. At the core of Kimura's argument lies the alliances and cooperation that take place within and between regions and centers. Later, Kimura (2013) developed his argument that alliances and the cooperation of various political actors in both the center and the peripheral regions served as the basis for territorial changes. In pursuit of this end, he investigates two territorial splits, one between Riau in Sumatra and the Riau Archipelago, the other in Papua, which divided into two provinces. Aspinall (2013: 39) argues that the underlying motive behind creating new regions is "often to provide a slice of patronage resources for the bureaucrats, political bosses, and networks that dominate the areas" affected. Therefore, it is relevant to consider the claim by Malley (2009: 141–2) that "the process of creating new provinces and districts clearly has played a role in shifting political power from Jakarta to the regions, and in changing the distribution of power among regions".

The scholarship on communal and ethnic violence in Indonesia has increased since the fall of Suharto's New Order. These conflicts took place in many parts of the country, such as in Maluku and parts of Kalimantan (Bertrand 2004; Kingsbury and Aveling 2003; van Klinken 2007a), where regional elites are on the rise in the fields of bureaucratic, economic and identity politics (Schulte Nordholt and van Klinken 2007: 2). Bertrand (2003: 3) argues that ethnic violence in the late 1990s can be partly explained by analyzing Indonesia's national model and its institutionalization during the New Order. He maintains that the 1990s created a critical moment in Indonesia's post-independence history, during which political changes provided openings to a renegotiation of the elements of the national model, which include ethnic groups' access to and representation in the state's institutions. He underlined the relative importance of political institutions in shaping the development of ethnic identity, their use in political mobilization, and their function as a means to negotiate group claims (Bertrand 2004: 9). He further argues that conflicts involving ethnic groups as participants or victims occurred at a critical juncture in the late 1990s. These conflicts, he reports, occurred between 1996 and 1998, and involved Dayaks who fought and victimized Madurese, and Chinese Indonesians who were the target of riots. He explains these ethnic conflicts in terms of Dayak marginalization (Bertrand 2004: 49–59) and Chinese-Indonesian exclusion (Bertrand 2004: 50–70). In an almost similar fashion, van Klinken (2007a) discusses the post-authoritarian communal violence that took place in Maluku, North Maluku, Poso (Central

Sulawesi), West Kalimantan and Central Kalimantan. He argues: "we need only two factors to identify those places prone to communal violence" (van Klinken 2007a: 12). According to him, these factors are part of the process in which there exists an increased number of workers in the non-agricultural sector and a high reliance on the state to help the economy absorb these workers.

The importance of natural resources to understanding diversity in elite political behavior is elaborated in Sakai (2003), Erman (2007) and Morishita (2008). By comparing West Kalimantan, a region with rich forest resources, and East Kalimantan, a region rich in mineral resources, Morishita (2008) develops the argument that such differences in natural resources reflect the variant patterns of local-national relationships. Her important contribution can be seen in her emphasis on natural resources as an independent variable when explaining the dynamics of local politics in Kalimantan. More importantly, she argues that profits from natural resources and the structure of resource-related industries help the degree to which central government control over those resources defines the relationship between local politics and the central government. National political leaders still maintain their agenda in mineral-rich regions because they are very important to the national economy. They continue to assert their political influence through local elections. In contrast, Morishita continues, national elites have adopted different strategies in forest-rich regions. The national political elite, she claims, left control over the regions to local power holders.

The demise of Suharto's authoritarian regime provides a window of opportunity for local elites called *putra daerah* (children of the region) to accrue benefits from natural resources in their regions. In order to enjoy access to forest resources, the *putra daerah* in West Kalimantan invoke local group membership and social and ethnic identity (McCarthy 2007: 161). McCarthy underscores that this political movement, which advanced local power, should be understood in the wider context of political economy. Under the auspices of the New Order regime, he continues, local people living in various villages resented the way outside interests superseded *adat* property rights. More importantly, he continues, resource extraction took place without providing sufficient funding for local infra-structure development. In short, McCarthy argues that *putra daerah*, who felt that they did not receive a fair share of the revenue sharing of extracted natural resources, now saw opportunities to capture benefits. Decentralization gave rise to what van Klinken (2007b: 149) refers to as "sultanship". In his opinion, sultanship has perhaps become a symbol of local identity and become a part of the communitarian turn in Indonesian politics since the fall of Suharto. Van Klinken claims, "identities are being revived or invented at a great rate, especially at the district level" (2007b: 149). The revival of *adat* property rights is also argued by Tyson (2010: 2–3), who contends that in the "transitory process of decentralization, local constituencies (particularly 'traditional' villagers) are engaging in familiar political struggles that challenge the legitimacy of the state and extractive sector, focusing primarily on land tenure". He goes on to mention that the framework of decentralization provided a procedural and normative basis for the revival of *adat* (Tyson 2010: 41).

The literature discussed above underscores the enormous attention paid to decentralization policies and their influence on local political dynamics. To be sure, these works are very important for providing an understanding of the new socio-political dynamics that developed after the fall of the authoritarian regime in 1998. In this, they pay serious attention to the dynamics of local politics. This turn is also understandable because past scholarship on Indonesia generally evaluated national politics at the expense of local politics. The new scholarship obviously fills in the lacuna left by previous research. Scholars working on decentralization believe that it would be better to understand Indonesia's political dynamics by analyzing changes at the local level. They assume that the dynamics of local politics can be contained at the local level. Missing from their scholarship should be the political networks that mediated between the center and the country's localities. The works of Kimura (2007 and 2013) and, to some extent, Tyson (2010) are exceptions. Kimura's assumption of political coalitions to evaluate political dynamics at the local level could not be separated from national political competition. For him, coalitions are "defined as a group of individuals and organizations that work together toward a common objective" (Kimura 2013: 15). In his treatment of coalitions, he rarely mentions trust among different actors at three different territorial levels: national, regional and local. In this sense, his work is relatively different from the argument advanced in this book. The presence of a coalition is necessary for Kimura, as he evaluates two competing interests at play in the creation of new provinces: one group that opposes such creation, while another that works to make new provinces a reality. Only by cooperating with national-level politicians who share similar security or political agendas, the local actors see a higher probability of making a new province. In an almost similar fashion, Tyson (2010: 113) illustrates the ability of one *adat* community to build a web of supporters extending from the provincial capital

Makasar (South Sulawesi) to Jakarta and beyond. However, the type of alliance among these actors proposed by Tyson differs much from the one discussed in this book, which emphasizes the crucial importance of networks of politicians tied together by mutual trust and benefit, even while Tyson mainly emphasizes a loose web of NGOs.

The present book develops its argument around the emergence of political networks that span Indonesia's regions—not necessarily its periphery—and the center of politics in Jakarta. These political networks are very fluid but at the same time can be transformed into a solid political entity, as long as they are bonded by the shared interests of the network's actors. They can also be supported by similarities in ethnicity, ideas, geographical location or educational attainment.

Changes in the Indonesian Political Economy

Earlier studies of the Indonesian economy and politics have tried to analyze the nature of the New Order government by looking at Suharto as the center of power. There are two views that operate within the study of the Indonesian political economy. The first one expressed by various scholars asserts that the fate of the country's economy and politics heavily depended on the behavior of state officials rather than societal actors, and that the future of political initiatives rested with the state rather than society (Emmerson 1976; Jackson 1978; Robison 1986; MacIntyre 1990). While these studies provide significant insights into the New Order government, they pay little attention to the bureaucracy. They do not address questions regarding the foundation of the New Order government by specifically looking at the relevance of networks and institutions, even if to some extent a few of these studies touch on the notion of networks and institutions (as Robison and MacIntyre's did). Robison describes networks of politicians and businesspersons who controlled the Indonesian political economy, but he does not deal seriously with the notion of networks as the foundation of the Suharto government, assuming that such networks were already in place. On the other hand, MacIntyre mainly discusses institutions in the sense of organization. He refers to business associations and their capacity to influence the process of policymaking in the New Order. What is missing is a full treatment of the process of policymaking to show the relationship between the government and business sector.

The second consensus highlights the personal approach, in that scholars treat Suharto as a patron to his clients. One example of this

argument states that Suharto should be considered as a "relatively autonomous" policymaker (Liddle 1992: 800). With his autonomous power,
Suharto "has emphasized patron-clientism" (Liddle 1992: 802). While
listening to the suggestions of technocrats led by Widjojo Nitisastro on
economic matters, Suharto gave special opportunities—trade and manufacturing monopolies, credit facilities and government contracts—to
his clients. In return, those businesspersons, like those personally close
to Suharto, expressed their gratitude by contributing to the coffers of
Suharto's private foundation. This type of research sees Suharto only
as the main player in both the economy and in politics. While this is
correct, scholars take the nature of Suharto's power for granted, as if it
were not worthy of study. Liddle looks only at Suharto's networks in
Jakarta, when in fact his networks reached into the provinces and shaped
economy and politics there, as this book demonstrates.

The literature on Indonesia's transition phase offers different interpretations. Though some of the literature tries to account for the Indonesian
political economy in the post-Suharto era, the discussion is largely con-
fined to the changes experienced by the New Order state under Suharto.
This chapter considers some examples of such works, specifically by
insiders and observers of various schools of thought on the Indonesian
political economy.

Kartasasmita and Stern describe Indonesia's economy as one that
seemingly had a record of successful economic growth. They argue that
this growth

> was aided by the government's centralized decision making coupled
> with strong analytic and economic insights of the technocrats, which
> allowed political leadership to respond decisively and appropriately to
> emerging problems ... But this crisis [1997] would expose not only
> the economic frailties but also the growing weakness of a political
> regime that held unchallenged power for some 30 years (Kartasasmita
> and Stern 2015: 8).

Important to their analysis is that, over its long period in power, Suharto's
New Order regime had become captive to the demands of the very limited
number of economic elites who circled around him, including members of
his family. Those who were members of this economic elite increasingly
opposed any meaningful extension of the economic reforms already in
place. Inconsistencies in economic policies were rooted in the erosion of
political support for the measures proposed by the economic policy team.
These scholars explain that the erosion of political support resulted in

the failure to extend economic reform. It will later be clear that Suharto had full control over economic policy. They gave an example of how Suharto bypassed the regulation of a highly regulated bank. Kartasasmita and Stern (2015: 31) point out the case of Bank Duta, which was close to the president and his associates. According to them, malfeasance by some of its officers caused Bank Duta to suffer serious losses in 1990. Kartasasmita and Stern explain that the bank was rescued thanks to a confidentially arranged private inflow of capital that contravened both banking and capital market regulations. The authors believe that the needed funds were arranged by Liem Sioe Liong and Prayogo Pangestu, two leading Chinese-Indonesian businessmen, and Mohammad Hasan, a timber tycoon and close friend of the president—each of whom were rumored to have contributed US$240 million. In return, according to the writers, these tycoons gained much political power.

A different political network that centered on Suharto's family could be found in lucrative business opportunities, such as in infrastructure, mainly the toll roads that circled Jakarta. Davidson (2015: 71) details the political network that centered on Siti Hardiyanti Rukmana, Suharto's first daughter. He claims that this network controlled the development and ownership of several main toll roads in Jakarta.

Kartasasmita and Stern (2015) believe that Suharto was in fact able to maintain institutions that benefitted himself and his close allies. They discuss support of the centralist state structure, which placed the president at the center of political decision-making and in strong control of all branches of government. They mention that technocrats adopted various economic reforms in several economic areas, such as banking, capital market, currency and taxes. However, they maintain, Suharto did not allow any serious debate that might have led to changes in the constitution, which served as the foundation for political activities. In this context, therefore, it would be understandable that Suharto was reluctant to support economic reforms and protected Liem Sioe Liong, Prayogo Pangestu and Mohammad Hasan. These tycoons were core members of Suharto's network, and their interests were treated as priorities. Kartasasmita and Stern explain that the weakness of the political regime was in fact that Suharto's economic measures were adopted to protect his interests and the interests of his cronies. Suharto was only too willing to defend the interests of people close to him; or to put it in a different way: Suharto only wanted to protect those who were members of his networks.

Scholars such as Richard Robison and Vedi Hadiz offer interesting interpretations of the transition that has been occurring in Indonesia since the fall of Suharto. They explain it by saying that some politico-bureaucrats have been able to reorganize their businesses and remain powerful, thus transforming themselves into oligarchs. They explain that the New Order government operated like an incubator that nurtured oligarchs. Yet, according to them, it was Suharto who was the quintessential oligarch. Suharto and his extended family started to appear in the business scene during the 1970s when banking, finance, public utilities and infrastructure were opened to private investors. These scholars explain that the *yayasan*, the charitable private foundation set up by Suharto, played a key role in facilitating this. In the 1980s, one saw Yayasan Dharmais and Dhakab hold shares in various business entities such as Bank Duta and Nusamba. However, those oligarchs survived the fall of Suharto. According to these writers, there are two scenarios with regard to oligarchic power:

> First, significant sections of the New Order oligarchy could continue to survive on the basis of new alliances and money politics and thus reconstitute within a new, more open, and decentralized political format. Second, although oligarchy and predatory forms of power survive, old forces may be swept aside by new coalitions of political entrepreneurs and business interests, many of them regional and local. In reality, both the old and new intermingle and overlap in everyday politics in newly powerful political parties and parliaments, at both the national and local level (Robison and Hadiz 2004: 225).

Although Robison and Hadiz mention national and local politics, they tend to see them in decentralized Indonesia as separate units without any substantial linkage. They explain that politics on the local level operate like politics on the national level. Several years later, one of the writers, Hadiz, maintained his view that "local power is thus but another arena of contestation among a range of interests concerned with the forging of economic and political regimes that would govern the way wealth and power are distributed" (2010: 3). He mainly argues that entrenched local predatory interests have been able to seize the agenda of good-governance reforms and decentralization in order to maintain their social and political dominance. Though the account of politics and the economy in decentralized Indonesia as described by Robison and Hadiz (2004) is important for our understanding of Indonesia, they do not ask how political actors in the provinces have developed links with the center.

Andrew MacIntyre analyzes the Indonesian political economy by stressing the distribution of veto authority regarding economic policies. MacIntyre argues that Suharto wielded de facto veto authority within and throughout the Indonesian political system (MacIntyre 2001: 93). Although the president and parliament both held nominative veto power, in reality Suharto's party, Golkar, dominated the parliament, and therefore the parliament preferred to vote in favor of Suharto. MacIntyre argues that in this political environment no one could block Suharto's decision on a particular policy. Later on, MacIntyre states that while Indonesia's political architecture provided for an extreme concentration of decision-making power, in the past this structure helped policymakers to respond quickly to emerging problems, leading to swift and often very appropriate policy responses (MacIntyre 2003: 91). However, this same political structure also led Indonesia into a long and deep crisis; predicting policy was difficult because it depended solely on Suharto. While this interpretation offers a good account of the Indonesian political economy, it takes for granted Suharto's power; therefore, it does not adequately explain why the president defended economic policies that benefited his cronies. For MacIntyre, this happened because veto authority rested solely with Suharto. This interpretation is interesting from an institutional perspective; however, it looks at only one foundation of Suharto's power, namely Golkar. In fact, Suharto was able to concentrate power because he effectively managed the country's military and regional politics through various political networks.

Another type of political economy study should address natural resource conflicts and the emergence of illegality in the country. After decentralization policy had been implemented for about seven years, Duncan (2007) concluded that there were a number of factors determining how groups were influenced by the new policies and their implementation, including the potential of their natural resource base, their levels of political organization, and the ability of local leaders to work effectively and honestly within the new political frameworks created by regional autonomy. More importantly, Aspinall and van Klinken (2011: 22–3) proposed the argument that, after the collapse of the New Order government, "illegality by the state officials is as central to the way the state operates in Indonesia as are the formal rules and bureaucratic structures that constitute the state on its surface". These authors do not merely mention ordinary practices of illegality by state officials. They assert that illegality was able to take place as part of a set of collective, patterned, reorganized and collaborative actions linked to the competition for political power and access to state resources. They contend that understanding illegality is relevant to the view of the state as less a bureaucratic machine and more a locus of power.

Why does the Papua case not fit the argument developed in this book? It seems that local political actors on this big island preferred to fight for the establishment of a new province. The ability to create a considerable political coalition developed in Papua. The presence of political connections among elites in Papua, however, does not satisfy the qualification for political networks, as this book mentions. This political connection helped to make a new province in Papua. In the making of the new provinces, Kimura (2013: 107) suggests that "actors at the local level, particularly local elites who had clear interests in seeing provinces created, worked together with national-level actors to make new provinces a reality". The creation of new provinces in Papua could not be separated from the intra-elite conflict at the national level which was very clear under President Abdurahman Wahid, who was elected in 1999. President Wahid's approach to the ongoing problem of Papua was to find a win-win solution by allowing Papua's elites to form the Papua Presidium Council (Presidium Dewan Papua), which seemed to be opposed by security and the MPR (Bhakti, Yanuarti and Nurhasim 2009). Wahid's liberal approach met the opposition of Megawati, who was elected as president to replace Wahid in 2000. Megawati held strong views on the unitary state of Indonesia, and therefore in a bid to maintain unity of the state she proposed a provincial split in Papua with Inpres (presidential instruction) No. 1/2003. Working on the tensions fueled by Papuan nationalism, which was compounded by mass migration, economic marginalization and the brutal behavior of Indonesian security forces (Chauvel 2010: 312), some of the elites at the national level tended to agree with Megawati's proposal. Megawati's proposal fell in line with several local actors who wanted to see a new province (Kimura 2013: 122). In short, the coalition of political elites in Papua pursued control of a territory rather than significant shares of particular natural resources.

It would be worthwhile to mention that there is a multinational company in Papua by the name of Freeport Indonesia that is owned mainly by the US-based company Freeport McMoran. Like any other foreign company operating in Indonesia, Freeport is subject to divestment of its shares to Indonesian nationals as stipulated in article 24 of the Contract of Work IV signed by the company and the government in 1991. The first part of divestment seems to have been created in 1991 when Suharto was in power. Only those who had close connections with the center of power in Jakarta had access to this divestment of shares (Leith 2003: 68–76; Kartasasmita 2013). After the fall of Suharto, divestment of Freeport's share took place in 2001, but this regulation was cancelled by Government Regulation No. 20/1994, which stipulated that a foreign company can own its subsidiary shares up to 100 percent. As explained above, local elites in Papua seemed to be more interested in fighting to possess a new territory as the result of splitting the previous province into two different political units. They seem to have recognized the possibility of being elected to new political offices.

Having discussed various works on decentralization and political economy, it is necessary to link them with political networks. The existence of political networks and their importance to understanding the rise of local political actors, discussed in the previous chapter, mentions the existing political networks in Indonesia that span quite a long time, from early in Suharto's rule to his fall. This chapter discusses various works that evaluate local socio-political dynamics that were the consequences of decentralization policies as well as the democratization process. Some of the above-mentioned works offer an understanding of how socio-political dynamics at the local level take place. In addition, this chapter discusses the scholarship on political economy in a country dominated by a circle of elites surrounding Suharto when he was in power. Some argue that the political connections that existed under Suharto penetrated the local level of politics after decentralization was introduced. These works are very useful to understanding the dynamics this created, but only at the local level of politics. Empirical study, which this book is based on, finds different occurrences of the strong linkages of political actors situated at the local level to power holders at the center of the political game in Jakarta. This book now proceeds to discuss the capacity of local political actors to develop networks, as the ensuing chapters will show in great detail, by analyzing three cases that operate within the boundaries of the new post-Suharto institutional arrangements. These political networks are relatively important to local actors, because they potentially increase their political bargaining power. As these cases demonstrate, the political networks of local politicians would likely define the outcome of any dispute. Looking at the conflicts between the central and provincial governments regarding the control, extraction and ownership of regional resources, we can deal specifically with the novel pattern of politics, which from its initial stage of formation grew in relevance to provincial-level politics, especially in relation to its links with power holders in Jakarta.

CHAPTER 3

Indonesia in a Time of Transition

This chapter briefly seeks to explore the relevant discussions that aid our understanding of the nature of transition in Indonesia. Also, it analyzes the Indonesian government under Suharto by employing the concept of institutions and networks. This chapter on political context is important, because all the conflicts under study in this book took place during this moment of political change. It observes that the changes in political institutional arrangements that occurred during this transition created incentives for various political actors and operated at different levels of government.

Power Structures and Governance

It is common knowledge that the New Order lasted for three decades starting in 1966. Therefore, it is necessary to understand the political and economic foundations of the government under the New Order. There are several questions to be answered in order to comprehend this regime. Why did the New Order survive for three decades? What was the foundation of its ability to stay in power for so long? Pabottingi (1995: 225) explains: "incumbents and supporters of the New Order argue its legitimacy on two key grounds: political stability and economic development". His argument seems to be correct, in that the endless political battle in the previous government's parliamentary system and Guided Democracy, both under Sukarno, created deep political instability that made it unable to provide tranquil time to think about development and that even threatened the survival of the government. His logic is simple: that economic development could only be possible where there is political stability. In addition, the strength of the New Order was buttressed by Suharto's role as the center of political patronage among competing political actors

54

and by his ability to manage them. Crouch (2010: 5) claims that "despite internal rivalries among his supporters Suharto's authority under the New Order had been such that he was able to foster formation of more-or-less cohesive political, social and economic elite during these three decades of his rule".

Political stability under the New Order was closely connected to the central role played by the military. At the core of this political stability lay the implementation of the concept of the military's "dual function", which accorded the military two political functions—namely, security and socio-political functions. This concept, rooted in the 1950s when the political role of the military was established during the chaotic period of parliamentary democracy, was expanded during the New Order to become the country's primary socio-political institution. This dual function is closely associated with the historical role played by the military during the struggle for independence, Indonesia's most difficult political crisis, a role that proved critical to saving the nation from disintegration (Said 2001: 2–21). However, the important role of the military in Indonesian politics did not originate from its numerical strength, given that it is relatively small in comparison to the Indonesian population; instead, it developed thanks to the way it effectively penetrated the process of policymaking from the very top level of government to the lowest. Shiraishi (1999: 74–5) maintains that the Indonesian military "possesses what can be called structural power resulting from its monopoly of the state's coercive power, its institutionalized role in the political process, its domination of the Indonesian intelligence community and its reach all the way down to the village level". By his account, an estimated 14,000 military personnel held posts outside the formal military structure by the early 1990s.

With this dual function, the military had the right of representation in the National Parliament (DPR) and the People's Consultative Assembly (Majelis Permusyawaratan Rakyat or MPR). The military also held seats in the provincial and district parliaments (DPRD). Its members also doubled as appointees to civilian posts in the government, serving as cabinet ministers, ambassadors, provincial governors and district chiefs, and occupying the top ranks of the bureaucracy at various level of government. It is not surprising that Suharto used the military networks to achieve his goal; in return, the military proved to be his loyal supporter.

Outside the military, Golkar is perceived as one of the political pillars that upheld the New Order. Golkar was the formal vehicle for political networks supporting the New Order government. At the top of the party hierarchy sat Suharto, who served as its de facto decision-maker. As the chairperson of Golkar's Supervisory Council (Dewan Pembina)—which was composed of serving and retired ministers, the commander of the armed forces and other senior members of the country's ruling elite—he held the ultimate right to set policies and veto them, as well as approve and dismiss the party executive board including the party chair (Tomsa 2008: 38).

The political alliances and networks forged among the elites with the military and Golkar provided political stability for the New Order government for three decades. Political stability provided a ground for Suharto to achieve economic goals. As mentioned above, Suharto inherited a country with a chaotic economic situation. One of his main tasks was to draw a map of the country's economic development. In order to develop the economy, Suharto depended upon technocrats from the Faculty of Economics, University of Indonesia, led by Widjojo Nitisastro. There were other technocrats who worked under the president, including Emil Salim, M. Sadli and Ali Wardhana. However, Suharto trusted Widjojo to formulate economic development of the country, especially in the beginning of his rule up until the early 1990s. Suharto knew Widjojo and other economists from the University of Indonesia and the Staff and Command School of the Army (Seskoad) in Bandung, which was headed by Colonel Suwarto in the middle of 1960s (Sadli 1993: 39). After working for more than ten years, the Indonesian economy improved. Indonesia's economy under the New Order had performed well thanks to the oil bonanza that gave the country an average annual rate of economic growth of more than 7 percent from 1968 to 1981; a per capita gross national product of 4.3 percent a year; and a reduction in poverty from 60 percent in the 1970s to around 15 percent in the 1990s (Schwartz 2000: 57–8).

Up to this point, it is safe to say that Suharto could fully manage the decision-making process, which also means that he had ample room to create institutions based on his wishes. In doing so, Suharto depended on political support from the military and Golkar, and to some extent the technocrats. Power in the New Order government was solely in the hands of Suharto; only he had the power of veto in deciding policy.

The New Order State Reconsidered: Institutions and Networks

The political economy of the New Order government can be understood from the perspectives of institutions and networks, because Suharto played a crucial role in shaping them. Both of them were outcomes of the enormous power he wielded through three channels: Golkar, the bureaucracy and the military. Through these channels, Suharto could—and did—set the parameters of behavior for the members of his networks.

Under the New Order government, Suharto constructed institutions through his power as the president as well as through his ability to control Golkar and the military. His ability to exert power over Golkar and the military were a major battle for Suharto if he wanted to forge institutions that would accommodate or promote his interests both economically and politically.

Golkar has long received support from the military. The connection between these two could be traced back into the late 1950s when the military backed the idea of its members having parliamentary representation. The military even welcomed Sukarno's decision in 1960 to grant functional group seats in the DPR-GR on the basis of article 2 of the 1945 Constitution, which refers to *golongan-golongan* (groups) and their representation in the People's Consultative Assembly or MPR (Nishihara 1971: 17). Their purpose at the time was to prevent the spread of support for the PKI (Indonesian Communist Party). It first initiated and controlled the anti-PKI labor movement through SOKSI (the All Indonesian Organization of Socialist Functionaries). Over the years, the connection between the military and Golkar grew closer. In 1966, in his capacity as first minister of defense and security, Suharto ordered the commander of the army, navy, air force and national police to provide maximum facilities for the development of the joint secretariat of Golkar (Sekber-Golkar) at national and regional levels. This political measure was important to Golkar, "so that its sense of mission could be achieved. Suharto also emphasized that Sekber-Golkar should always be accepted as the real brother of the Armed Forces" (Rasyid 1994: 165).

In the years that followed, Suharto's control over Golkar became more apparent. In 1978, at the National Congress (Munas) in Bali, Suharto decided to create and legitimize the existence of the Supervisory Council (Dewan Pembina) and to chair this powerful body within Golkar. This power was expanded in 1983, when the Munas decided to give full authority to the chief of the Dewan Pembina to freeze or dispose of any member of Golkar's central executive board. In his capacity as Dewan Pembina's chief, Suharto was given the right to appoint members of Golkar's central executive board as well as to suspend them. It is no surprise that DPR members from Golkar all fell under the control of Suharto.

Since the early life of the New Order, the military was under Suharto's control. On 1 October 1965, Suharto took effective command of the army. As the most senior officer in Jakarta and with direct control of troops, he asserted his authority. The other generals with whom he had a personal connection accepted his authority. Then he used this authority to appoint the members of the general staff. By the beginning of November 1965, the army's general staff consisted almost entirely of officers handpicked by Suharto (Crouch 1978: 229). In the periods that followed, Suharto expanded the role of the military by filling civilian posts with military personnel. Clear examples of this tendency include such posts as the governorships of various provinces, mayoral posts throughout the country, and seats in parliament. Some of the ministerial positions in the New Order government were also filled by the military. For example, in the 27-member cabinet appointed by Suharto in July 1966, six ministers were drawn from the army and another six, including the service commanders, were drawn from the other branches of the armed forces (Crouch 1978: 241).

In the early 1990s, Suharto still controlled the civilian bureaucracy by inserting military personnel. It has been estimated that, during this period, some 14,000 military personnel continued to hold posts outside the formal military structure (Shiraishi 1999: 73–86).[1]

Suharto appointed some members of the armed forces to the DPR and the MPR. From 1971 to 1992, Suharto appointed 100 military men to serve as members of parliament, whose membership totaled 460. In 1997 Suharto reduced that number to 75 out of 500. Suharto controlled the dynamics of the national parliament through his direct appointments of armed forces members, not to mention through Golkar.

With his control over Golkar, the military and the parliament, Suharto could easily engineer the drafting of policies. This book looks at several institutions that were designed to serve Suharto both in politics and the economy. Examples of these institutions include Law No. 3/1973 on Politics, Law No. 5/1974 on Regional Government, Law No. 8/1971 on Pertamina and Law No. 11/1967 on Mining. These examples are important because they offer a picture of how institutions in Indonesia were created and maintained. Equally important, these institutions were designed to conform to Suharto's rules.

---

[1] Another scholar, Ryaas Rasyid, reported that by January 1992 about 6,745 active and 7,855 retired military personnel occupied non-military jobs in the government at the national and regional levels (1994: 109).

Table 1. Number of military members who occupied non-military posts

No	Title	Number (%)	Number (%)
	Central Government	1977	1980
1	Ministers, chair of state agencies	17 (42.5%)	19 (47.5%)
2	Secretary General	14 (73.6%)	14 (73.6%)
3	Inspector General	18 (29.5%)	18 (29.5%)
4	Director General	15 (78.9%)	15 (78.9%)
5	Chair of non-ministerial state agencies	8 (44.4%)	8 (44.4%)
6	Secretary of Ministers, Assistant Ministers	21 (84%)	21 (84%)
	Total	76 (53.5%)	76 (53.5%)
	Chief of Regional Governments		
7	Governor	19 (70.3%)	19 (70.3%)
8	Regents/District Chief	136 (56.4%)	137 (56.6%)
9	Mayor	19 (31.6%)	20 (33.3%)

Source: Appendix 5 in Nugroho Notosusanto, ed., *Pejuang dan Prajurit: Konsepsi dan Implementasi Dwifungsi ABRI* (Jakarta: Pustaka Sinar Harapan, 1985).

These institutions formed the backbone of Suharto's control of regional politics and economy. Here, politics and economics were very difficult to separate because they were so deeply interrelated.

Table 2. Pillars of the New Order government and their impact on central-regional relations

Institutions	Issues	Ties for Creating Network
3/1973	Political parties (3 parties)	Golkar, dominant
5/1974	Local administration (appointment)	Bureaucracies, military, Golkar
11/1967	Mining (larger share for central government)	Golkar, military
8/1971	Pertamina (share revenue for central government)	Golkar and military in the regions

Source: Author's field research.

Through Law No. 3/1975, Suharto simplified the political life of the country by allowing only three political parties to compete in every election: Golkar, PPP (the United Development Party, an Islamic-oriented Party), and PDI (the Democratic Party of Indonesia). Even though Suharto had passed this law in 1975, he had already grown preoccupied with the idea of streamlining political parties as early as 1971. At that time, Indonesia had about 20 political parties, most of which originated in the Sukarno government. When Suharto delivered a speech during the induction of new DPR members on 28 October 1971, he suggested that DPR party groupings should become the basis for future party simplifications (Rasyid 1994: 166). Suharto invited the political parties[2] to the presidential palace, where he explained his proposal to simplify the number of political party factions in the DPR from ten to three plus a faction from the military. He already expressed his opinion that in the next election (1977) only three political parties would compete: Golkar, PPP and PDI. In January 1973, Islamic oriented parties like PPP and nationalist secular parties like PDI were founded. It was clear from this episode that Suharto had imposed his rule over the other political leaders of the country. Indeed, he could adopt this decisive political measure precisely because of his position as the leader of the state supported by both the military and Golkar. After overhauling and streamlining the political parties, Suharto's government achieved its goal of controlling the political life of the country. This further underlined the superiority of the government over political society. In practice, Golkar benefited from the situation because it was part of the government.

Law No. 5/1975 on Local Administration should be contextualized in the broader context of the central-regional governmental relationship under the New Order regime. These relations go back to the beginning of the 1970s, when the Suharto government tried to exert political control over the regions. In this new institutional arrangement, Suharto gave the minister of home affairs the authority to manage the fiscal matters of the region. In 1974, under the Ministry of Home Affairs, Suharto established an office called the Inspectorate General for Development (Irjenbang), with the goal of controlling the implementation of the five-year plan in the local level. This office was particularly important because the central government provided routine subsidies in the form of grants to the regional governments, which covered wages and salaries and other running expenses (Booth 1989: 191). These subsidies comprised various Inpres programs. These subsidies were made possible because the regional government received only a small income, and because many of

---

[2] Suharto invited the secular-nationalist PNI, as well as IPKI (League of Supporters of Indonesian Independence), Murba, the Catholic Party and the Christian Party. The Islamic-oriented parties were the NU (Nahdlatul Ulama), Parmusi, PSII (Islamic Union Party of Indonesia) and Perti. Then, of course, there was Golkar.

the lucrative tax items went to the central government. As an outcome of this policy, many of the provincial governments depended on grants from the central government: 75 percent of their routine revenues and 78 percent of their development revenues came from the central government, such as in 1983 and 1984 (Devas 1989: 22). In short, the central government's control over sources of income created absolute dependency among regional governments.

On the political front, Law No. 5/1974 marks another milestone in Suharto's growing ability to consolidate power. Even though the law ostensibly addressed local administration, in reality the central government under Suharto assumed almost all initiatives in development programs, from design and implementation. To make the situation clear, Suharto formulated an extremely conservative interpretation of decentralization, as it was not in his interest to give up his power to regional politicians. Indeed, he planned to control all the governors in order to secure his policies, thus guaranteeing that his economic goals would not face resistance from people in the regions. The president was forced to diminish the involvement of regional politicians in political and economic affairs. Even though Law No. 5/1974 stipulated that gubernatorial candidates, municipal mayors (*walikotamadya*) and district heads (*bupati*) were elected by the local assemblies (DPRD), they were appointed by and responsible to the president at the final stage of decision-making (Rasyid 1994: 122). With this, Suharto minimized the initiative and creativity of regional government officials. After all, Suharto measured their performance in terms of how closely they could follow the directions given by the central government.

Law No. 11/1967 on Basic Mining was also important to the Suharto government's efforts to attract foreign investments. The relevance of this law to creating a hospitable environment for foreign investors was located in the institution of Law No. 8/1971. Suharto's government enacted these laws in response to the demand of foreign investors operating in the mining sectors. These laws were drafted with the single intention of abolishing the previous ones, Law No. 78/1958 on Foreign Investment and Regulation No. 37/1960 on Basic Mining, which were considered inhospitable to foreign investors.

The effort by the international financial community and foreign investors to pressure Indonesia to relax its investment climate relates to the making of Law No. 11/1967 on Basic Mining. Under the Sukarno government, foreign investors experienced difficulties caused by policies begun in 1957 when the nationalization of foreign firms commenced

(Crouch 1978). This policy disconnected Indonesia from the international economy. As a result, trade and investments were in decline. By 1965 the government was unable to service its debt of some US$2.5 billion, while the central bank was unable to honor letters of credit. In 1966, debt repayments were estimated to total about US$530 million, exceeding the projected official foreign-exchange earning of US$430 million (Hill 1996: 65). Suharto was also aware that his only option for realizing this pressing goal was constrained by who or what controlled investment resources and production units, and what instruments policymakers had at their disposal to gain access to these resources (Winters 1996: 63). Guided by technocrats trained in US universities—mainly the University of California, Berkeley—Suharto prepared to attract foreign investors. At that time they were targeting US investors, so they sought to establish a close and supportive relationship with international donors, mainly those from the International Monetary Fund (IMF). Both parties then sought a constructive new engagement. One of the technocrats vividly remembers this personal relationship:

> The relationship with the IMF and the World Bank had been friendly from the beginning in 1967 ... The relationship between the IMF and World Bank at one hand, and the "economic technocrats" on the other hand, was also based on a sympathetic understanding and trust between the Widjojo group at the Indonesia end, and personalities such as Bernie Bell (World Bank) at the other ... There was something unique in the chemistry between different personalities in the game that is difficult to explain and rationalize ... These remarkable relations with the Bank and Fund remain even today (Sadli 1989: 6–7, quoted in Hill 1996: 79).

After having secured international support, Suharto prepared an "Indonesian investment conference" to be held in Geneva in November 1967. The chairperson of the foreign investment team, M. Sadli, played a key figure thanks to his ability to explain the tenets of the foreign investment law to some of the leading American mining companies.[3] At that time, Suharto and his team of technocrats were desperate to win new investment, and they were willing to receive anything in return. A US company

---

[3] Attendees at the conference were Shell Oil, Standard Oil of California, US Steel, International Nickel of Canada, Bechtel Indonesia, Union Carbide, Freeport Sulphur and Alcoa (Winters 1996: 68).

named Freeport Sulphur, the predecessor of today's mining giant Freeport McMoran Copper and Gold, became the first foreign company to sign a contract with the Suharto government. Ali Budiardjo, who was the secretary general of defense, director general of national development, and assistant to Prime Minister Djuanda under Sukarno, engaged with Freeport to assist with the contract negotiation.

The central government under Suharto signed an agreement with Freeport in Jakarta. This agreement intentionally excluded the region of Papua from involvement. Consequently, the income from mining operations was split between Jakarta and Freeport based on contract production sharing (CPS). At the initial stage of investment in the late 1960s, Freeport was willing to invest US$1.226 billion. In return for this investment, Jakarta fulfilled the needs of Freeport: it awarded the company a highly favorable contract, the riches of Ertsberg, and the Indonesian military to protect them (Leith 2003: 14). In 1993, when Freeport had to divest, its shares went to Suharto, through the Nusamba foundation chaired by M. Hasan (Leith 2003: 74–5).

Looking at these events, it is clear that Law No. 11/1967 was the by-product of the politics and economy of the times. In tackling the problems of Indonesia's economy, Suharto apparently wanted only to gain the confidence of the international finance community. In order to achieve that goal, he was willing to protect their investments for 30 years, that is, the life of contract, even though at that time there was no clear indication that Suharto would run the government for such a long period of time.

Law No. 8/1971 on Pertamina was also the product of the Suharto government's dealings with foreign investors, this time in the oil sector. This relationship has had a long story that can be traced back to the days of the Dutch colonial government. Law No. 8/1971 was a continuation of previous regulation, though within this particular law the Suharto government wanted to have more room to control the contract. By using Ibnu Sutowo, the former minister of mines under Sukarno and the director of Pertamina, President Suharto tried to accomplish this goal. In concrete terms, he wanted changes made to the scheme for sharing income between the central government and foreign investors, from that of contract of work (CoW) to that of contract production sharing (CPS). Ibnu Sutowo faced this matter when he was struck by the friction between the government and the three largest foreign investors in the oil sectors—Shell, Stanvac, and Caltex—friction that in his view had resulted in losses for both sides. Ibnu found difficulty in implementing his envisioned

CPS scheme for two reasons. First, the minister of mines at that time, Bratanata, preferred to sign a contract with foreign investors that relied on the old CoW scheme. Second, the foreign investors, mainly the big ones like Shell, Stanvac and Caltex, also preferred to work on the basis of a CoW because it gave them more room to manage the operation of oil companies and, most importantly, earn more profit.

On 19 January 1967 Suharto, in his capacity as chairperson of the Presidium Cabinet, managed to place Ibnu in a good position to control oil operations. It started when Suharto instructed Minister Bratanata to approve the CPS scheme. Suharto gave instructions to separate the directorate general of Migas (Directorate General of Oil and Gas) from the Ministry of Mines (later Ministry of Energy and Mineral Resources), and to place the oil and gas agency directly under the Presidium Cabinet. Then, on 11 October 1967, Suharto replaced Bratanata with Sumantri Brodjonegoro, a chemical engineer and professor in the University of Indonesia. In July 1968, Suharto allowed Sumantri to merge Permina and Pertamin to become Pertamina (Perusahaan Negara Pertambangan Minyak dan Gas Bumi Nasional, or the State Oil and Natural Gas Mining Company). On 28 August 1968, a decree was enacted that put the merger into effect. Suharto designated a new board of directors and appointed Ibnu Sutowo as president-director.

In 1971 Suharto proposed a new law, and he directed the minister of mines to prepare a draft. On 1 January 1971 the Pertamina Law (Law No. 8/1971) was enacted. This law established a new company— Pertamina—in place of P.N. Pertamina. Suharto retained ultimate authority, and the Government Council of Commissioners reported to him. The president had the power to appoint and discharge council members (Bartlett III 1972: 325). In 1971 the central government, with Pertamina as its representative, and Caltex signed the CPS. With power in the hands of the central government, it was clear that the provinces got nothing from this contract. The income was split between the central government and Caltex only, leaving Riau with no share of the income.

From the examination of four different laws in whose making Suharto was deeply involved, it is clear that power was very important to the making of new institutions. Through his power, Suharto created new institutions in place of the old ones. No other politician of the region was able to challenge the president openly. Such dependency of regional politicians was an outcome of Law No. 5/1974 giving Suharto the power to appoint and dismiss local officials.

The combination of institutional arrangements and political networks served as Suharto's power base. Having controlled these elements, Suharto was able to determine the political careers of regional politicians and to intervene decisively in the economic affairs of the region.

Instituting New Regulations

The collapse of Suharto in 1998 provided a fertile ground for relaxing the political institutions that govern politics. After Suharto had gone from the political scene, the demand to replace political institutions with new ones that accommodated the voice of the people grew stronger. In addition, there was also a demand to abolish the centralistic system of politics. These two demands would be completed with the introduction of two policies in this country: new political institutions and decentralization. The introduction of new political institutions eased the way for new political parties to begin competing in elections. The change in political regulation by way of Law No. 2/1999 on Elections boosted the number of political parties in the country. A total of 48 political parties qualified for the June parliamentary elections. All parties agreed to democratic political processes and to follow the rules of the game drafted under the presidency of Habibie, Suharto's successor. The parties divided into two blocks. The first block, the opposition, was secular-nationalist, which consisted of Golkar, the incumbent, and PDI-P (Indonesian Democratic Party-Struggle, a continuation of PDI except that Megawati was chairperson). The bond in this group lay in the separation between religion and government. It also emphasized ethnic and religious diversity. Megawati Sukarnoputri represented PDI-P, and she was popular among the poor, both urban and rural. Habibie represented Golkar, which had lost many of its members. Under Habibie, Golkar tried hard to convince the population at large that the party had changed, having democratized its structure and discarded its connection to Suharto; they tried hard to project the image of a party willing to reform. Habibie's effort gained some success, in that some modernist Muslims in Java and some of the population outside Java supported his party.

The second bloc was a Muslim bloc that consisted of 18 political parties, each of which identified itself as Islamic. These parties had different political stands vis-à-vis the relationship between religion and government. However, the largest Islamic parties—such as PAN (the National Mandate Party, a party for modernist Muslims) led by Amien

Rais—proposed agendas of social justice. PAN was strongly connected to the Islamic modernist organization Muhammadiyah. Another Islamic party, the National Awakening Party (PKB, a party for traditionalist Muslims) led by Abdurahman Wahid, enjoyed strong traditional Muslim support mainly in Java, and proposed a similar agenda of reform, calling for the eradication of corruption, collusion and cronyism (abbreviated in Bahasa Indonesia as "KKN").

The result of the June 1999 election pointed out that Megawati and her party PDI-P gained the most votes compared to other parties, and thus Megawati naturally was seen as the one who would replace Habibie as president. However, her votes, which totaled around 30 percent, were not enough to win the majority in the parliament. Naturally, it seemed that she should seek a partner and form a coalition—but with whom could she make it? This was a difficult question. She could not align with Golkar, because PDI-P was established primarily to challenge Golkar. She could not forge a coalition with the Islamic parties, because promoting her as a presidential candidate would be anathema to them. She could not even forge a coalition with Abdurahman Wahid, her close friend. Analyzing this difficulty, Amien Rais cleverly proposed the establishment of a political group named "Central Axis", comprised of Islamic parties, and promoted Abdurahman Wahid as the alternative presidential candidate to both Habibie and Megawati. Golkar and Central Axis reached an agreement that promoted Wahid as presidential candidate, after Golkar rejected the nomination of Habibie. The MPR elected Wahid president. Before that, Amien Rais was elected as the chairperson of MPR and Akbar Tanjung as the chairperson of DPR. Considering that it was impossible to ignore Megawati, as her party gained most of the votes in the election, she was appointed vice president.

This short discussion of the transfer of political leadership suggests two conclusions. First, the election results revealed that only seven political parties would have a role in the national parliament (see table 1). With this change, state building also took a different trajectory from that followed under Suharto. There was no single party with a dominant voice in the national parliament. With seven political parties competing to gain votes, it would be very difficult to garner a majority vote in the parliament. A coalition was thus the only feasible choice for any president seeking to create a stable government. Second, the process of policymaking in the coalition government has taken a different route from that of Suharto. There was no single person that held a veto like Suharto did and no political party that held majority power like Golkar did. There were now two agencies that held veto power: the president and the parliament (backed by political parties). Considering this fact, the process of policy-making became much more difficult, time consuming, and in need of political solutions.

Table 3. Indonesian parliamentary election, 7 June 1999

Party	Key Figures	Seats Won in DPR	Percentage Shares in DPR
Indonesian Democratic Party of Struggle (PDI-P)	Megawati	153	30.1
Golkar	B.J. Habibie	120	24
National Awakening Party (PKB)	Abdurahman Wahid	51	10
United Development Party (PPP)	Hamzah Haz	39	7.8
National Mandate Party (PAN) and Justice Party Coalition	Amien Rais	41	8
Army-Police	Wiranto	38	7.8

Sources: National Election Committee (Komisi Pemilihan Umum).

The decision-making process under Abdurahman Wahid might be a good example of ineffectiveness in the making of economic policy. Wahid's decision to form a "government of the whole" was reflected in the fragmentation of economic decision-making authority within the cabinet between a number of competing ministers and an outside advisor, culminating in the embarrassing suspension of IMF support in late March 2000 (Haggard 2000: 124).

The idea for political restructuring to reformulate central and local government relations can be traced back to March 1998, when President Suharto created the Coordinating Ministry for Development Supervision and Administrative Reform as part of an endeavor to recognize the emerging demand for reform. He appointed Hartarto to fill the post. Hartarto was not a new face to Suharto, as he had served as the minister of industry in the past. But Suharto trusted him. Soon after being appointed, Hartarto engaged the senior staff in his office to discuss decentralization. After this discussion, he ordered his staff to prepare a draft of a revision of Law No. 5/1974 (Turner and Podger 2003: 12). The regions, after learning that the central government had started to weaken, demanded decentralization. The dissatisfaction of the regions found momentum when some of the resource-rich provinces such as Riau, Aceh and East Kalimantan appealed for a fair distribution of revenues (Tadjoeddin, Suharyo and Mishra 2001). Hartarto was instrumental in dealing with the demand from the regions. When Habibie took over the presidency, he retained Hartarto as coordinating minister for development supervision and administrative reform.

President Habibie also appointed Syarwan Hamid, a reform-minded military man, to serve as the minister of home affairs. Syarwan's role was important in persuading Suharto to step down as president. On 18 May 1998, in his political position as one of the chairpersons of the MPR—the highest political body under Suharto's government—Syarwan suggested Suharto resign. Habibie recognized Syarwan's role in pushing the president to step down. As the new president, Habibie did not hesitate to give Syarwan the important duty of managing domestic political affairs. Equally important, Habibie and Syarwan were connected to ICMI (Ikatan Cendekiawan Muslim Indonesia or the Association of Indonesian Muslim Intellectuals). Syarwan was among the generals who had very close relations with the association.

Syarwan Hamid was the person in charge of changing the entire political system in the Habibie government. In his first six months, Habibie confronted formidable obstacles since he inherited the presidency from Suharto, and he had been portrayed as Suharto's best student. Habibie had longstanding relations with Suharto, and in fact his political emergence is associated with the Council for the Study and Implementation of Technology (Badan Pengkajian dan Penerapan Teknologi, BPPT). In order to convince people that he could break with the past, Habibie embarked on a plan to change political laws and the laws on local administration.

In order to meet the demand for revising political regulations, on 1 July 1998 Syarwan Hamid appointed Ryaas Rasyid, a professor in the government's Institute of the Science of Government (Institut Ilmu Pemerintahan, IIP), as Director General for General Governance and Regional Autonomy. The role of Ryaas could be located in the political context of 1995, when Suharto ordered the Indonesian Institute of Science (LIPI) to conduct a study of the electoral system. One year later, LIPI produced a report that was submitted to Suharto. The report suggested some drastic changes for the elections in 1997, because it found

Indonesia in a Time of Transition

three distortions in the conduct of past elections. First, the government was too dominant, as reflected in the structure of the election committee. Second, elections would not be undertaken fairly because of the bias on the part of the election committee in favor for Golkar. Golkar's six wins in a row were very difficult to dissociate from the complicity of the government bureaucracy in mobilizing voters and in acting as an electoral political machine for the one in power. Government officials at various levels served as election officials and Golkar functionaries at the same time. Third, non-governmental political parties with any aspirations different from that of the New Order were suspected of disloyalty (Haris et al. 1998). Suharto's government rejected this finding. The election of 1997 was conducted in a manner similar to the past, and Golkar won the election. However, in May 1998, confronting the demand for change in the middle of an economic crisis, Minister of Home Affairs Hartono appointed a team of experts led by Ryaas Raysid to propose changes in the laws and regulations governing the elections (King 2003: 47; Turner and Podger 2003: 13). It is said that in the middle of the crisis and prompted by popular opposition, Ryaas in his capacity as professor of IIP under the Ministry of Home Affairs approached Minister Hartono to propose changes in the election laws that would bring about democracy, accountability to the people and efficient management (Turner and Podger 2003: 13). In the weeks before Suharto's resignation, Hartono issued a ministerial decree calling for the formation of a team to prepare three political laws.

The newly established government under Habibie considered the existence of Ryaas's team as relevant to its efforts to convince people that the new government was different from that of Suharto. Faced with the pressing issue of making the new government look good and democratic, Syarwan Hamid appointed Ryaas Raysid as the director general of general government and regional autonomy. With his new position, Ryaas received an order from Syarwan not only to rewrite the laws that govern elections but also Law No. 5/1974, in addition to drafting a law on fiscal balance. Ryaas established a team[4] that he tasked with writing the law on regional autonomy that would replace the old one, Law No. 5/1974. Smith (2008) draws a similar conclusion to this study, saying that the team was crucial to pushing forward decentralization policies.

---

[4] The members were Ryaas Rasyid (chief), Afan Gafar, Andi Mallarangeng, Ramlan Surbakti, Anas Urbaningrum, Luthfi Mutty, Koswara, Djohermansyah Djohan and Rapiuddin Hamarung.

Ryaas Rasyid, as the architect of the regional autonomy law, had the idea of writing a new law on regional autonomy. The basic feature of the draft was the extension of political authority and administrative authority to the autonomous regions—in this case, the provinces and the districts or regencies. It meant that people in the regions were given the right to elect their political leaders. Other than that, Ryaas planned to give the regions more political authority to write and control their own policies.[5]

When the draft of the decentralization regulation was debated in the DPR, Ryaas Rasyid had already expressed his vision of decentralization. As early as February 1999, Ryaas disclosed that the central government under Habibie recognized the long frustration of the resources-rich provinces over receiving a fair share of the income earned from their natural resources. At the same time, Ryaas understood that poor provinces still needed the help of the central government. Therefore, a fair distribution of income seemed to be the first concern for the director general.[6] Another concern was the appointment of governors and mayors elected by the regional parliaments (DPRD) at the provincial and district levels. Regarding income distribution, Ryaas had not found a formula at that time; however, he assured the regional governments that they could manage their own resources as long as they were in accord with existing law. In order to prevent a separatist movement, Ryaas proposed the implementation of more autonomy at the district or municipal level.[7]

In May 1999, when a draft of the decentralization law was passed by the DPR, Ryaas fulfilled his promise to change the structure of governance in Indonesia. Law No. 22/1999 on Regional Autonomy states that the country's district chiefs were responsible not to the provincial governor but to the district-level DPRD. Likewise, governors would be elected by provincial DPRD. That said, the central government still wanted the keep the governor functioning as a representative of the central government in order to coordinate matters they deemed too difficult for districts to properly handle, such as the coordination of roads connecting the country's many districts.[8]

---

[5] See book by Djohermansyah Djohan 2003: 8.

[6] Ryaas Rasyid, interview; see "Soal otonomi daerah, kita realistislah ...", *Tempo*, 1 Feb. 1999, p. 64.

[7] Ryaas Rasyid, interview; see "Kalau mereka tak sanggup diganti saja", *Media Transparansi*, Mar. 1999.

[8] "Masih ada kuasa pusat", *Tempo*, 3 May 1999, p. 34.

Indonesia in a Time of Transition

While planning to write the new law on regional autonomy, Syarwan Hamid was also asked by president Habibie to prepare for an election that would be held in the middle of 1999. Again, Syarwan relied on Ryaas Rasyid to prepare laws that would govern these elections. To do the job, Ryaas established a team of seven members, named the "Team of Seven", all of the members academics from various universities, such as Ryaas Raysid (Institute of Science of Government, IIP); Ramlan Surbakti (University of Airlangga); Andi Mallarangeng (University of Hasanudin); Djohermansyah Johan (IIP); Lutfi Mutty (IIP); Anas Urbaningrum (Muslim Student Association); and Affan Gafar (University of Gadjah Mada). Four members graduated with PhD degrees from American universities, namely Ryaas Rasyid (Hawai'i), Ramlan Surbakti (Northern Illinois), Andi Malarangeng (Northern Illinois) and Affan Gaffar (Ohio State). Thus, they had the credentials necessary to write such laws. Their shared backgrounds and lines of thought made it easy for them to convey their ideas on paper. Due to their education, all the Team of Seven were preoccupied with idea of a democratic Indonesia—Ryaas, for example, wrote his dissertation about the prospect of democracy in Indonesia. The other members, except Anas, kept in close contact with Ryaas in the IIP. Within this context, then, Ryaas was in a good position to lead the team. As mentioned earlier, the people from LIPI had already identified the distortion of existing laws and practices that favored Golkar. Therefore, Ryaas was confronted with the task of eradicating those distortions and preparing laws that effectively govern fair and more democratic elections.

However, Syarwan Hamid had already set the parameters for the new laws, which he had done in response to the findings of the LIPI team. Syarwan proposed three distinct ideas. First, non-partisan or independent persons should be appointed to an election committee (KPU) that would work on behalf of the Ministry of Home Affairs.[9] In this context, the role played by the Ministry of Home Affairs was merely that of a secretariat. Second, a team established to select political parties, which would be eligible to compete in the 1999 elections, was established. This would be a very difficult task because about 140 parties had been established since May 1998 to compete in the elections, although not all of these parties were yet eligible to participate. This independent team

---

[9] Interview with Syarwan Hamid; see "Seharusnya partai sudah punya calon presiden", *Forum Keadilan*, 22 Mar. 1999, p. 77.

included eleven members: Nurcholish Madjid (noted Muslim scholar), Adnan Buyung Nasution (lawyer), Miriam Budiardjo (senior political scientist, University of Indonesia), Kastorius Sinaga (sociologist, University of Indonesia), Adi Andojo (former judge), Andi Mallarangeng (political scientist, University of Hasanuddin), Mulyana W. Kusumah (NGO for election watchdog), Affan Gafar (political scientist, University of Gadjah Mada), Eep S. Fatah (political scientist, University of Indonesia), Anas Urbaningrum (HMI, Muslim Student Organization) and Rama Pratama (student activist from University of Indonesia). Syarwan tried to be credible by appointing personalities such as Nurcholish Madjid, Adnan Buyung and Miriam Budiardjo. Rama and Anas were crucial in accommodating the student activists that propelled demonstrations all over the country. It was clear that none of those members were from the political parties.[10] Third, Syarwan also proposed a reduction in the number of military personnel in the DPR/MPR to only 38 (from that of 75 under Suharto). He also proposed the neutrality of the civil service.[11]

When the draft enacted by the DPR became the country's election law, Syarwan Hamid relaxed the rules on the establishment of political parties. With Law No. 3/1999, a political party could be created with a minimum of 50 members. The number of political parties mushroomed. It was very dramatic change since the New Order only allowed three political parties to exist.

With the changes in the regulation of political parties, many began to compete for offices at central and regional levels. About 48 parties competed in the 1999 elections, though only five political parties dominated the scene: they were PDI-P; Golkar; PPP; PAN (National Mandate Party); and PKB (the National Awakening Party).

Up to this point, it was clear that the Habibie government was only able to change three of the four regulations that governed the central and regional relationship under Suharto. Law No. 22/1999 and Law No. 25/1999 replaced the previous Law No. 5/1974. Governance in Indonesia dramatically changed as the center handed more function and power to regional-level government. Law No. 3/1999 altered the political landscape by allowing many political parties to compete for power. However, Law No. 11/1967 on Mining was still in place. Even though Law No. 8/1971 on Pertamina had been changed, it changed only the company's status,

---

[10] "Sebelas tokoh menguak parpol", *Forum Keadilan*, 8 Feb. 1999, p. 89.
[11] Interview with Syarwan Hamid; see "Kalau Presiden enggak mau, mati saya", *Forum Keadilan*, 8 Feb. 1999, p. 90.

from a state-owned company into an ordinary one. Law No. 22/2001 on Oil and Gas mentioned that Pertamina still retained its right to deal with foreign investors through the contract production sharing during the transition process.

The Nature of Decentralization

Decentralization policy, initiated by the Law No. 22/1999, drastically changed the political architecture of Indonesia. This particular policy was designed to change Indonesia from a centralized government to a decentralized one. The process of decentralization, which had been designed in a good manner, in fact could not be implemented as planned because of the transfer of power at the national level, which had happened in such a short time (World Bank 2003). With this quick transfer of power, the process of decentralization would not go smoothly.

One of the reasons for the country to adopt a decentralization policy was likely political pressure from resource-rich provinces such as Riau and East Kalimantan to gain a greater share of revenue from their natural resources. Local politicians in these provinces saw an opportunity to voice their demand once the national government's ability to control their resources weakened. The resignation of Suharto in 1998 was followed by a serious breakdown of central and local relationships. President Habibie, Suharto's successor, was keen to hear the voices from the region.

Despite several attempts to address the issue of decentralization, Law No. 22/1999 had been the most serious effort at decentralization. It was issued only after the 1997 economic crisis and the collapse of Suharto's New Order administration. The law devolved its "authority rather than its functions to lower levels of government like the local governments. The central government devolved some of its authority to local governments and provinces. However, the central government remains responsible for national defense, international relations, justice, security, religion, and monetary and fiscal policies."[12] To maintain its authority, the central government also maintains its organizations in the regions. The central government maintains some policy functions, including national planning, intergovernmental fiscal policies, state administration, human resource development, natural resource conservation and national standardization. The provinces coordinated among the local governments

---

[12] Law No. 22/1999, article 7 (1).

and carried out functions that affect more than one local government. Law No. 22/1999 clearly stipulates that there was no hierarchical link between the province as an autonomous region and the regencies and cities. However, the governor (not the province) continued to carry out deconcentrated tasks on behalf of the central government, and acted as the central government's representative in the regions. The governor still had power to supervise local governments. Implementing regulations (Government Regulation No. 25/2000) further clarified the roles of the central and provincial governments, which include the setting of standards for the delivery of public services. The local governments carried out all functions except those allocated to the center and the province. The local governments must deliver services in sectors such as health, education, public works, environment, communications, agriculture, industry and trade, capita investment, land, cooperatives, and manpower and infrastructure services. Local governments might return to their provinces the functions that they cannot perform.

New Networks, New Institutions

Observations from micro studies unravel two different types of political networks. As mentioned in the previous chapter, political networks are based, at least, on interpersonal ties and mutual trust. The first type of political network is a connection based primarily on ethnicity. The second type is a political network based on educational background. Both types of political networks share common objectives. The examples of West Sumatra and Riau confirm this tendency. For example, political actors who are involved in a dispute in West Sumatra are Minangkabau. They have a common interest in opposing the central government's plan to privatize Semen Padang. The network involved here comprises people who are ethnic Minangkabau; none of the members claim any other ethnicity. Political actors in Riau engaged in a dispute with the central government are Malays from Riau; they were unable to create network. To compare, a careful observation of another network constructed by politicians in East Kalimantan reveals a different pattern. Even though the governor of East Kalimantan represents the interests of East Kalimantan, he actually does not belong to any ethnic group that originates in East Kalimantan; he is in fact Sundanese. Another political actor is Javanese and operates from Jakarta. However, they share a similar background in the military, where high-ranking officers received similar training and ideas regarding the concept of the unitary state of the Indonesian republic. This point is made clear by pointing out the relationship between governor and political actor in Jakarta. This type of non-ethnic based network was created based on a common educational background and the shared objective of controlling the coal company, Kaltim Prima Coal.

These two types of networks, ethnic and educational, worked on a common ground. Age, in the sense of shared generational experience, is essential for interconnecting members of a network. Political actors of the same age share similar experiences. Age is relevant because the members of a network may share a similar language. Every political network involves communication processes by way of information exchange that spread messages from one actor to another through shared languages. This shared language acts as an epistemic reference for members of a network. This refers back to the argument by Knoke (1990: 11–12) that members of a political network are linked directly to one another by way of intense communication. Putting Knoke's explanation into the context of Indonesian politics, members of Suharto's network experienced mutual ties through the political language crafted by Suharto. The local political actors of the three provinces mentioned above reveal that almost all of them were in their late fifties to early sixties. They started their careers as politicians in the regions at a time in the 1970s when Suharto was just beginning to take control of politics and worked in Suharto's government in various capacities.

Interpersonal ties are also a mechanism for binding members of a network in the Indonesian context. Recalling the definition of ties advanced by Granovetter (1973: 1361) it would be clear that a tie can be characterized by a combination of shared time that stresses emotional intensity, intimacy (mutual confiding) and reciprocal services. This definition describes interpersonal ties only in terms of emotional intimacy. In the Indonesian context, interpersonal ties are far more complex. Interpersonal ties could also be built because of a similar agenda, a belief in a particular economic school of thought or even a similar training in a governmental program. Consider the technocrats who wrote Indonesia's policies for almost three decades under Suharto. They shared interpersonal ties because of their shared beliefs in market economics, and received training from either the Faculty of Economics of the University of Indonesia or the University of California at Berkeley.

In the Indonesian political context, however, interpersonal ties are relevant because they offer a cogent way of understanding the emergence of provincial political actors. At first, it is necessary to say that the Suharto government provided institutional arrangements in which most of bureaucrats, military officers and Golkar members at various levels could meet and connect. These bureaucrats, military personnel and politicians might meet at some event designed by the president; or they would meet and come to know each other in a course to educate local officers run by the central government.

Interpersonal ties were possible because the local politicians were members of Golkar, the bureaucracy or the military. In the 1980s, the governor of Riau was a retired general and a bureaucrat within the New Order as district chief of Kampar. The governor of East Kalimantan was a retired general; his background links him with a retired general operating in Jakarta. The CEO of Semen Padang was connected to a powerful politician from the Minangkabau ethnic group, and they shared similar experiences working in Semen Padang.

After discussing both institutions and political networks, it is safe to mention that changes in the institutions did not necessarily alter the political networks. The emergence of local politicians as a new force is better explained in terms of their capability not only to maintain the links they established under Suharto's government but also to exercise their ability to expand their networks under different institutional arrangements. Under the Suharto government, these politicians used their links to respond to the wishes of the president and to survive after he was gone. They mainly employed networks to advance their own interests. The political networks did not collapse, even after Suharto's departure. Under the New Order, political networks shared the same feature, the president, on which all networks focused as the political center. Figuratively, Suharto was the web's spider. However, when the spider disappeared, the web remained intact. This web was transformed into smaller networks with many hubs that linked together many nodes that operated independently. The post-Suharto government featured many networks with weak centers, even if sometimes these centers also operated as hubs that connected many nodes. For example, the political network in West Sumatra operated independently from that in East Kalimantan. These politicians also connected different political actors in Jakarta, who also operated independently from the influence of presidents Habibie, Wahid and Megawati.

These regional politicians could also expand their links by connecting with different political actors, in Jakarta and the regions, who did not participate in the networks. It is clear in the cases of KPC and Semen

Padang that political parties were important for linking provincial politicians with politically important people in Jakarta and other regions. Golkar indeed served as a seedbed for political actors in West Sumatra as well as for expanding their political networks in Jakarta with other Golkar politicians through a powerful actor from this region. For the governor of East Kalimantan, for example, PDI-P played an important role because it linked him with SOE Minister Laksamana Sukardi.

In conclusion, the discussion above unravels the change from centralized to decentralized Indonesia. The political architecture of the Indonesian government was profoundly altered in 1999 when the Habibie government introduced various regulations such as Law No. 22/1999 on Regional Autonomy and Law No. 3/1999 on Political Parties. While Suharto had the ability to arrange institutions to suit the prerogatives of his rule, the post-Suharto government had a diminished ability to organize or control such institutions to accommodate their interests. The governments under Abdurahman Wahid and Megawati had to work within and through institutions that were not always supportive of them because some of these institutions were organized by the Habibie government. These leaders found it difficult to maintain the cohesiveness of the central government. With a less powerful Golkar and the growing role of new political parties such as PDI-P, PKB and PAN, it became almost impossible to form a majority in parliament and more broadly in government. Since the passage of these new regulations on regional autonomy and political parties, successive central governments have had very little means to control the politics and economies of the regions. On the contrary, these new regulations paved the way for local politicians to emerge and establish new networks.

CHAPTER 4

Your Mine or Mine: The Divestment Process in East Kalimantan

Introduction

This chapter focuses on a conflict related to the coal multinational company that had to divest its shares to Indonesian participants. It is an intriguing, complex case study, the crux of which lies in a conflict concerning the decision of the Ministry of Energy and Mineral Resources to engineer the divestment process. The governor of East Kalimantan openly expressed his intention to control the coal company by buying its divested shares. On the surface, it seemed natural that a governor could make manifest his interest to buy the shares, as all other Indonesians had a similar right to do the same. However, careful observation reveals that the governor was not merely following the normal procedure for buying shares, but was also adopting various political measures to achieve his goal. The governor insisted to both the Ministry of Energy and Mineral Resources and multinational corporations that he was entitled to be treated as having an exclusive right to buy the divested shares of Kaltim Prima Coal (KPC, a holding company incorporated in Indonesia owned by a group of foreign investors from Britain and Australia). This meant that first priority to buy these shares should be given to him. In response, the Ministry of Energy and Mineral Resources and KPC strongly resisted his move.

This case offers much illuminating material on the political networks of a provincial political player from the region and how such networks have shaped politics and business since the breakup of the New Order regime. It also shows that this novel pattern of politics was in its initial

78

stage of formation, with the increasing relevance of provincial-level politics and its deep connection to politics in Jakarta. Such a pattern is clear: the governor of East Kalimantan, Suwarna Abdul Fatah,[1] successfully managed to create political networks on a personal level with powerful politicians in Jakarta, such as Laksamana of PDI-P, who was also the SOE minister, and retired general Mutojib, a former intelligence officer under Suharto. In addition, Suwarna also extended this personal network by involving other regents in the province. The governor intended to create this political network in order to improve his political strength to oppose both Minister of Energy and Mineral Resources Purnomo Yusgiantoro and KPC. The political networks formed by Suwarna moved beyond his ethnic group, geography and education. In the provincial level his political networks were weak because, as a Sundanese, he had no means to mobilize the Dayak, an important indigenous ethnic group in East Kalimantan. It should be made clear that Suwarna would only have had a small opportunity to engage in this conflict had he not received multi-layered political support from both the center and the region.

Another crucial point is that the dispute created an unfavorable situation for foreign investors who operated in the region like KPC. The increasing importance of provincial politics coincided with the new demand of provincial politicians to have a right to own shares of KPC. This new demand hardly existed in the New Order state, as Suharto had silenced local elites. When the central government was less successful in finding a workable solution, at least in the eyes of the foreign investors that were closely tied up with the coal contract, the multinationals felt unsafe and threatened.

This chapter first looks briefly at the fundamental pillar of New Order government under Suharto and how he established institutions to gain control of politics in the province of East Kalimantan. It then discusses the politics of the province after the collapse of Suharto's government before it turns to a brief description of the KPC, to which the central government granted the coal mine in Sangatta, East Kalimantan. The next section charts the rise of the province's governor as a major political actor. The section that follows discusses the governor's dispute with the central government and, later, KPC.

---

[1] He was born into a Sundanese family on 1 Jan. 1944 and graduated from the military academy in 1966.

Establishing the Context: East Kalimantan under Suharto

East Kalimantan contains 211,440 kilometer square meters of territory, one-and-a-half times that of Java island, and is home to around 2.5 million people. Around 44.51 percent of its population consists of migrants from the provinces of East Java, South Sulawesi, South Kalimantan and Central Java. The Javanese, who came from both East and Central Java, are the largest ethnic group, comprising 29.55 percent of the population. After that, the Buginese of South Sulawesi comprise 18.26 percent; the Banjarese of South Kalimantan 13.94 percent; the indigenous Dayak 9.91 percent; the Kutai people 9.21 percent; and the province's remaining various ethnic groups 19.13 percent (East Kalimantan Statistical Bureau 2001: 5). The Javanese are concentrated in the three regencies and cities of Samarinda, Balikpapan and Kutai. They came to the province for two reasons: transmigration and employment provided by the timber and mining booms of the 1970s. Other regencies such as Pasir are home to Buginese and Banjarese. The Dayaks reside in interior areas such as Kutai.

During his long reign from 1966 to 1998, Suharto established institutions for controlling political and economic processes to his benefit. He directed the political process from the center out, extending his reach across the entire country by establishing institutional arrangements and creating political alliances. These institutional arrangements were deeply associated with the military and with Golkar, the dominant political party.

Through his rule over the military and Golkar, Suharto controlled the appointment of provincial governors, district chiefs and mayors. For this purpose, he instituted Law No. 5/1974 on Local Administration. In this law, although the candidates for governors, mayors or district chiefs were elected by the regional parliaments (DPRD), they were appointed by President Suharto at the final stage of decision making and thereafter responsible to him.[2] With his control over the election process, Suharto made regional government leaders depend on him politically.

In addition to that, Suharto also controlled the flow of funds to the regions by means of allocating lucrative taxes to the central government and then channeling some of the funds to the regions. Regional income (PAD) was far from sufficient to run the government. All the provinces had to rely on was a subsidy from the central government for about 60 percent of their operating expenses (Kuntjoro 1995).

---

[2] Article 15 of Law No. 5/1974 on Local Administration.

These political and fiscal arrangements were the factors that then pushed forward the formation of political alliances between Suharto and the governors. It would be safe to claim that all the governors were political allies of Suharto, and they depended on him for their political careers. As a consequence, governors responded to the wishes of Suharto instead of the local population, being politically accountable to him only.

The combination of such institutional arrangements and political connections created a political economy that revolved around Suharto. This enabled the president to determine the fate and political careers of regional politicians and intervene decisively in the economic affairs of regions.

This was apparent in the political structure of the economy in East Kalimantan. It was borne out by the 1978 defeat of Wahab Sjahranie,[3] a prominent local elite,[4] in his bid to maintain his governorship. Wahab was unable to compete with Ery Supardjan, commander-in-chief for Kalimantan territory, appointed governor by Suharto in 1978, and a Javanese (Magenda 1991: 91). With the appointment of Ery Supardjan, the role of the local elites started to decline politically. After that, Golkar dominated the political scene with an average vote of 55 percent in the elections held between 1982 and 1997. It was in this context that in the 1980s Suharto granted a concession to Kaltim Prima Coal to mine in the province. His rule defined the coal contract between KPC and the government in the sense that the central government received the entire 13.5 percent royalty from KPC sales, plus corporate tax. East Kalimantan received only a small portion of KPC revenue in the form of a regional development tax and land rent.

Post-Suharto Kalimantan

The introduction of new institutions such as the laws on regional autonomy and political parties created new arrangements in politics and fiscal

---

[3] Wahab Sjahranie was born into a Banjarese aristocratic family in Rantau, South Kalimantan. In 1937 he graduated from HIS (Hollandsche Inlandsche School, a primary school for natives); then in 1941 he went to work in the Opleiding Bestuur (Ministry of Education under the Dutch administration). From 1947 to 1950 he worked within a unit of Division I in the Indonesian Navy. Between 1950 and 1960 he held various jobs in the army, one of them as the commander of a battalion in Kandangan. He was deputy to the sixth assistant to the army chief of staff. From 1967 to 1978, he served as governor of East Kalimantan Province.

[4] The term "local elite" here refers to those who descended from aristocratic families in both East Kalimantan and South Kalimantan.

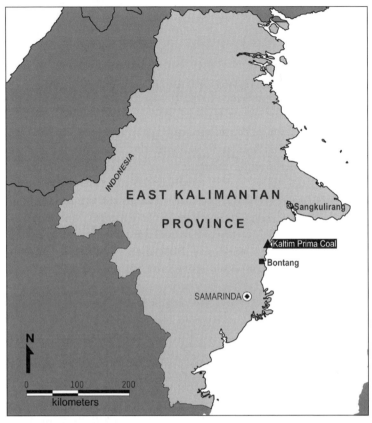

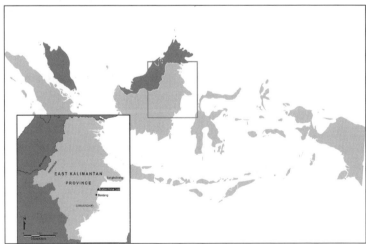

Map 1. East Kalimantan

relations. Law No. 25/1999 abolished the privilege of the president to appoint governors. This new law also made the provincial parliament powerful due to its new authority to elect the governor and the governor's accountability to the assembly. At the same time, the governor was responsible to the president, because the governor represented the central government in the region.

The new rules on political parties in Law No. 2/1999 offered regional political actors an opportunity to set up new parties other than those that already had existed during the Suharto period, such as Golkar, PPP (United Development Party), and PDI (Indonesian Democratic Party). Both old and new parties competed in the 1999 election, and the results of the elections in 1999 dictated that five political parties would dominate the political scene on both the central and regional levels: PDI-P (Indonesian Democratic Party-Struggle), Golkar, PPP, PKB (National Awakening Party) and PAN (National Mandate Party). The parliament and political parties thus began gaining strength vis-à-vis the executive.

The political landscape at the national level was reflected at the regional level. In 1999, PDI-P outperformed Golkar by garnering 33.8 percent of the vote.[5] PDI-P won 17 seats out of 45 seats in the provincial legislative body. The secretary of the PDI-P's branch in East Kalimantan, Soekardi Jarwo Putro, has ever since been chairing the provincial legislative body. It seems that PDI-P received votes from mainly Javanese migrants residing in Samarinda (33.2 percent of its total votes in East Kalimantan) and Balikpapan (37.3 percent of its total in East Kalimantan). Other than that, PDI-P received votes from the Dayak group in Kutai (38.6 percent of its total votes in East Kalimantan). Furthermore, the Javanese who reside in East Kalimantan are mainly from East Java, one of the strongholds of PDI-P. In Samarinda, Balikpapan and Kutai, the voters shared urban characteristics and were aware of the politics of Jakarta; Golkar was thus discredited. The Dayaks, who are mostly Christian (Nanang 1998: 2), supported PDI-P due to their religious affiliation. The religious leaders in the Dayak communities mobilized their members to vote for the PDI-P through various churches and the association of Dayak communities.

The combination of massive changes on many fronts broke the political and economic structure established by Suharto. The relationship between the center and the region, as indicated by the relationships

---

[5] "Sebuah Pelajaran yang Sangat Pahit", *Kompas*, 3 Feb. 2004.

among the various offices of central government and the provincial governors, had also been altered. As mentioned earlier, the governors were no longer accountable and responsible to the president only; they now were answerable primarily to the provincial parliaments, the political bodies that elected them. The political connections created by Suharto also disappeared and were replaced by more diverse political networks that may have centered on political parties.

The realm of central government authority was weakest at its periphery. Here, it would have to deal with the rise of local elite politicians, such as the governor of East Kalimantan, Suwarna Abdul Fatah.[6] With the rise of the governor, the central governing body, in this case the Ministry of Energy and Mineral Resources, had to negotiate and bargain with or even, to some extent, accommodate the interests of the local elite. Such a situation is characterized as a symptom of a weak state (Migdal 1987, 1988; Abinales 2001).[7]

The dispute over the divestment of KPC is located in the wider context of the break-up of the old structure of the political economy. This structure of political economy centered on Suharto. In this context, scholars argue that the fall of Suharto "merely opens the door to a fresh round of struggles to reshape and to redefine economics and politics" (Robison and Hadiz 2004: 27). However, it did open the door to a fresh round of struggle that mainly involved the players incubated during the New Order days, players who may be considered oligarchs (Robison and Hadiz 2004: 40–66, 187–217). Furthermore, these scholars admit that such struggles took place at the regency level where local politicians developed political capability and tried to reshape politics and economics in their locality (Robison and Hadiz 2004: 245–7). In an almost similar fashion, Choi (2011: 102) contends that political competition at the local level has allowed entrenched local elites to enhance their power. Research points to those political players who operate mainly in a regional context and possess the ability to control the local economy through such activities as protection rackets, illegal gambling and prostitution. In controlling those economic activities, scholars add, the local politicians hardly needed support from Jakarta. These scholars, however, pay less attention to the

---

[6] See footnote 1.

[7] Migdal (1988: 9) argues that the state becomes weak whenever local strongmen are able to capture state agencies and resources. They limit state autonomy and capacity, thus causing weakness in the state.

interconnections between politics on the local level and the politics of Jakarta when trying to understand the behavior of local politicians. It is in fact necessary to expand the scope of analysis and discuss the provincial politicians who were able to develop political networks that extended to those wielding power in Jakarta. As this case points out, there were new players from the provinces and others in the process of emerging. More importantly, these new players were able to secure political support from powerful politicians in Jakarta through networks.

This case sheds light on the development of Indonesian politics and economy by looking at the provincial politicians who managed to craft political networks. Although the governor of East Kalimantan, Suwarna Abdul Fatah, met with little success in achieving his goal of controlling KPC, he was capable of creating networks that strengthened his political bargaining position in the conflict that arose over the KPC divestment process. Since the beginning of the conflict, he needed to forge a political network, because he seemed well aware that he would deal with coal mining under the legal control of the central government. Other than that, Suwarna had to consider the behavior of the multinationals that wanted to protect their source of income. Confronted with this situation, the governor was left with little choice if he wanted to control coal mining except to strengthen his political standing by linking up with powerful politicians in Jakarta who shared an interest in controlling KPC.

Suwarna's initiatives and his ability to establish political networks are new developments in the context of Indonesian politics and economy during the post-Suharto period. Equally important is his readiness to take advantage of the process of political opening and decentralization. Therefore, Suwarna's effort to connect politics in the province with the politics of Jakarta's offers up material for a discussion about political networks and the new patterns of Indonesian politics and economy.

Calibrating the Relative Strength of KPC

In 1982, the country experienced a decline in oil production and oil price. This had major consequences on foreign-exchange receipts and government revenues. This was because oil revenues constituted the greater part—around 70 percent—of foreign-exchange inflow and government revenues.[8] In order to respond to the situation, government technocrats—

---

[8] Government Statement on the Draft State Budget for 1983–84 to the House of People's Representatives, Government of Indonesia, delivered by president Suharto.

86   *Networked*

one of them M. Sadli,[9] the minister of mines at the time—adopted a
market-friendly approach to the mining industry.[10] Before the introduction of such a policy, the coal mine sector was operated mainly by the
state-owned company, small domestic operators and cooperatives, which
produced only between one million to four million tons per year (Prijono
1990: 519). Substitution of coal for oil was part of a bigger strategy of
diversification of domestic energy usage in order to enable more oil to be
preserved for export.

Two multinational corporations owned KPC: Rio Tinto of Anglo-
Australian company[11] and BP International of the UK.[12] Rio Tinto of
Anglo-Australian company had been conducting mineral explorations in
Indonesia since 1970. In 1976, it entered into an agreement with BP of
Britain to conduct a joint exploration for coal throughout the country,
which they carried out between 1976 and 1978. As a result of this
exploration, the two multinational companies responded to the government's invitation and submitted a tender for an area centered on the
small town of Sangatta in Kutai (Dolinschek 1990: 530). Then, in
December 1978, Rio Tinto and BP International entered into a coal
contract in the Sangatta area with Perum Tambang Batubara (Batubara),
the state coal company. The two parties signed their coal agreement on
8 April 1982. In 1996, Batubara was replaced by the Ministry of Energy
and Mineral Resources.

KPC is a company incorporated in Indonesia. In the late 1970s,
Rio Tinto and BP International each owned 50 percent of its shares.

---

[9] Sadli was a part of a group of technocrats who were educated in the US, mainly at
the University of California, Berkeley. See Shiraishi 2002: 1–3.

[10] This market-friendly approach is a legacy of the neoclassical economics of the 1970s,
which in the 1980s influenced three important nations—the US (Reagan), the UK
(Thatcher) and West Germany (Kohl)—whose leaders embraced this policy. The
OECD, World Bank and IMF also supported this neoclassical approach. During the
1980s the World Bank and IMF both imposed additional policies on Indonesia based
on its tenets.

[11] Rio Tinto had invested US$1.2 billion in 2003 (email correspondence with one of
the vice directors, 12 Feb. 2004). Rio Tinto's operation in Indonesia accounted for 4
percent of its net earnings, approximately US$60 million. See Rio Tinto Ltd, *Social
and Environment Review* (Melbourne, 2000), p. 4.

[12] BP controls interest in Indonesia of about US$6 billion in various companies
("Investasi BP di Indonesia mencapai US$6 miliar"), *Bisnis Indonesia*, 26 Jan. 2004.
BP is Indonesia's largest offshore oil and gas operator and the main natural gas sup-
plier to its largest domestic market. BP conducted a project for a gas plant amounting
to US$2 billion. See "BP in Indonesia—Sociologists Before Geologists?", *The Economist*,
29 June 2002.

KPC initially invested about US$570 million in operations covering 790,000 hectares.[13] Construction started in January 1989 and ended on 1 September 1991. KPC's main asset has been the government's 30-year concession of mining rights to an area of 90,000 hectares. Up to 2001, KPC had opened about 30,000 hectares of land for its coal production with an average annual production of 15 million tons. In short, the power of KPC derived from its capital invested in the Indonesian economy.

KPC's agreement with the Ministry of Mining and Energy formed the legal framework in which the firm operates. It also defined a package of tax and other conditions, including divestment. KPC's obligations, as stated in the coal contract, were as follows:

1. an operating period of 30 years (article 10);
2. the application of an income tax at 35 percent during the first 10 years of operation and 45 percent thereafter (article 11);
3. the obligation to provide 13.5 percent of all coal mined to the government of Indonesia free of charge (article 11); and
4. the obligation to progressively offer for sale at market value a total of 51 percent of corporate shares to the Indonesian participant(s) (article 26).

During the period from 1991 to 2001, KPC exported 116.7 million tons of coal (see figure 1), with Europe taking 28 percent, Japan 25 percent, Taiwan 16 percent, other Asian countries 21 percent, the US 6 percent and the domestic market 4 percent. This data reveals not only KPC's strength in producing coal but also its worldwide marketing network.

The significance of KPC in the Indonesian economy reveals itself in the form of its fiscal obligation to the government through the payment of royalties and dividends. As governed in article 11 of the coal contract, KPC had to pay a royalty of 13.5 percent from its net sales per year and to pay for dividends from its annual net profit amounting to 35 percent to 45 percent. The total royalty payment by KPC to the government for the period from 1991 to 2001 amounted to US$499,287,040—an average annual payment of US$45,389,730. From 1995 to 2000, KPC on average paid royalties and dividends amounting to US$80.8 million annually. This figure was larger than that of other contractors such as

---

[13] Interview with Anang Rizkani Noor, External Relations Officer of PT Rio Tinto Indonesia, 14 Aug. 2003.

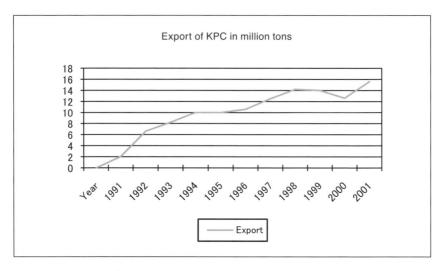

Figure 1. Export of KPC in million tons
Source: KPC presentation to DPRD, 5 July 2001. Adapted from Lembaga Penyelidikan Ekonomi dan Masyarakat Universitas Indonesia 2002.

Arutmin, a coal company operating in South Kalimantan, which paid royalties amounting to US$35.2 in 2002.[14]

The Rise of Governor Suwarna

The governor of East Kalimantan, Suwarna Abdul Fatah, spent his career mainly within the military, and he served in various posts until 1994. That year, he entered political life as the deputy governor of East Kalimantan. In 1998, he was appointed governor with political support mainly from former commanders of Military Area Command (Kodam) Tanjungpura.[15] Later on, Golkar and PDI-P also supported him. Decentralization and other political policies had provided an impetus for

---

[14] Data for net sales of PT Arutmin can be obtained from www.miningindo.com [accessed 25 Oct. 2004].

[15] He became governor with the support of Military Area Command (Kodam) Tanjungpura in 1998, after his term as vice governor ended. With the installment of a new parliament in 1999, he cultivated political support from important political parties in the region like PDI-P and Golkar, both of which were instrumental to his reappointment as governor in 2003. Golkar's local leader Syaukani and PDI-P local secretary Sukardi Jarwo Putro have been his close allies. Chief Kodam of Tanjungpura was mainly from Java, like Mutojib, Namuri Anoem, Muchi PR and Zainuri Hasyim.

Suwarna to voice his concern over the divestment of KPC even in the national scene, yet according to the new regulations, he did not have any particular legal standing for claiming his interest. The space to maneuver for Suwarna was opened up when he received information of the divestment process around 1999.[16] Up to November 1999, the provincial government had been short-listed by KPC as one of the parties that would be given the opportunity to buy the equity of the company.[17]

The invitation from the central government stated clearly that it was the province, and not Suwarna himself, that was short-listed for the opportunity to purchase KPC. Therefore, as will be discussed later, Suwarna could only use his office to challenge the central government. This was clear when Suwarna had to use the provincial government enterprise— *perusahaan daerah* or *perusda*—to set up a joint-venture company. Yet the possibility that Suwarna could benefit from his effort to purchase the equity of KPC on behalf of the province might still have arisen. Such a benefit would have appeared in the form of a commission fee, had the province successfully purchased the equity of KPC.

The source of Suwarna's bargaining power was the coal-mining site. This site could not be transferred to other places. The source of his power therefore resided in the immobility of extractive resources (Moran 1974). He could translate this immobility directly into power because KPC had already been in operation for some time in East Kalimantan. The possibility of a KPC withdrawal was nil due to its massive cumulative investment in the country.

Another source of Suwarna's power was his ability to seek political support by establishing political alliances at the national level. In November 2000, he entered into an agreement with Mutojib, the former commander of Tanjungpura territory in Kalimantan. Later, this agreement cemented his efforts to acquire KPC equity. This meant that Suwarna renewed his political connection to the former commander. He met with

---

[16] Interview with Syaiful Teteng, secretary of the East Kalimantan government. He was involved deeply in the dispute regarding the divestment of KPC shares. The interview was conducted in Samarinda on 9 Sept. 2003. *Gatra* also revealed that it was David Salim who in 1996 provided the information to the provincial government. See "Kemelut pertambangan Batubara: Baku Sikut Juragan tambang", *Gatra Weekly Magazine*, 2 Apr. 2002.

[17] Letter from KPC to Minister of Energy and Mineral Resources Susilo Bambang Yudhoyono, dated 16 Nov. 1999, signed by Philip Strachan (of Sangatta Holding Ltd) and Peter Vider (BP International).

Mutojib in Lemhanas, a government-security think tank, and since then they have maintained a close relationship.[18] Mutojib was Suwarna's senior in Lemhanas and in the military service. He graduated from the National Military Academy in 1962 and served as the chief of intelligence service BAKIN (Badan Koordinasi Intelijen Nasional, National Intelligence Coordinating Body) under Suharto. He previously held various positions, such as chief commander of Kodam Tanjungpura in Kalimantan and governor of Lemhanas. Suwarna and Mutojib strengthened their political connection by establishing a company called PT Melati Intan Bhakti Satya (MIBS), which was a joint venture between PT Intan Bumi Inti Prasada (PT Intan), where Mutojib was acting as commissioner, and the East Kalimantan-owned enterprise PD Melati Bhakti Satya (PD Melati).[19] Mutojib also connected Suwarna to David Salim, nephew of prominent Indonesian tycoon Sudono Salim,[20] who provided substantial capital to purchase shares of KPC. This joint venture not only provided Suwarna with political standing but also financial backing. In particular, MIBS intended to purchase all 51 percent of KPC's equity.[21] In short, Suwarna was able to renew and enlarge his political networks due to his connection to Mutojib.

Then Suwarna and Mutojib, with financial backing from David Salim, entered into an agreement that gave PT Intan 45.9 percent shares and the province 5.1 percent.[22] However, Suwarna later demanded more shares for the province, as he had to convince other chiefs of districts in the province to support his proposal. In July 2002 the composition of shares changed, and the province now received 10.2 percent. Since then, the governor has acted as a representative of MIBS on behalf of the joint venture.

Suwarna approached Laksamana Sukardi, the minister of state-owned enterprises (SOE), who was already involved in the process of KPC's divestment through Perusahaan Tambang Batubara Bukit Asam (PTBA),[23]

---

[18] "Berebut Batubara Kalimantan", *Tempo*, 16 June 2002, p. 71.

[19] Deed of Agreement before notary Esther Mercia Sulaiman, which means the venture has a legal basis.

[20] He perhaps acted as a broker with international capital such as Batavia Investment Management; see "Berebut Batubara di Kalimantan", *Tempo*, 16 June 2002, p. 72. However, only limited information relates to him. Until the dispute was over, he remained in the dark.

[21] Deed of Agreement, Policy over Dividend clause, p. 10.

[22] Look also for confirmation from Said Safran, former secretary of the East Kalimantan government ("Baku Sikut Juragan Tambang", *Gatra*, 2 Apr. 2002).

a state-owned enterprise specializing in the coal industry, which was under his supervision. In July 2002, the central government divided 51 percent of the equity of KPC into two main parts: 20 percent for PTBA and 31 percent for the local government of East Kalimantan. The involvement of PTBA provided a way for Laksamana to take part in the process of divestment. In mid-September 2002, Suwarna saw his efforts bear initial fruit. Laksamana stated that he was ready to involve himself in the proposed consortium—comprised of PT Intan, PTBA, PD Melati and a company belonging to the East Kutai regency by the name of Perusda for Mining and Energy (Pertambangan dan Energi Kutai Timur, PEKT)—to buy 51 percent of KPC's equity.[24] The consortium, named MIBS, was formed on 8 November 2002 in order to pursue benefits for Suwarna and Laksamana. With this consortium, Suwarna hoped to control KPC, and Laksamana could solve his problem. He would buy only about 4 percent of the shares of KPC because he learned that PTBA did not have enough funds to purchase the entire 20 percent of the shares. Suwarna and Laksamana agreed that 10.2 percent, which was already allocated for East Kalimantan, would be divided into two parts, where the central government (PTBA) would receive 3.98 percent shares, and East Kalimantan province (PD Melati) and PEKT 6.22 percent.[25] In this consortium called MIBS, PT Intan would receive 40.8 percent of the total shares.[26] They also agreed that PT Intan would be involved in

---

[23] Perseroan Terbatas Tambang Batubara Bukit Asam (PTBA) is a state-owned enterprise specializing in coal-mining operations. It was established in 1981 and publicly listed on the Jakarta Stock Exchange in 2002. PTBA is the country's fifth-largest coal producer. In 1990 PTBA merged with Perum Tambang Batubara. It possesses about 17 percent of Indonesia's coal reserves. PTBA is currently exploiting two mining areas, one in Tanjung Enim (South Sumatra) and the other in Ombilin (West Sumatra). PTBA is under supervision of the Ministry of SOE.

[24] "Pemerintah Optimis Divestasi Akan Tuntas", *Bisnis Indonesia*, 11 Sept. 2002.

[25] The calculation was based on a ratio of 20:31; therefore PTBA would receive 3.98 percent ($20/51 \times 10.2$ percent), and PD Melati and PEKT would receive 6.22 percent ($31/51 \times 10.2$). The 6.22 percent portion for PD Melati and PEKT was divided based on a ratio of $40:60$; therefore, PD Melati would receive 2.49 percent (6.22×40 percent) and PEKT would receive 3.72 (6.22×60 percent).

[26] Article 1, Memorandum of Understanding, Perusda Melati and Perusda East Kutai, signed by Ismet Harmaini (PTBA), Mandurdi (Perusda Melati), Wahyu Setiaji (Perusda East Kutai) and Mutojib (PT Intan), dated 8 Nov. 2002. Minister Laksamana Sukardi approved this agreement in his letter to the board directors of PTBA (letter number: S-300/M-MBU/2002, dated 12 Dec. 2002 and signed by Laksamana Sukardi). PT Intan would receive a large amount of shares because it provided the funds.

the partnership and could join the negotiator team;[27] moreover, that the negotiator team would scrutinize KPC with due diligence.[28]

Laksamana's decision to support Governor Suwarna's proposal to purchase the equity of KPC might be related to the bigger political effort by PDI-P to approach the governor and to the financial constraint he had to face. In late July 2002, Megawati, after listening to a suggestion by Minister of Energy and Mineral Resources Purnomo Yusgiantoro, who was in charge of the divestment of KPC, to block Suwarna's intended effort to control the multinational. Megawati thus ordered PTBA to purchase 20 percent of KPC's equity. Minister of SOE Laksamana Sukardi was fully aware that the government lacked fresh funds to acquire KPC equity—20 percent would amount to US$164.4 million—and it would be difficult to find people who could, or would want to, finance the purchase.[29] Only by establishing an alliance with Governor Suwarna could Laksamana find a way to resolve his problem of providing a significant amount of fresh funds.

Governor Suwarna was important to the national PDI-P strategy of maintaining an alliance with the military. Megawati and PDI-P secretary general Soetjipto decided on 22 May 2003 to throw their support behind Suwarna's candidacy for a second term as governor at the expense of PDI-P East Kalimantan chairperson Imam Mundjiat. Megawati intended to send a clear message that her party was ready to cooperate with the military. Megawati sent her aides Theo Syafii and Agnita Singedikane to discuss the matter with the provincial chapter of the party and concluded that PDI-P would support Suwarna with 12 of the 17 votes that the party held.[30] In June, Suwarna was reelected governor with a majority of 24 votes (53 percent) out of a total of 45 votes.[31]

In addition to connections with national figures, Suwarna also entered into a political network with the chief official of the district of East Kutai, where the KPC mine site is located. In late April 2001,

---

[27] The team was comprised of Roes Aryawijaya from Minister Laksamana's office, Syaiful Teteng from the East Kalimantan provincial government and Wahyu Setiaji from the East Kutai regency government.

[28] Article 3, Memorandum of Understanding among Minister of SOE, Government of East Kalimantan and Government of East Kutai.

[29] Minister Laksamana's statement as quoted in "Bumi sudah setor dana akuisisi KPC", *Koran Tempo*, 2 Aug. 2003.

[30] "Mega Restui Suwarna?", *Kaltimpost*, 28 May 2003.

[31] "Suwarna jadi gubernur lagi", *Kaltimpost*, 3 June 2003.

Governor Suwarna managed to gain initial support from Regent Awang Faroek Ishak. By July 2002 they had entered into an agreement, after settling their dispute over who had the right to represent East Kalimantan vis-à-vis the central government. After disputing representation for about one year, they finally agreed to increase the equity allocation of the province from 10 percent out of 51 percent (5.1 percent) to 20 percent (10.2 percent) in MIBS. The regent would receive 60 percent of 10.2 percent and the province 40 percent.[32] As a result of this agreement, Faroek wrote a letter of support on behalf of Governor Suwarna to Minister Purnomo.[33] Regent Faroek was critical of Governor Suwarna because Faroek could have chosen not to join the governor. The governor knew that the regent could move on his own to fight the central government. The only incentive that could be offered by the governor to the regent was to raise the shares composition and increase the community development fund. Both of them were aware that they would face difficulties if they moved on their own. They agreed that PT Intan must provide community development funding of US$7 million if MIBS purchased all 51 percent of KPC's equity.[34]

Suwarna received political support from Syaukani,[35] district chief of Kutai Kartanegara. Though Syaukani's political influence was probably important and went beyond the scope of his district, due to his strong connection to Golkar of which he had been a member since 1978, he had no claim on the mining because it is located in East Kutai. His reason

---

[32] Memorandum of Understanding between Governor East Kalimantan and Regent East Kutai, dated 25 Mar. 2002, signed by Governor Suwarna and Regent Awang Faroek Ishak; Agung Firmansyah, *Divestasi saham KPC: memperjuangkan hak rakyat Kalimantan Timur* (Jakarta: Forum Indonesia Tumbuh, 2003), p. 56; press release of East Kalimantan Government, n.d.

[33] Letter of Regent of East Kutai, dated 27 Apr. 2001, signed by Awang Faroek Ishak, no. 236/541/BUP-KUTIM/3/V/2001.

[34] The provincial government approached several companies, including Prabowo Subianto's company and Bumi Resources; however, they had been defeated by PT Intan, which increased its shares to the province from 10 percent to 20 percent; in contrast, PT Bumi Resources offered only 5 percent.

[35] Syaukani was born in Tenggarong on 11 Nov. 1948. He graduated from Jember University, a local university in East Java, in 1978. After that, he began his political career in Golkar, in which he served as the chief of the Golkar youth organization AMPI beginning in 1978; chief of Golkar in Kutai between 1993 and 2001; and chief of the local parliament in Kutai for two periods before serving as the district chief. For further information, see M. Amir P. Ali, *Syaukani: Di tengah kancah kepemudaan dan otonomi daerah* (Kuta Kartanegera: Ombak, 2003).

for supporting Suwarna was that it was his only chance to acquire shares in KPC. After considering that Suwarna received political support from Mutojib, Laksamana and Awang Faroek, Syaukani had little chance to wage his own battle.

Dispute between the Ministry of Energy and Mineral Resources and the Governor

Minister of Energy and Mineral Resources Purnomo was assigned to conduct the process of KPC's divestment as stipulated in the coal contract. According to article 26 of the contract, KPC had to divest its equity to Indonesian participants. This regulation was formulated with the intention of offering Indonesian businesspersons a chance to operate a large coal-mining operation through a partnership with large multinationals. At the beginning of the 1980s, the Indonesian government was aware that Indonesian companies had limited access to technology, capital and the international market—access that such a partnership would provide.

Although Purnomo received the task of divesting KPC equity, he and KPC both doubted that Suwarna met the qualifications of a potential majority shareholder. He and KPC shared the belief that Suwarna did not have enough funds to purchase 51 percent of KPC's shares, worth US$419 million. Indeed, this amount was far greater than the entire provincial budget of IDR517.83 billion, or US$5.17 million.[36] Purnomo and KPC believed that Suwarna, even with David Salim's involvement, still lacked fresh funds to finance the purchase. They acquired relevant information stating that neither David Salim nor Suwarna had any substantial experience in the coal industry. This was the most relevant reason why Purnomo and KPC sought to impede Suwarna. While David Salim had been doing business in the property sector, Suwarna was a politician with a military background. Considering these facts, Purnomo and KPC concluded, the future of KPC would not be very promising if it went to Suwarna and David Salim. Finally, they considered the trust and relationship that they had built over the last three decades. Through the operation of KPC, under the management of Rio Tinto and BP, the central government regularly received funds. Purnomo thought that KPC would be the best partner for the central government in terms of providing a continuous flow of income into its coffers in the form of royalties and taxes.

---

[36] Government of East Kalimantan, *Nota penjelasan perhitungan APBD propinsi Kalimantan Timur*, 1999/2000.

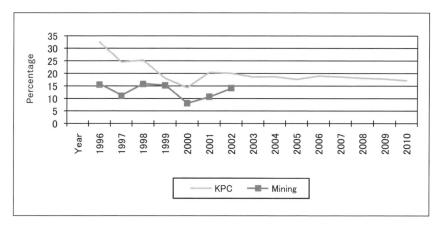

Figure 2. Comparison of net-profit margin between KPC and mining
Source: Confidential Report of Bahana Securities to Ministry of Energy and Mineral Resources; KKEDS to Minister of Energy and Mineral Resources; and PriceWaterHouseCooper Survey on the Indonesian Mining Industry in 2002 and 2003. (Note: Figures for KPC in 1996–2000 are actual, while the rest are projected. The figures for mining are actual.)

The dispute was characterized by Suwarna's effort to control KPC by gaining majority ownership. For Governor Suwarna, controlling KPC meant gaining profit. KPC had an average net profit margin (NPM) of 20 percent after 2001 (see figure 2), which was far better than the less than 15 percent NPM of the entire mining industry for the period from 1996 to 2002. If the province had purchased 2.49 percent of KPC shares, KPC would have generated dividends for the province of about US$3 million per year on average between 1995 and 2000.[37] Though PT Intan would benefit the most if the consortium had purchased the entire 51 percent equity, Suwarna seemed quite happy with the allotment of shares. He knew that PT Intan provided all the necessary funds by borrowing from international lenders.

Figure 3 indicates that if the rate of profit were stable for the next ten years, the governor could have acquired a nominal profit amounting to an average of US$3 million per year for the duration of the coal contract simply by holding 2.49 percent of KPC equity.

---

[37] This number is calculated based on an agreement of the East Kalimantan government, PTBA, and the East Kutai regency on shares proportion if they could purchase 51 percent of KPC shares. In this proportion, the province would have gotten 6.2 percent (31/51 × 10.2 percent). The 10.2 percent share would have constituted the portion for all three of them. 6.2 percent multiplied by net profit gives the dividend.

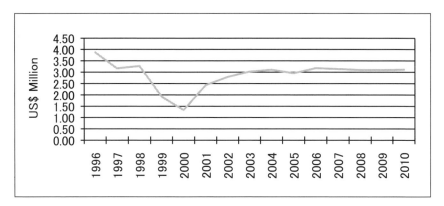

Figure 3. Dividends for province's 2.49-percent share
Source: Confidential Report of Bahana Securities to Ministry of Energy and Mineral Resources, KKEDS to Minister of Energy and Mineral Resources, 2002.

The real conflict between Suwarna and Purnomo began in November 2001 when the governor filed an administrative lawsuit in Jakarta State Administrative Court. Suwarna challenged the validity of several decisions by Purnomo to defer the divestment of KPC equity. He argued that the minister was blocking the process,[38] because until late 2001 there were no signs of a permanent solution as to how to proceed. The governor also questioned the ministry for its lack of decisive political measures to solve the chaotic divestment regulation.[39] The governor asked the court to direct the minister to instruct KPC to sell 51 percent of its equity to the provincial government for US$419 million. Because of the legal suit, Purnomo had to continue the divestment process, and this allowed more room for Suwarna to get involved in it.

Although Suwarna maneuvered to find room to work for the divestment, Purnomo in fact remained influential within the context of the dispute. By making use of his authority as the minister in charge of the divestment, he carefully limited Suwarna's choices. Purnomo, aware of the necessity to accommodate the demands of the province, sent a clear signal that he intended to comply with Suwarna's wishes. Nevertheless, Purnomo had systematically intended to place him as simply one of the

---

[38] As said in press release obtained by *Bisnis Indonesia*; see "Pemda Kaltim gugat menteri ESDM", *Bisnis Indonesia*, 21 Nov. 2001.
[39] "Gugatan hukum Kaltim tak berdasar", *Bisnis Indonesia*, 26 Dec. 2001.

company's shareholders, while he carefully engineered KPC to stay on as a majority shareholder. To this end, Purnomo adopted three political measures.

First, in responding to Suwarna's legal suit, mentioned above, Purnomo decided to continue the divestment process. Having done so, however, he preferred to make a huge concession to KPC, instead of Suwarna, by agreeing to the price of US$8.22 million for each one percent of equity or US$822 million for 100 percent of KPC equity.[40] The price was very close to the one proposed by KPC at the very start of the divestment process. At the beginning of the process, the Ministry of Energy and Mineral Resources and KPC had not yet settled on a price. In 1999, the ministry had considered KPC's offer of US$200 million for 30 percent of the shares as very expensive. The minister proposed a price of US$145 million.[41] In 2001, when KPC had to divest its 51 percent equity, a multinational proposed a price of US$889 million for 100 percent of the shares or US$453.39 million for 51 percent.[42] Purnomo bid US$320 million for a 51 percent stake.[43] The price of the shares fluctuated, as the negotiation experienced a deadlock that lasted almost a year. In the end, Purnomo had to agree to the price offered by KPC in order to block Suwarna.

Second, Purnomo demanded that Suwarna "fully, finally and unconditionally withdraw, remove or cease" all legal claims as a requirement for the continuation of the shares offer.[44] By doing this, Purnomo left the

---

[40] "Kepercayaan Investor tambang kembali pulih", *Bisnis Indonesia*, 13 Mar. 2002.

[41] As mentioned by its president director of PT Timah, Erry Riyana Hardjapamekas, in "Timah Batal Beli 30 percent Saham KPC", *Bisnis Indonesia*, 24 Nov. 1999.

[42] This price was offered by Lex Graefe in "KPC Ajukan Nilai Kapitalisasi US$889 juta", *Bisnis Indonesia*, 4 Oct. 2001.

[43] "Pemerintah Hargai 51 percent Saham KPC US$320 juta", *Bisnis Indonesia*, 6 Oct. 2001. In fact, the ministry relied on three scenarios to determine shares prices. The first option called for a 44-plus-7 percent model. This decision was based on an agreement reached on 26 Oct. 2000, in which 44 percent of KPC's shares were valued at US$257 and 7 percent were calculated from 7 out of 100 percent (US$889), worth US$62 million. In the first option, 51 percent of KPC shares were worth US$319 million. The second option called for a 37-plus-14 percent model, which calculated based on the price agreed for 37 percent of shares on 26 Oct. 2000, US$216 million, with the remaining 14 percent calculated on the basis of the median price of US$889 million (100 percent shares).

[44] Framework Agreement between Government of Indonesia and KPC, dated 5 Aug. 2002, clause 5.1, p. 10.

decision to Suwarna. If the governor wanted to continue the process of divestment, he had to withdraw all legal charges; if he did not, the divestment would stop. This situation was a dilemma for Suwarna. He had intended to use the legal charges to weaken Purnomo's political standing. However, he had no choice but to withdraw his charge against KPC.

Third, one month after Purnomo decided to split the shares of KPC into two parts, he exerted another form of pressure on Suwarna. Purnomo and KPC entered into an agreement under which the 2001 offer of divestment of 51 percent equity in KPC was to be implemented. This agreement was an attempt to influence the divestment process and to protect the interest of KPC by stating several conditions that Suwarna would have difficulty accomplishing in his position as the buyer of the equity. The framework defined the criteria of the buyers, such as Indonesian participants, and sought proof to demonstrate that the buyers could provide the necessary funds to buy the shares.[45]

Dispute between the Governor and KPC

A scholar said, "there is one and only one social responsibility of business —to use its resources and engage in activities designed to increase its profits so long as it stays within the rules of the game" (Friedman 1982: 133). This position reflected the main objective of KPC in gaining profit from coal operations as the multinational stayed within the rules of the game. Even in attempting to justify its interest, KPC preferred to keep to the various regulations that defined the coal operations. When Suwarna insisted that the province had the exclusive right to become the shareholder, KPC preferred the legal road to protect its position. This section analyzes the dispute between Suwarna and KPC. The large part of this conflict centered on the interpretation of the contract, and the other part on the legal steps adopted by KPC.

With no substantial legal standing to be involved in the process of divestment, Suwarna initially offered a controversial interpretation of the coal contract, stating that the province had priority as the first buyer of KPC equity. Suwarna went on to explain that his interpretation should be considered by KPC. When KPC emphatically denied that the province must be granted majority shareholding, it led to a dispute, which can be grouped into three clusters: legal disputes, the framework agreement, and due diligence process.

---

[45] Ibid., clause 3, pp. 7–8.

Legal Disputes

On 17 July 2001 Suwarna lodged a lawsuit against KPC[46] over the alleged failure of the multinational company to carry out its divestment obligations under the coal contract.[47] With this charge, Suwarna systematically sought damages worth US$776 million for past and future dividends that the province would have received from KPC if the divestment had occurred according to the original coal contract and the province had held 51 percent of the shares. In addition, he sought exclusive rights to buy the entire 51 percent.

In seeking damages of US$776 million, the governor argued that the province had a right to the natural resources in its territory.[48] To strengthen his claim, he stated that KPC's operation was designed only for the benefit of its shareholders.[49]

In seeking exclusive rights, Suwarna expressed the opinion that the government owns the mineral resources. He referred to Presidential Decree No. 49/1981, article 26 of the coal contract, and the provision of Law No. 11/1967 on the Basic Provisions of Mining that states the government holds authority over and ownership of mineral resources.[50] Suwarna based his argument on article 10 of Law No. 11/1967, stating that the minister could appoint another party as contractor. Suwarna argued that KPC was a contractor to the government of Indonesia. Then he claimed, "a contractor had no right to determine or even to select the Indonesian participant" in the divestment process.[51]

Having established the arguments that KPC, as the contractor, had no right to select the Indonesian participant in the divestment process, Suwarna tried to argue that the province was also a part of the government. He adopted a definition of government that included the province in the coal contract.[52]

---

[46] Lawsuit registered in the District of South Jakarta; court number 350/Pdt.G/2001/ PN Jaksel, dated 17 July 2001.

[47] KPC, case overview, available at http://www.kaltimprimacoal.co.id/legal_overview. cfm [accessed 4 Feb. 2004].

[48] Lawsuit of East Kalimantan Province as represented by its law firm Dermawan Nugroho & Co., case no. DN/tb-mp-is/079/III/02, dated 12 Mar. 2002.

[49] Ibid., p. 27.

[50] Ibid., 17 July 2001, p. 6.

[51] Ibid., p. 7.

[52] The coal contract states: "*government* means government of the Republic Indonesia, its Ministries, Departments, Agencies, Intrumentalities, Regional, Provincial or Districts Authorities [italics added]". See also Reply of Lawsuit No. 350/Pdt.G/PN Jaksel, dated 12 Mar. 2002, signed by East Kalimantan provincial lawyer Ibrahim Senen, p. 6.

100   *Networked*

Under this pressure, KPC prepared careful responses by means of deploying interpretations that ran counter to the arguments levied by Suwarna. The company denied the accusations of the governor on the two points of the divestment and the exclusive rights of the government as an Indonesian participant. As for divestment, KPC and its shareholders shared the opinion that KPC "has no obligation to sell, transfer, or divest shares".[53] KPC maintained that it had an obligation to offer its shares to Indonesian participants. It made its position on the matter clear by trying to distinguish between the obligation to sell, transfer or divest and the obligation to offer shares. KPC also referred to article 26 of the coal contract, yet stressed that it had an obligation to ensure that shares "are offered ... to the government or Indonesian nationals or Indonesian companies controlled by Indonesian nationals".[54] Contrary to the governor's position that sought a complete process of divestment until all the shares were sold, KPC adopted the opinion that it was obliged only to ensure the offering of shares.

As for Indonesian participants, KPC maintained the argument that the government, including the province of East Kalimantan, had no exclusive rights. The province was not the only prospective purchaser but instead merely the holder of the status of a single interested purchaser.[55] To support its position, KPC claimed it had already fulfilled its obligation to offer shares to Indonesian participants in 1998, 1999 and 2000 in full consultation and agreement with the Ministry of Energy and Mineral Resources. While offering the shares, KPC was also of the opinion that it was waiting for the government to agree on the shares price.

The dispute ended on 29 July 2003, after the central government made a decision to split 51 percent of KPC's shares into 20 percent for the central government and 31 percent for the local government. As a condition for the divestment, the company demanded that the provincial government withdraw its legal suit. KPC argued that it could not conduct the divestment process because the law did not allow the company to do so, particularly when the asset in question was placed under an

---

[53] Response from KPC as presented by its lawyers Lubis, Santosa and Maulana, dated 19 Feb. 2002, signed by T. Mulya Lubis, Leylana Santosa and Fredrick Pinakunary, p. 10.
[54] Response of KPC, dated 19 Feb. 2002, p. 29.
[55] Ibid., p. 30.

order of seizure.[56] Governor Suwarna then wrote a letter to the panel of South Jakarta District Court for revocation of the lawsuit against KPC, and the court granted his petition.[57]

The Framework Agreement

Noke Kiroyan, the CEO of KPC, and Purnomo signed the framework agreement on 5 August 2002. In the earlier part of this chapter, the agreement was mentioned in relation to Purnomo's attempt to block Suwarna. This sub-section looks at the agreement from the perspective of KPC when it had to face opposition from Suwarna. The agreement was an additional explanation to deliver on the divestment process. It aimed at providing detailed procedures and conditions for implementing the KPC share offer. Noke Kiroyan supported it and commented that the "twin principles of business-to-business and win-win solution advocated by the minister from the outset have finally led us to the conclusion of the Framework Agreement".[58] KPC used the agreement as a means to protect its interest. KPC might welcome Suwarna as new shareholder, but the governor would have to follow the terms and conditions set out in the framework agreement.

The framework agreement states that the government of Indonesia or a state-owned company involved in mining may have shares of not less than 20 percent, and that the provincial government of East Kalimantan, the regency of East Kutai or companies owned by them may have shares in aggregates of not less than 20 percent. It also stipulates, "the government of Indonesia will ensure that all the offered shares will not be held through a single entity and that the assignees will act independently of each other and not in concert or as a group".[59] Later on, the management of KPC insisted on two important points: "the qualified buyer to reveal its sources of funding; and that shares will not be held by a consortium

---

[56] Opinion presented by KPC legal adviser Fredrick Pinakunary, email correspondence, 8 Jan. 2004.

[57] Determination of South Jakarta District Court regarding case no. 350/Pdt.G/PN, Jaksel, dated 1 Aug. 2002, signed by presiding judge IDG Putra Jadnya.

[58] Address of president director of PT Kaltim Prima Coal on the signing of the framework agreement with the minister of energy and mineral resources on 5 Aug. 2002, as published by KPC's internal magazine, *Kabara*, Sept. 2002, p. 2.

[59] Framework Agreement between Minister of Energy and Mineral Resources and KPC, dated 5 Aug. 2002, signed by Purnomo Yusgiantoro and Noke Kiroyan, article 3.2 (b).

which comprised of perusda owned by East Kalimantan or East Kutai governments".[60]

In the following month, Governor Suwarna filed a lawsuit against KPC in the court of Samarinda, the capital of East Kalimantan, to annul the framework agreement. Suwarna knew that his chance of owning the majority of KPC shares were better if he could work for the annulment of the framework agreement. Siding with Suwarna, the court handed down two decisions: first, it attacked the very foundation of the agreement's existence as a legal document that governed the divestment process by concluding that it was illegitimate;[61] second, it therefore ruled that the agreement be annulled.[62]

In response, KPC wrote a complaint letter to the court of Samarinda questioning its decision to annul the framework agreement. KPC stated that the decree was a mistake from a legal perspective; that the court of Samarinda had no legal foundation for an annulment; and that this matter was beyond the jurisdiction of the court.[63] But this complaint had no legal implication because it was not intended as a legal step.

In January 2003, Minister Purnomo intervened in the legal dispute by writing a letter to the court of Samarinda arguing that it had no authority to issue a decision to annul the agreement. The minister insisted that any dispute must be settled by way of a proper mechanism set out in the coal contract through an international arbitration body.[64] The legal matter remained unresolved[65] as the parties involved preferred to continue the process. Moreover, both KPC and the minister of energy and mineral resources still based their actions on the framework agreement for procedures regarding the share offer.

---

[60] Attachment of letter from KPC, dated 13 Feb. 2003.

[61] Decision of the court Samarinda, East Kalimantan, no. 118/Pdt.P/2002/PN.Smda, dated 4 Dec. 2002, p. 13.

[62] Ibid., p.18.

[63] Letter written by law office Lubis, Santosa & Maulana to the chairperson of the Samarinda court, no. 0206/LSM-FP/L/XII/2002, dated 17 Dec. 2002, signed by T. Mulya Lubis and Fredrick J. Pinakunary.

[64] "KPC Tolak Due Diligence oleh Perusda Kaltim", *Bisnis Indonesia*, 7 Jan. 2003. *Bisnis Indonesia* obtained a letter, no. 4016/SJN.H/2002, written by Minister Purnomo to the court of Samarinda.

[65] Information from interview with Fredrick Pinakunary, legal adviser of KPC, 12 Aug. 2003.

Due Diligence

Since January 2003, due diligence emerged as a main bone of contention between KPC and Suwarna. Due diligence is a general term for the proper process of evaluating a transaction. KPC argued that, as indirectly stated in the framework agreement, it had the right to conduct due diligence on potential buyers. Suwarna argued that the perusda, the company that represented his interest, had the right to conduct due diligence.

On 13 February 2003, KPC wrote a letter to Purnomo. It revealed that Purnomo had proposed that the company consider allowing further exclusivity for PTBA and the perusda to accept and complete the purchase of KPC's shares. Here, Purnomo still maintained his position that 51 percent of the shares of KPC must be divided into two. In replying to this proposal, KPC was pleased to take advice from Purnomo. The position of KPC was clear: it agreed to "an extension of the central government offer process; re-instatement of the perusda into the central government offer process; and due diligence by the perusdas on KPC".[66]

Using the available opportunity, Suwarna wrote a letter to KPC demanding that the perusda conduct due diligence on KPC. Suwarna demanded that KPC must provide all the necessary documents and information with regard to the divestment process for a thorough examination under the due diligence process.[67] If Suwarna allowed evaluation of KPC, he would have been in a better position to judge the overall performance of the company. Suwarna preferred that his party, the potential buyer, conduct an evaluation of the seller.

KPC replied by sending a letter. The letter states the following:

> Under the terms of the Framework Agreement, GOI may assign part of its offer to the Indonesian Province of East Kalimantan, the East Kutai Regency (kabupaten), or companies owned by them, subject to certain agreed criteria. KPC is not aware of those criteria having been satisfied or of the GOI having made an assignment of the share offer to your Company. As a consequence all we can do at this time

---

[66] Letter from KPC to Ministry of Energy and Mineral Resources, dated 13 Feb. 2003, signed by Lex Graefe and Murray Easton.

[67] Letter of Perusda Melati Bhakti Satya, number: 94/A/MBS/2002, dated 6 Nov. 2002, signed by its director Mandurdi, Samarinda, East Kalimantan. Perusda Pertambangan dan Energi of the East Kutai Regency government also wrote a letter, number 46/A.3-PPEK/XI/2002, dated 6 Nov. 2002, signed by its director Wahyu Setiaji, Sangatta, East Kalimantan.

is to pass a copy of your letter and this letter in reply to the Secretary General of the Ministry of Mines and Energy for his consideration.[68]

This letter clarifies the position of KPC to deny the due-diligence process. The argument put forward by KPC states that it was not aware that the central government had transferred its right to the share offers to the perusda. The process of due diligence for KPC by the perusdas never materialized.

The Response

As mentioned before, KPC responded to particular sources of pressure from Suwarna. However, even as early as April 2003, KPC saw signs of danger on the horizon when the authority shifted from Purnomo to Laksamana. Roes Aryawijaya, the chief of the divestment solution team who was also working under the supervision of Minister Laksamana, had threatened KPC by revoking the legal base of KPC as the contractor and by threatening to stop its coal-mining operations on the grounds that KPC denied due diligence on KPC by two perusda that represented the interests of the province.[69] In addition to that threat, Laksamana warned KPC of the closure of its operations because of its failure to fulfill its obligation to divest the company's equities.[70]

At this crucial time, the shareholders of KPC, BP[71] and Rio Tinto, suddenly in mid-July 2003, transferred their entire ownership to PT

---

[68] Letter from Kaltim Prima Coal to President Director Perusda Melati Bhakti Satya, dated 12 Nov. 2002 and signed by director Lex Graefe.

[69] *Tim penyelesaian divestasi saham 51 percent PT Kaltim Prima Coal, Laporan kemajuan proses divestasi 51 percent Saham PT Kaltim Prima Coal*, 21 Apr.–12 June 2003. The existence of this document and its recommendation was claimed by the chief of the team, Roes Aryawijaya; see "Ijon Laba, Berbuah Masalah", *Tempo*, 10 Aug. 2003, p. 124.

[70] "Kaltim Prima Coal dianggap default", 2 June 2003.

[71] BP controls interests in Indonesia valued at about US$6 billion, including various companies such as PT Petrokimia Nusantara, PT Amoco Mitsui Indonesia PT Polytama Propindo. Now concentrated on the Tangguh project in Papua, it reached a verbal agreement in Jan. 2004 to extend its contract in the Terang Sirasun oil field in East Java ("Investasi BP di Indonesia mencapai US$6 miliar", 26 Jan. 2004). As stated by Satya Widha Yudha, BP Indonesia vice president for government and public affairs, the company took the view that coal mining was not BP's core business ("Govt Proves Sale KPC shares", *Jakarta Post*, 23 July 2003).

Bumi Resources[72] (Bumi hereafter) for US$500 million, cheaper by 40 percent than the divestment price of US$822 million. They defended their move to sell their interest in KPC. BP vice president in Indonesia, Nico Kanter, argued that this greatly reduced price was due to the fact that the US$412 million for 51 percent of the firm was a 2001 valuation, and circumstances had changed since then, particularly the price of coal. (The international coal price according to Japan Benchmark for June 2003 was around US$36/ton. The average annual price in 2001 was around US$33/ton.)

Rio Tinto defended the decision to sell its shares by saying it was a transaction to transfer the parent companies, not those of KPC.[73] Yet, it would be clear that for the next ten years Rio Tinto and BP would lose a projected profit of US$1,202.03 million, or US$601.01 million each.[74] The move by KPC to allow losses of future income was a clear signal of its frustration with the overall situation surrounding the divestment process.[75] In addition, Lex Graefe stated: "we were not happy with the slow (divestment) progress, and were not happy with a number of disputes ... we would much rather that the divestment process was more straightforward, that there were not a lot of legal issues".[76]

Other than the reason put forward by Rio Tinto, BP was the driving force behind the deal because it wanted to get rid of its last mine and concentrate on the liquefied natural gas (LNG) business. In the sale

---

[72] Bumi Resources started as Bumi Modern in 1973 and became a major player in the hotel and tourism sector. In 1998, however, the company, citing adverse economic conditions, shifted its core business to oil, natural gas and mining. At the time of the transaction, Bumi had only IDR3 trillion in assets and a liability amounting to IDR4 trillion. Bumi Resources, which operates in the mining sector, is listed on the Jakarta Stock Exchange. Aburizal Bakrie, who controlled 2 percent of shares, is a prominent businessperson and political figure from Golkar. At the time of this research, he followed Golkar's convention to nominate a presidential candidate that would represent the party for the election of 2004. In 2001, Bumi acquired PT Arutmin, a coal company in East Kalimantan, worth IDR1.2 trillion, by issuing bond ("Kembali ke Titik Nol", *Tempo*, 3 Aug. 2003, p. 132).

[73] As said by Anang Rizkani Noor, spokesperson of Rio Tinto Indonesia; see "Bumi pinjam dana ke Bank Asing", *Koran Tempo*, 23 July 2003.

[74] Calculated based on projected profit by Salomon Smith Barney, Bahana Securities and KKEDS, the number is the mean.

[75] This impression is derived from an interview with Anang Rizkani Noor, deputy director for communication at Rio Tinto Indonesia, 7 Aug. 2003.

[76] Interview with Lex Graefe, *Jakarta Post*, 30 July 2003.

process, BP's vice president for Indonesia Nico Kanter stated that Bumi Resources approached BP in London with an offer to both owners of KPC. At the time, BP had planned to sell its stakes in KPC and found no takers.[77] In Indonesia, BP had already started selling its investment in 2002. For example, BP sold shares in PT Petrokimia Nusantara that it had bought from Suharto's son Sigit Hardjojudanto to a relative, Sudwikatmono, in early 2004. The main reason given was that BP wanted to concentrate on the new liquefied natural gas (LNG) project and maintain only a small proportion of shares in select companies like Amoco Mitsui Indonesia[78] and Polytama Propindo.[79] BP's annual report for 2003 mentions only the Tangguh LNG project in West Papua.[80] BP recognized that Indonesia was still the world's main producer of LNG, and the Tangguh project would reinforce this market-leading position.

The transfer of KPC's ownership to Bumi involved an exchange between Aburizal Bakrie,[81] who owns a 2.12 percent shares in Bumi,[82] and shareholders of KPC. Bumi got a US$404 million loan to finance the purchase. Singapore's United Overseas Bank and Credit Suisse First Boston provided US$318 million, Australia's Macquarie Bank US$46 million, and Leighton Financial around US$40 million.[83] The possibilities for Bumi to obtain funds from international lenders were open, as KPC had been a profitable business entity. Moreover, Rio Tinto and BP had acted as guarantors for Bumi in order to obtain funds from international lenders.[84] The shareholders of KPC stated, "Rio Tinto and BP will work with PT Bumi Resources to ensure a smooth transition of ownership and are ensuring that there will be no impact on service to customer".[85]

By siding with Aburizal Bakrie, BP and Rio Tinto were hoping to get political protection in two forms. First, they intended the sale of KPC to receive political protection from possible attacks from Suwarna.

---

[77] "Why BP Had to Wash Its Hands off Coalmining after Two Decades", *The Times*, 22 July 2003.
[78] BP holds 45 percent together with Mitsui Chemical of Japan.
[79] BP holds 10 percent, while Nissho Iwai of Japan holds 10 percent, and Tirtamas Majutama holds 80 percent.
[80] BP, Record of Annual Result, London, Feb. 2004, p. 7.
[81] He was a candidate for president at the Golkar Party convention and was defeated.
[82] "Aburizal Bantu Bumi Beli KPC", *Koran Tempo*, 25 July 2003.
[83] "Bumi Gets $404 Loan to Close Deal", *Jakarta Post*, 14 Oct. 2003.
[84] "Kembali ke titik nol", *Tempo*, 3 Aug. 2003, p. 132.
[85] Press Release of PT KPC, 21 July 2003.

Second, they had intended to receive political protection for their entire interests in the country over the long term. Total BP interest in Indonesia was valued at US$6 billion and spread out over many projects. British minister for energy Brian Wilson, who visited Indonesia in November 2001, said that BP had committed a total of US$11 billion in investments, with US$1.9 billion in current capital to spend on Indonesian projects. Rio Tinto's operation in Indonesia accounted for 4 percent of its earnings, approximately US$60 million,[86] and its investment accounted for US$1.2 billion.

After selling its business interests in the country, BP concentrated on its newly established Tangguh project.[87] BP had planned to invest US$3–4 billion in the development of the Tangguh liquefied natural gas (LNG) project in West Papua's Bintuni Bay.[88] It already had sunk some US$600 million into the project.[89] It was a big project, and BP needed assurances in terms of political protection for a very long period, at least over the 30-year life of the contract and project. In the Suharto era, BP had adopted a strategy of cultivating close ties with politically powerful personages. It moved closer to Suharto's circle by befriending his son and other relatives.

Rio Tinto also had stakes that needed protecting. It was involved in various mining operations around the country, one of the most important assets being Freeport MacMoran in West Papua. In this company, Rio Tinto had first encountered Aburizal Bakrie when Freeport had to divest shares and Aburizal bought them. Through this encounter, they established mutual trust. When Rio Tinto and BP wanted a local partner, they specified several requirements such as experience in coal operations, trustworthiness and political power. Aburizal met all these criteria. The

---

[86] Walhi, "Undermining Indonesia" (Jakarta: WALHI and Friends of the Earth Report, 2003), p. 4.

[87] LNG Tangguh is operated under a production-sharing contract with Pertamina. Shareholders of Tangguh are: BP Plc (50 percent); Mitsubishi Corporation (16 percent); Nippon Oil (12 percent); British Gas (10.8 percent); Kanematsu Group (10 percent); and Nissho Iwai (1.1 percent); data from database of *Bisnis Indonesia*. The project was initiated in 2002 and aimed at starting production in 2006. It already had a commitment from Fujian Province in China to supply 2.5 million tons LNG, 1 million tons to SK Power and POSCO for the next 20 years. See the Tabura Newsletter for the Tangguh Project, Oct. 2003. Tangguh would become the third LNG project in the country after Arun and Bontang.

[88] "BP and the Tangguh Test", *Inside Indonesia*, Apr.–June 2002.

[89] "BP in Indonesia: Sociologists Before Geologists?", *The Economist*.

future political standing of Aburizal Bakrie looked like it would be increasing with his move to establish himself as a presidential candidate and then to join the presidential convention in the Golkar Party for election in 2004.

As already anticipated by BP and Rio Tinto, in early September 2003 Suwarna went to Jakarta and met president Megawati to express his disappointment over the sale of KPC to Bumi. In this meeting, the governor still insisted on the possibility of the province obtaining 31 percent shares as decided by the central government in July 2002.[90] However, no conclusion was reached.

Before Governor Suwarna went to Jakarta, he issued a press release on 6 August 2003, stating: "our aim is one: divestment of 51 percent of KPC must be done".[91] The next week, the governor asked whether this transfer of equity was valid without approval from the government of the Republic of Indonesia.[92] He went on to say that based on the coal contract, KPC was only a contractor that obtained a permit to mine through a mining authorization issued by the central government. He stated that if the transfer of equity was valid without approval from the government of Indonesia, did it mean that foreign investors granted a right from the government could freely sell their equity?

The next day, Suwarna attacked KPC and Bumi. His point was to question whether the transaction between KPC and Bumi was a pure business deal free of backroom dealings.[93] Suwarna continued by questioning whether the transfer of assets was correct, and to question why BP and Rio Tinto did not fulfill their obligation to divest KPC's equities and sell them to the government. Did Bumi finish the divestment of 51 percent of KPC's equity? On 11 October 2003 Bumi completed the acquisition of KPC from BP and Rio Tinto by paying a total of US$500 million, including the assumption of its debts.[94] But Suwarna had faced

---

[90] "Setelah kambing makan sapi", *Tempo*, 14 Sept. 2003, p. 138.
[91] Press release of the East Kalimantan Government as published in *Media Indonesia*, 6 Aug. 2003.
[92] Ibid., 12 Aug. 2003.
[93] Press release of the East Kalimantan Government as published in *Sinar Haparan*, 13 Aug. 2003.
[94] "Bumi Resources Concludes Purchase of KPC", *Jakarta Post*, 11 Oct. 2003. After that, Bumi became the owner of KPC, and Edie S. Hudaja was appointed president director of KPC, replacing Noke Kiroyan.

a great loss when the newly appointed East Kutai Regent Mahyudin[95] entered a new agreement with Aburizal Bakrie through Bumi to divest 18.6 percent[96] of KPC's shares, which the regency was appointed to purchase at the price of US$104 million.

Furthermore, Minister Purnomo formed the opinion that the transaction was valid.[97] The national parliament (DPR) also held the opinion that the divestment of KPC was completed following the agreement to give 18.6 percent of shares to East Kutai Regency.[98] In January 2004, the regency government obtained a loan worth US$25 million to purchase the equity of KPC,[99] while an additional loan was still in under negotiation between the regency and a UK-based financier. Given these events, the governor lost his battle in trying to control KPC's shares.

Conclusion

This case study has been lengthy and rather complex. What has been the main element of the story? Briefly, the story centered on a new political player: East Kalimantan Governor Suwarna Abdul Fatah. The case highlights Suwarna's ability to develop into an important political player trying to shape the politics and economy of the province. To do so, he heavily relied on political networks that involved politicians in Jakarta and lower local elites on the regency level. Such personal connections, which were based on converging interests, emphasized the emergence of a new pattern of politics in which the province was linked to Jakarta.

People like Suwarna could only possibly emerge as important political players because of their capability to forge political networks with

---

[95] Mahyudin was born in Tanjung, South Kalimantan on 8 June 1970 and graduated from the Engineering Faculty of Lambung Mangkurat University in Banjarmasin. He was the deputy regent of East Kutai from 2001 to 2003. He replaced Awang Faroek Ishak in May 2003 when Faroek decided to compete for the East Kalimantan governorship, which meant he had to resign his position as the regent of East Kutai. Mahyudin is chairperson of Golkar branch in East Kutai. Since he is from Golkar, there was a possibility that he would side with Aburizal Bakrie.

[96] This number is calculated from 60 percent out of 31 percent of KPC's shares, because the remaining 20 percent is allocated to PTBA.

[97] "Pemerintah setuju penjualan 18.6 percent saham KPC ke Kutim", *Bisnis Indonesia*, 18 Oct. 2003.

[98] "Long Haul Sells Shares of PT Bumi", *Bisnis Indonesia*, 11 Dec. 2003.

[99] "East Kutai Obtains Loan from the US to Buy KPC's Shares", *Bisnis Indonesia*, 15 Jan. 2004.

those wielding power at the center of politics in Jakarta. As a consequence, Suwarna was able to voice his interest on the national level, and even openly challenge decisions of the central government. He was undeniably the product of the decentralization and democratization processes that started to take root in 1999. Since the departure of Suharto, the rules of the game have been changing, and as this study shows, the political networks created under these long periods remained intact. This pattern should be clear in Lemhanas, the central government think tank that conducted courses for high officers around the country, and the place where Suwarna met Mutojib. In late 2000, Suwarna cultivated his personal relationship with Mutojib in order to wage a battle with the central government. The governor's political networks expanded by involving persons with relevant power on the national level, particularly in the context of the divestment process, such as Laksamana Sukardi. This political link then connected Suwarna to other politicians from PDI-P. On the regional level, Governor Suwarna successfully managed to consolidate power by connecting with other powerful politicians such as Syaukani and Awang Faroek.

The emergence of Suwarna paved the way for the rise of a new pattern of politics characterized by interconnectedness between the center and the region through a network of politicians and their overlapping interests. This interconnection also reflects the increasing importance of politics on the provincial level in relation to both Jakarta and other regencies and cities in the province.

Another source of Suwarna's power lay in the mining location sites of Kutai Regency. Suwarna was able to make these places a source of power and to use it to bargain with the central government and multinationals. In the New Order's state, the mining sites were the source of power Suharto could tap in order to bargain with foreign investors, especially if they had already invested heavily in the extractive sector of the country. After the collapse of the New Order state, Suwarna began to learn the significance of the mining sites in his administrative region; therefore, according to him, he could also use them to bargain with both the central government and foreign investors. While Jakarta is the legal owner of the mining sites, Suwarna thought he or his province must also have rights to it. Therefore, he demanded a portion of the shares in KPC.

Ironically, Suwarna's failure to obtain stocks from selling KPC's shares is due to political networks that worked *against* his interest. These political networks connected local politicians who wanted to own shares in KPC with the national businesspersons-cum-politicians who wanted to have a local partner.

Faced with the twin challenges—the rise of provincial elites and the vulnerability of the political and economic structure—KPC strategically employed a classical method, making an alliance with political power. Logically, the foreign investors tended to seek political protection for their overall investment in the country, especially in the long run. For sure, the chance for Rio Tinto and BP to withdraw from the country was unlikely, because they each had—and still have—a massive investment in extractive sectors such as LNG in Papua. Because the introduction of decentralization policies and political parties allowed political parties to become important players, KPC tended to side with businesspersons who were politically connected to relatively strong political parties for long-term political protection. Business figures such Aburizal Bakrie, with strong connections to Golkar, could offer political protection to shareholders of KPC. Here, political parties took over Suharto's role of offering viable long-term protection.

CHAPTER 5

The Conflict over the Privatization of Semen Padang

Introduction

This chapter looks closely at the dispute over the privatization of Semen Padang, a state-owned cement enterprise located in West Sumatra, which had to undergo privatization because its parent company, Semen Gresik,[1] another state-owned cement company, was ordered by the central government to do so. This led to the dispute over privatization that involved the central and provincial governments, as well as, to some extent, multinationals.

The case of Semen Padang offers an example of how the breakup of an institutional arrangement established by Suharto paved the way for the emergence of provincial politicians on the national political stage through the establishment of political networks. It exhibits the way political networks could be forged around friendship, ethnicity and, to some extent, affiliation to a political party.

The introduction of democratization and decentralization policies provided a means for a provincial politician such as the CEO of Semen Padang, Ikhdan Nizar,[2] and the deputy speaker of the provincial assembly,

---

[1] Both Semen Gresik and Semen Padang are state-owned enterprises. In 1995, Semen Padang was merged with Semen Gresik.

[2] Ikhdan Nizar was born in Bukittinggi on 30 July 1943. He graduated from local primary school and Padang senior high school, and in 1972 he graduated from Bandung Institute of Technology (ITB). His career started in Semen Padang in 1974, and he has since worked as director of research and development in Semen Gresik (1988–95); CEO of Semen Baturaja (1995–99); and CEO of Semen Padang (1999–2003).

112

Titik Nazif Lubuk,[3] to rise to power. Through these institutions, they boosted their political strength by creating political networks with capable politicians in Jakarta, in this case with Azwar Anas,[4] the CEO of Semen Padang in the 1970s and governor of West Sumatra from 1977 to 1988. Most of these provincial politicians had been cultivating personal connections with each other since the days of Suharto, so the networks were already in place.

As the case of Semen Padang shows, with the rise to power of these provincial politicians, the power of SOE minister[5] Laksamana Sukardi[6] to engineer privatization was challenged. Laksamana had to carefully consider the political strength developed by both Ikhdan Nizar and Titik Nazif Lubuk.

The Semen Padang case provides a good case for understanding the political and economic situation in Indonesia after Suharto. First, the case unveils the capability of provincial politicians to develop political power depending on the personal relationships established mainly under the auspices of the Suharto government. These networks linked these provincial politicians to relatively powerful politicians at the center of the country's politics: namely, Jakarta. Second, with their rise to power, these provincial politicians challenged the central government's economic policy to privatize Semen Padang. Third, the case illustrates that the deep and unresolved political fight between the central and provincial governments deterred the establishment of a stable new political-economic structure to suit their new power. Instead, their dispute encouraged disorder.

---

[3] Titik Nazif Lubuk was born in Bukittinggi on 7 Oct. 1947. She received her entire education in Padang and graduated from the Foreign Language Academy in 1970. She served as a provincial parliament member from Golkar during 1972–79 and 1999–2004, where she served as the deputy speaker. She has also been active in local women's organizations.

[4] Azwar Anas was born in Padang on 2 Aug. 1931. He was educated in Padang through high school and graduated from Bandung Institute of Technology in 1959. He was CEO of PT Pindad (1969–70); CEO of Semen Padang (1970–77); Governor of West Sumatra (1977–87); Minister of Transportation (1988–93); Coordinating Minister of Social Affairs (1994–97); and Member of the Supreme Advisory Council (1998–2000).

[5] The Ministry of SOE was established by the late Suharto government in 1998 as a response to the crisis, but under Abdurahman Wahid's government it was dissolved. The Megawati government revived the ministry and appointed Laksamana Sukardi from PDI-P as its minister.

[6] Laksamana Sukardi was born in Jakarta on 1 Oct. 1956. He graduated from the Bandung Institute of Technology in 1979.

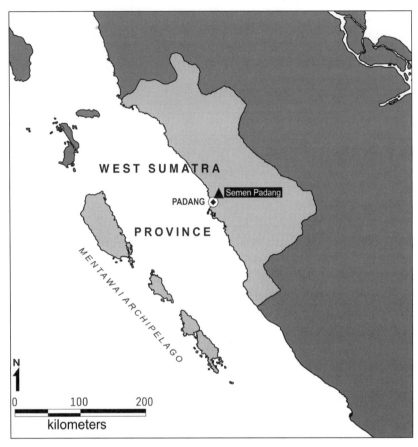
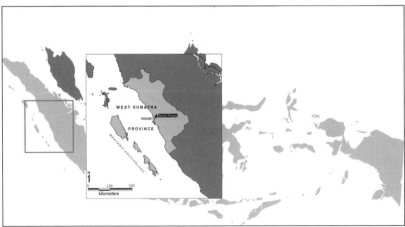

Map 2. West Sumatra

It revealed that economic policy had been politicized, as both parties heavily employed political measures to defend their political and economic interests instead of honoring the existing rules of the game.

This chapter first looks briefly at the fundamental pillar of the New Order government under Suharto and how he established institutions to control politics in the province of West Sumatra. Then the chapter discusses the present political situation in the province as the outcome of both decentralization and democratization. Last, it addresses Semen Padang in the context of the changing political and economic situation. The next section charts the rise of Ikhdan Nizar and Titik Nazif Lubuk as major political actors; the section after that discusses the dispute between the central government and provincial politicians.

Context

West Sumatra's Integration into the New Order

West Sumatra is home to 68.44 percent of all Minangkabau (Suryadinata and Nurvidya 2003: 52). Political parties based on religious alignment had influenced the structure of politics in West Sumatra during the early life of the republic. Islamic political forces controlled the region. The modernist Muslim groups (Muhammadiyah) were close to Masyumi, the modernist Muslim political party. The older traditional groups were close to Perti (Pergerakan Tarbijah Islamiah, Islamic Education Movement). The result of the 1955 election reflected those forces: Masyumi won the election with 48.89 percent of the vote, followed by Perti with 27.80 percent, with the rest of the vote divided among small parties.[7]

The influence of Islamic political parties weakened when the Sukarno government successfully eliminated the regional rebellion of the PRRI (Revolutionary Government of Indonesian Republic) in 1957 (Kahin 1999). Waged to set up a revolutionary government in Sumatra headed by Sjafruddin Prawiranegara, the rebellion was joined by some leaders who originated in West Sumatra. This episode with the PPRI left the elites of West Sumatra with an uneasy feeling about the label "rebel". In the early 1970s Suharto further weakened the influence of Islamic political parties by consolidating them into a single political party, the United Development Party (PPP).

---

[7] From Lembaga Ekonomi dan Kemasyarakatan Nasional (Leknas), 1971, as quoted in *Kompas*, 31 Jan. 2004.

In the beginning of his reign, Suharto controlled West Sumatra through the military and the government bureaucracy. Additionally, Suharto appointed the leader of the Minangkabau in order to bring the region's *adat* and religious organizations closer to Jakarta. A component of this political scheme was the role played by Saafroedin Bahar, the president's commissioner of Semen Padang between 1998 and 2003. In 1969, Saafroedin Bahar was appointed the chairperson of the Golkar branch, after which he succeeded in weakening the political parties by incorporating most of their influential members into this government organization (Kahin 1999: 256).

These measures significantly changed the behavior of regional elites in West Sumatra vis-à-vis Jakarta. Regional elites since then have wanted to benefit from their relations with Jakarta. Given the serious consideration that the region would not benefit if it opposed the central government, regional elites changed their behavior from opposition to one of full cooperation. As far back as the 1970s, regional elites of Minangkabau were ready to cooperate with Golkar. Baharuddin Dt. Rangkayo Basya (Amal 1993: 156–7) reminded other political elites to prevent rebellions like that of the PRRI from occurring again in West Sumatra. Baharuddin's position as the leader of the Forum of the Adat Association of Minangkabau (LKAAM)[8] was important, since he formally led the entire body of ethnic leaders. His readiness to fully cooperate with the central government meant that all ethnic leaders in Minangkabau wanted to cooperate with the central government. Baharuddin argued that only by cooperating with the central government's political party, Golkar, could West Sumatra prosper economically and become politically stable. He pointed out the cases of some West Sumatran elites who supported the PRRI rebellion and alienated the province in the eyes of central government. Such alienation put the province in a situation where it was allocated fewer funds for development.

The first governor of West Sumatra, serving from 1958 to 1964, Kaharoeddin Rangkayo Basa, was chief of the police force in West Sumatra, where he successfully helped the central government under Sukarno to outmaneuver the PRRI rebellion by way of supporting the military attack

---

[8] LKAAM is Golkar's political wing and is used to consolidate ethnic leaders. LKAAM turned out to be the political vehicle in West Sumatra used to help Golkar's effort to gain votes in every election under Suharto. In fact, it was designed to prevent a communist movement. Captain Saafroedin Bahar was its first secretary.

led by Colonel Achmad Yani.[9] However, Kaharoeddin had to let his position go in 1964 when he refused to cooperate with the Sukarno government, which at the time tended to support both PNI and PKI. He refused because he was close to and helped Colonel Ahmad Yani to silence the PRRI. Kaharoeddin's closeness to Ahmad Yani meant the governor was aligning with the political attitude of the military against siding with Sukarno. Colonel Ahmad Yani was sent by General A.H. Nasution, army chief of staff, to fight the PRRI. He was a Javanese officer and commanded troops from the Brawijaya and Diponegoro divisions of East and Central Java.

Golkar started to cultivate its political domination here in 1971 and Suharto had to thank the role played by three governors: Harun Zain, Azwar Anas and Hasan Basri Durin, who served between 1966 and 1998. At the beginning of the New Order government under Suharto in 1966, the role of Governor Harun was crucial because he had to persuade the West Sumatran people to support the government after the region had experienced a bad episode with the PRRI. Suharto's assignment for Harun was to secure political support for the New Order government. Harun's background included his work as a technocrat of West Sumatran origin, though he was born and raised in Jakarta; he received his economic training at Berkeley; and he was a member of the prestigious Economics Faculty at the University of Indonesia, where he enjoyed an excellent reputation.[10] Suharto appointed Harun because of his background as both the leader of a Muslim student group (HMI) that opposed the communist student movement (CGMI) in Padang and his personal capability as an economist. Harun performed his assignment well, as evinced by the result of the first election conducted under the Suharto regime, which at that time was seeking political legitimacy. West Sumatra under Governor Harun Zain gave the victory to Golkar with 63.2 percent of the votes. The election in 1971 became a turning point for the elites in West Sumatra, when they pragmatically began to support Golkar. At the same

---

[9] For details on Kaharoeddin Rangkayo Basa, see Hasril Chaniago and Khairul Jasmi, *Brigadir Jenderal polisi Kaharoeddin Datuk Rangkayo Basa* (Jakarta: Pustaka Sinar Harapan, 1998).

[10] Harun was born in Jakarta on 1 Mar. 1927. He received his education from the Europese Lagere School (ELS), Jakarta (1942); Hogere Burgeije School (HBS), Jakarta (1942); Tju Gakku, Surabaya (1945); the senior high school in Blitar (1948); the Economics Faculty, University of Indonesia (1958); and the University of California, Berkeley (1960).

time, Golkar also used them for political mobilization. The explanation of Baharuddin Rangkayo Basa, the chief of LKAAM, mentioned above, strongly indicates the willingness of elites to cooperate with Golkar. Harun persuaded local leaders to both cooperate with the central government and also vote for Golkar. As a result, in 1977, Golkar won the election with 66.6 percent. When Harun Zain had to leave West Sumatra, Azwar Anas took over the post of governor and was able to secure another Golkar victory in 1982 with 60.4 percent.

When Harun Zain completed his term, he recommended a native West Sumatran, Azwar Anas[11]—then CEO of Semen Padang—as his replacement. Zain considered Azwar an able person due to his career within the government. Azwar was a Brigadier General, a chemical engineer, and a capable businessperson who had succeeded in restructuring the near-bankrupt Semen Padang and making it a profitable business. Azwar also had good ties with military officers in Jakarta. Thus, Azwar fulfilled Suharto's requirement for governor: he was from the military and loyal to the government. Two facts indicate his loyalty to Suharto: first, he supported the development program that Suharto designed. In 1984, his achievements were recognized when Suharto selected West Sumatra as Indonesia's most successful province in terms of carrying out his development plan, that is, according to Jakarta's criteria (Kahin 1999: 260). Second, Azwar sustained Golkar domination in the province by maintaining an average vote percentage above 60 percent. Again, in 1987, Golkar won the election with a vote of 78.7 percent. In doing so, Azwar made use of similar strategies that involved relying on bureaucracies and local leaders in the region.

At the center, Suharto fully weakened political parties to the point that they had to accept Pancasila, the state's ideology, as their foundation. The outcome of this measure on Islamic-based political parties was tremendous, since they were not able to maintain their Islamic character, which was their main appeal to voters in West Sumatra. Eventually, the influence of PPP weakened and dropped to about 16 percent in the 1987 elections. It was Golkar that gained the maximum benefit from this situation.

---

[11] Azwar Anas graduated from primary school in Bukittinggi (1944); junior high school in Bukittinggi (1948); senior high school in Padang (1951); and the Bandung Institute of Technology (1959). He also served in various ministerial posts under the Suharto government.

Conflict over the Privatization of Semen Padang   119

Governor Hasan Basri Durin secured the victory of Golkar with 91.15 percent of the vote in the election in 1997. He was a son of an Islamic religious teacher and joined the Ministry of Home Affairs after graduating from high school.[12] He served for several years in Jambi and then returned to Padang at the end of 1969 as secretary of the regional election committee for the 1971 election. Governor Harun appointed him mayor of Padang, and he served until 1983. In 1987, he was appointed assistant to the governor of West Sumatra. Also in 1987, the provincial councilors appointed him governor, replacing Azwar Anas, who gave him his full support. Durin was the head of LKAAM and used this position to help Golkar secure its victories in the elections. During the 1999 election, the first after Suharto's departure, Golkar still ruled the region, with 23.63 percent of the vote. Following Golkar were PAN (National Mandate Party) with 22.16 percent of the vote, PPP with 20.6 percent, and PDI-P (Indonesian Democratic Party of Struggle) with 10.92 percent.[13]

Other political parties had never challenged Golkar's influence in West Sumatra. Its long domination of 30 years created a pattern that allowed the vertical political mobility of governors. Each of West Sumatra's three governors, Harun Zain, Azwar Anas and Hasan Basri Durin, served the province for ten years, during which they secured Golkar domination in the region. Such an accomplishment suggests that the three governors performed well in the eyes of Suharto as well as the West Sumatran population. To the West Sumatran people, what was positive about it was that their three decades of work linked West Sumatra to the center and strengthened their ability to eliminate the negative feelings in a region that had once rebelled against the central government. In the end, people stopped being anti-Jakarta in attitude. In the eyes of Suharto, the ability of these governors to secure the political domination of Golkar over a long period of time shows that the West Sumatran people approved of their leadership. With such a high level of performance on the political scene, Suharto rewarded these governors with even higher political positions as ministers. Each of them had served as a minister under Suharto:

---

[12] Hasan Basri Durin was born in Padang Panjang on 15 Jan. 1935. He graduated from the Faculty of Social Sciences, Gadjah Mada University, Yogyakarta. He served as mayor of Padang, the capital of West Sumatra, for 11 years; district chief of Jambi for 2 years; and deputy governor for 4 years.

[13] General Election Committee 2000, as quoted in *Kompas*, 31 Jan. 2004.

For example, Harun Zain served as the minister for transmigration and the labor force; and Azwar Anas as the minister of transportation and co-ordinating minister for social affairs.[14] Later, in 1998, Hasan Basri Durin served as the state minister for agrarian affairs in the Habibie government.

But, Golkar domination, though still unchallenged after the fall of Suharto, still lost much of its former power. The vast network deeply embedded within the bureaucracy of West Sumatra and ethnic associations such as LKAAM served as the basis for Golkar's political mobilization. Prominent politicians such as Azwar Anas played a role in supporting the local elites who were mainly from Golkar in defending Semen Padang as a state-owned company. His role was important, because he was highly credited by both local leaders and members of the central government under various presidents—Habibie, Abdurahman Wahid and Megawati.

Semen Padang under Suharto and Its Aftermath

The life of the company known as Semen Padang began when Dutch officer Carl Christophus Lau found minerals in Padang. On 25 January 1907, after having conducted research, Lau sent a request to Amsterdam to set up a cement company. In 1910, he was granted permission to set up a cement factory called NV Nederlandsche Indische Portland Cement Maatschappij (NIPCM). This company, now the oldest cement factory in Indonesia, started production in 1913, with a capacity of 22,000 tons per annum. By 1939, production had increased to 172,000 tons per annum.

In 1972, in accordance with Government Regulation No. 7/1971, the status of PT Semen Padang[15] was modified. It became a limited state-owned company in which all shares were owned by the government of the Republic of Indonesia. The difference between PN Semen Padang and PT Semen Padang was that, in the former scheme, the entity acted

---

[14] Biro Penerbitan BK3AM, *Siapa mengapa sejumlah orang Minang* (Jakarta: Biro Penerbitan BK3AM, 1995).

[15] During the Japanese occupation of 1942–45, Asano Cement managed the company. In 1947 the Dutch regained the management and changed the name of the company to NV Padang Portland Cement Maatschappij (PPCM). As a result of Presidential Decree No. 10/1958, issued by Sukarno, the Indonesian government again took over the company on 5 July 1958. Government Regulation No. 135/1961 changed the status of the company to that of a state-owned company (PN Semen Padang).

as an agent tasked with developing manufacturing industry, while in the latter scheme, PT operated like a commercial company subject to commercial law, therefore as a competitor within the manufacturing industry. Table 4 shows the annual production of Semen Padang from 1996 to 2001.

Table 4. Semen Padang's production over the years

Year	Production (tons)
1996	3,344,489
1997	3,374,985
1998	3,464,024
1999	4,002,163
2000	4,501,845
2001	4,744,229

Source: Semen Padang, 2000, *Annual Report of Semen Padang* (Padang: Semen Padang); Semen Padang, 2001, *Annual Report of Semen Padang* (Padang: Semen Padang).

Three decades later, Suharto, through Ministry of Finance Decision No. S-326/MK.016/1995, ordered three state-owned companies—Semen Gresik, Semen Padang and Semen Tonasa—to merge under a single parent company named Semen Gresik. Such a consolidation was realized on 15 September 1995, and it changed the future of Semen Padang. At that time, Padang's elite, including Azwar Anas, did not challenge the decision, because they knew it was an order from Suharto (Padang Press Club 2001: 12). Under the guise of efficiency, Suharto intended to create a monopoly leading to control of the country's cement market. Since the mid-1980s, Suharto's family had interests in the cement industry as indicated by their shares in Indocement, a leading private cement maker (Robison 1992: 79). Suharto obviously controlled the cement market by controlling production, that is, the market's supply side.

After Indonesia was hit hard by the economic crisis of 1997, the central government entered into an agreement with the International Monetary Fund (IMF). One of the measures adopted by the government was the privatization of some state-owned enterprises (SOE) in order to control the budget deficit. In March 1998, Suharto established a new government body, the Ministry of State-Owned Enterprise. Its task was to privatize a range of SOEs.

In 1998, Habibie, who replaced Suharto, decided to privatize Semen Gresik as part of the structural reform of the country's economy.[16] The central government was committed to raising US$1 billion for the fiscal year 1998–99 from the privatization of seven large SOEs, including Semen Gresik.[17] Privatization was aimed at reducing the budget deficit of 8.5 percent of GDP in the fiscal year 1998–99.[18] In 1998, the Habibie government continued the privatization of Semen Gresik by inviting a strategic partner. After several rounds of bidding, the multinational company Cemex of Mexico (Cemex) was appointed partner, and it purchased 14 percent of Semen Gresik's shares for US$122.1 million. Nevertheless, due to political pressure from the province of West Sumatra where Semen Padang is located, Cemex was not granted permission to purchase more shares.[19] The multinational company purchased shares from the Jakarta Stock Market. Under this arrangement, the central government retained 51 percent of the shares, while Cemex 25 percent, and public investors in the Jakarta Stock Exchange retained 24 percent.

The Local Elites and Their Efforts: The Golkar Connections

Golkar had begun to penetrate local politics after 1966. The party established the Forum for Minangkabau Adat Associations (LKAAM). Saafroedin Bahar prepared for the establishment of an organization designed to mobilize political support for its local (*adat*) leaders.[20] Under the New Order regime, Azwar Anas was appointed governor of West Sumatra.[21]

---

[16] International Monetary Fund (IMF), Memorandum of Economic and Finance Policies (MEFP), 15 Jan. 1998, which outlined the need for privatization but did not mention which SOEs should be privatized. In the supplementary MEFP of 4 Apr. 1998, appendix IV, it states clearly that PT Sement Gresik must be privatized.

[17] "Target perolehan dana privatisasi BUMN direvisi", *Bisnis Indonesia*, 19 Dec. 1998.

[18] *Bisnis Indonesia*, 19 Dec. 1998.

[19] For more information on Cemex, see www.cemex.com; and Bersihar Lubis, *Who's Who Cemex* [Suntingan Dosa-Dosa Cemex] (Jakarta: Yayasan Swadaya Mandiri, 2001).

[20] Saafroeddin Bahar was born in Padang Panjang on 10 Aug. 1937. He graduated from Gadjah Mada University (UGM) in Yogyakarta (1955), and he earned his doctoral degree from UGM. He was an expert staff member for the Cabinet Ministry of Cabinet in 1995 and Lemhanas from 1983 to 1989; chairperson of Golkar in West Sumatra (1970–73); and chief of information for Kodam II Padang (1970–73). He played a crucial role in the creation of LKAAM.

[21] See footnote 11.

Azwar Anas received support mainly from the previous governor, Harun Zain, who thought he would be a candidate who could embark on economic development. Because he was a military officer, he had good connections in the military.

During his two terms as governor from 1977 to 1988, Azwar was able to develop the region on Jakarta's terms, mainly because he responded to the wishes of Suharto. His success in securing funds from Jakarta for development indicates this well. He accomplished this by implementing a Javanese village unit called the *desa* at the expense of the traditional extended village unit called the *nagari*. As the outcome of this policy, the number of desa villages increased from 543 (the number of nagari) to 3,138 (the number of *jorong*), plus 408 urban districts, or *kelurahan* (Kahin 1999: 258). As a result, West Sumatra received approximately six times its original allocation of government funds for the development of the region. Other than that, Azwar also helped the central government to integrate the region into the unitary state.

In the context of the privatization of Semen Gresik, Azwar Anas's role was that of a political supporter, because he shared the interests of provincial politicians from West Sumatra, who wanted to prevent the company's privatization. His political standing was more than enough to offer a counterbalance to the central government under Habibie, where Tanri Abeng was the SOE minister. After he successfully gained Suharto's trust due to his ability to integrate West Sumatra completely into the Indonesian unitary state, the president rewarded him with the post of minister of transportation, in which he served from 1988 to 1993. Later on, he managed to secure his political career by moving to Habibie's side in 1991 in order to support the establishment of an Association of Indonesian Muslim Intellectuals (ICMI).

Azwar was among the three ministers who supported ICMI. Moreover, internal politics within Golkar explain his ascendancy. He was already a member of the party's powerful central board, serving from 1988 to 1993. When Golkar held its congress in October 1993, Minister of Information Harmoko[22] was appointed its chairperson, while Habibie operated in the background (Schwarz 2000: 177; Vatikiotis 1993: 211).

---

[22] Harmoko and Habibie were Suharto's trusted politicians in 1993. See "Mencari ketua, menyiapkan suksesi", *Tempo*, 8 May 1993, p. 23.

Golkar adopted this move to place a civilian politician with Suharto's permission as a counterweight to the military. Under this political game, Azwar obviously sided with Habibie due to their mutual links to the ICMI. With his link to Habibie through Golkar and the ICMI, Azwar was rewarded with the high position of Coordinating Minister for People's Welfare in 1993.

Azwar was in a good position to offer protection to politicians who wanted Semen Padang separated from Semen Gresik. In fact, on various occasions, Azwar expressed his agreement with Ikhdan Nizar and Titik Nazif Lubuk, who advocated for a separation of Semen Padang from Semen Gresik. In 1998, with his authority as member of the DPA,[23] Azwar summoned the SOE minister at the time, Tanri Abeng, to his office and ordered him to stop selling shares of Semen Padang to Cemex. Azwar strongly argued that such a sale would diminish the government's ownership in the company. More importantly, Azwar protected the interests of Ikhdan Nizar and Titik Nazif Lubuk. Tanri listened to Awar's suggestions because of the latter's political standing, and also because the minister realized it would be very difficult to maintain opposition to Azwar—he was well aware that Azwar was close to Habibie. Therefore, he concluded it would be better for the minister to not openly challenge the former governor of West Sumatra.

The CEO and commissioners of Semen Padang were key players in the privatization of Semen Gresik, which included Semen Padang. Padang elites were led by Ikhdan Nizar, Semen Padang's CEO, and Saafroedin Bahar, its president commissioner. Ikhdan Nizar's career developed mainly within the structure of state-owned companies in the cement industry. He joined Semen Padang after graduating from Bandung Institute of Technology. In 1996, two years before he was appointed CEO of Semen Padang, he served as CEO of a much smaller cement factory, Semen Baturaja, an SOE located in South Sumatra. Saafroedin's political position was significant. He was involved in the creation of LKAAM in 1966. He served as its first secretary and then as its chairperson. In the 1970s he chaired the regional Golkar branch. In the 1980s he moved to Jakarta to serve as an expert for the Ministry of Cabinet secretary.

Ikhdan Nizar's long relationship with Azwar Anas worked as a glue that bound them together. They had, at different times, served as CEO

---

[23] DPA stands for Dewan Pertimbangan Agung (Supreme Advisory Council), a high political body whose task it is to offer advice to the president. Many of the members were former ministers such as Azwar Anas.

of Semen Padang. Ikhdan had worked under the supervision of Azwar in Semen Padang. Under Azwar's tutelage, Ikhdan learned that cement must be treated as a strategic commodity that should receive protection from the government. Azwar's argument should be understood in the broader context of the central government's policy of Import Substitution Industry (ISI) under the Suharto regime. Since the 1970s, the cement industry had been developed on an import substitution basis protected by a substantial tariff,[24] which was abolished only in October 1990 in response to a temporary cement shortage in the domestic market. Azwar directed Semen Padang when Suharto heavily protected various industries through the ISI strategy. No foreign investors or companies could enter this industry easily. Due to his experience in the cement industry in the past, Azwar judged that the best solution for Semen Padang would be to continue treating cement as a strategic industry protected by the government. Ikhdan picked up this argument when he defended the separation of Semen Padang from Semen Gresik. Equally important was Ikhdan's effort to renew his political relationship with Azwar early in 2000. His effort was relatively easy because he shared similar beliefs with Azwar on Semen Padang's management.

In Padang, Ikhdan depended on Titik Nazif Lubuk, the deputy speaker of the provincial assembly.[25] Titik was a local Golkar politician who had developed her political career in Golkar during the 1970s. She served as a member for Golkar in the provincial parliament, and from 1998 to 2004 served as the deputy speaker. The political position of Titik was quite important, as she could function as a bridge for the Golkar political network linking Padang and Jakarta. On the regional level, she had contact with mass organizations linked to Golkar such as Bundo Kanduang (a local women's organization) and LKAAM. Though Golkar was split on the national level, on the provincial level this split had little impact. After Akbar Tanjung[26] secured his position as the party's leader, its branch in West Sumatra sided with him. Local Golkar politicians

---

[24] Economic Intelligence Unit, *Indonesia: Industrial Development Review* (London: Economic Intelligent Unit, 1993), 136.

[25] "Gaya Ikhdan Nizar mencari dukungan", *Zaman*, 9 June 2002.

[26] Akbar Tanjung was born in Sibolga on 14 Aug. 1945. He finished primary school in Tapanuli, junior high school in Medan, and senior high school in Jakarta, before attending the Faculty of Engineering at the University of Indonesia. He joined the anti-Sukarno movement in 1966 and established various youth organizations related to Golkar. From 1988 to 1993 he was minister of sports and youth; from 1993 to 1998 state minister for housing; and from 1999 to 2004 DPR speaker.

like Titik Nazif Lubuk were willing to side with Akbar. On the national level, Titik had connections with Azwar Anas, who still exerted some political power due to his reputation in both Golkar and West Sumatra.

In 2001, Ikhdan Nizar started to resist the privatization of Semen Gresik after he learned that his managerial position would be in jeopardy if foreign investors dominated the management of the company. Ikhdan soon learned that the privatization of Semen Gresik was followed by the replacement of management executives with people working for Cemex of Mexico. In fact, Cemex placed two of its managers in Semen Gresik. Ikhdan's post in Semen Padang would be in danger with the privatization of Semen Gresik. To prevent his dismissal, Ikhdan pushed harder for the plan to separate Semen Padang from Semen Gresik.

Raw Materials

The immobility of raw materials for cement, such as limestone, provided Ikhdan with power. Immobility was thus turned into political leverage (Moran 1974). Ikhdan could easily hijack the operations of the Semen Padang plant by withholding its access to raw materials.

The raw materials for cement production in Padang were predicted to last for as long as 50 to 150 years.[27] One of the limestone deposits, located in Lubuk Kilangan, could supply the plant for another 50 years if it were to produce portland cement with an output of 6 tons per annum. There are also limestone deposits in other municipalities such as Padangpanjang (250 million m^3), Sawahlunto Sijunjung (7 billion m^3), and Paninggahan Solok (7.5 billion m^3). This abundance solidified Ikhdan's position of strength.

Political Targets

In 2001, Ikhdan Nizar began to openly oppose the privatization of Semen Gresik. When Minister Laksamana Sukardi pressed him to implement the plan, Ikhdan sent an early warning that there was the high probability of social chaos in West Sumatra.[28] He emphasized that such social chaos would damage the image of Semen Gresik. At the same time, he argued that the presence of international cement companies in the country was dangerous because they were buying up local cement factories at very low prices. He referred to global cement makers that were already operating

---

[27] "Divestasi Semen Gresik kontroversial", *Bisnis Indonesia*, 5 Dec. 2000.
[28] "Kegagalan spin off bisa picu chaos", *Bisnis Indonesia*, 24 Feb. 2001.

Conflict over the Privatization of Semen Padang   127

in the country, such as Holderbank of Switzerland, which had bought 12.5 percent of existing Semen Cibinong shares, and Heidelberger, which had planned to acquire 60 percent of Indocement shares. Ikhdan also claimed that Semen Gresik had been sold cheaply to Cemex. Instead of US$47, he argued, Semen Gresik should have been sold at the price of US$114.3 per ton capacity, a similar price paid by Cemex to buy Rizal Cement in the Philippines.[29]

By the middle of October 2001, Ikhdan Nizar concentrated his argument against the privatization of Semen Gresik on the national interest. He openly labeled privatization as the systematic looting of national assets by foreign investors. He insisted that such privatization was a mistake, because it would automatically transfer the plant and natural resources to foreign investors. Therefore, he emphatically called on the central government to reconsider the proposal to privatize the company. He defended his position by claiming that Semen Gresik, particularly Semen Padang, had the managerial capability to run the company.

Ikhdan secured political support from national politicians like Azwar Anas and members of the provincial elite like Titik Nazif Lubuk. Ikhdan then put his plan into action. He presented a detailed plan on how to buy back Cemex's shares in Semen Padang, thereby forcing Laksamana to restructure the plant's ownership. The first thing that Ikhdan did was to identify the exact number of shares of Semen Padang Cemex held, since Cemex owned Semen Padang indirectly through its ownership of Semen Gresik. He devised a formula to calculate the shares of Cemex in Semen Padang based on Cemex's proportional shares in Semen Gresik: the Indonesian government owned 51 percent; Cemex 25 percent;[30] and the public 24 percent. Then he concluded that the Cemex's equity in Semen Padang must total 83 million shares (given that the total number of shares of Semen Padang totaled 332 million units). The value of these shares amounted to IDR533.4 billion.[31]

Ikhdan's plan, however, could not be executed because the central government had no funds to repurchase Cemex's shares in Semen Padang. One of the most important reasons for the central government to privatize Semen Gresik was to have money to fill the gaps in its budget.

---

[29] Interview, Ikhdan Nizar, *Forum Keadilan*, 29 Apr. 2001.

[30] Cemex paid US$114.6 million or US$1.38/share.

[31] Tim Spin Off PT Semen Padang, *PT Semen Padang: Dari spin off menuju perusahaan kelas dunia* (Padang, 2001), 55. The calculation was based on the price of shares of Semen Padang in 1995, IDR 3,205.

Any expenditure that would hurt the stability of the budget, such as buying back Cemex's Semen Gresik shares, would be unacceptable.

The Maklumat Affair

The *maklumat* (declaration) affair refers to the takeover of Semen Padang by the provincial assembly led by Titik Nazif Lubuk on 31 October 2001. Although the maklumat was staged on behalf of the people of West Sumatra, it was formally signed by only five mass organizations: the National Council of Indonesian Youth (KNPI), the Indonesian Council of Ulama (MUI), LKAAM, ICMI, and the women's organization Bunda Kandung. KNPI, LKAAM and, to some extent, Bunda Kandung all have connections with Golkar. KNPI is a recruiting ground for Golkar; the chief of the LKAAM was a member of Golkar. Titik Nazif Lubuk was deeply involved in Bunda Kandung.

The takeover was the outcome of a meeting of the provincial assembly. It highlighted the tensions between Ikhdan and Titik Lubuk on one side and Laksamana on the other. The councilors in Padang issued a declaration that stated four points:

(1) From 1 November 2001, Semen Padang, upon the approval of the provincial government, will operate under the supervision of members of the West Sumatra provincial assembly. Eventually, Semen Padang will be separated from Semen Gresik and given back to being a state-owned enterprise run by the government of Indonesia;

(2) Administration, members of the governing body and workers of Semen Padang will report to the provincial government and provincial assembly of West Sumatra;

(3) Administration will circulate the content of this declaration to the appropriate organizations, including banks and creditors, confirming that the business will work normally;

(4) Additional practical matters that emerge will be solved in the proper manner in line with prevailing procedures.[32]

The unilateral takeover was aimed at preventing the further privatization of Semen Padang. When the central government sold shares of Semen Gresik to Cemex, it signed an agreement declaring that it would

---

[32] "Masyarakat Sumbar Ambil Alih PT Semen Padang", *Tempo Daily*, 18 September 2003, available at https://nasional.tempo.co/read/17191/masyarakat-sumbar-ambil-alih-pt-semen-padang [accessed April 2004]. Several local papers also wrote about these events.

have the right to execute the option to sell any remaining shares to Cemex only. The deadline for this "put option" was scheduled for late October 2001, and if central government were to execute its right, Cemex would have become the majority shareholder of Semen Gresik. In addition to preventing privatization, the takeover also served the purpose of consolidating Ikhdan and Titik's political power. After the event, they practically ran the entire company. Titik made it clear that from then on the central government, particularly Minister Laksamana, could not make any meaningful decisions concerning Semen Padang alone.[33] In short, Ikhdan and Titik would be involved in any decision related to the company.

Laksamana's Responses

From 2001 to 2004, Laksamana Sukardi was the minister of SOE under the Megawati government. He spent most of his career in the business sector as a professional, having started at Citibank where he rose to become the chief of its customer-banking unit in 1988. In 1993 he moved to the domestic conglomerate Lippo where he managed Lippo Bank,[34] serving as its CEO from 1994 to 1999. He got involved in politics in 1992 when he joined PDI (and later PDI-P) under Megawati. From 2001 to 2004, he served as the minister of SOEs with the task of privatizing some of Indonesia's state-owned enterprises.

Initially, Laksamana did not make any serious attempt to directly confront Ikhdan and Titik. Laksamana expressed his disappointment over the takeover and blamed the duo for violating existing laws. He had reasons for not taking serious measures against the two, however. He worked to avoid a collision with Golkar, a political ally in the coalition government under Megawati. Laksamana fully understood that Megawati, as the leader of PDI-P, needed the support of Golkar in order for the government to survive. Any rifts in the coalition would place the government in jeopardy.

In early December 2001, Laksamana proposed a deal with Ikhdan and Titik to buy back Semen Padang from Semen Gresik. After Laksamana sold its stake, the shareholdings of Semen Gresik would have been pegged

---

[33] "Maklumat wajib lapor", *Gatra*, Nov. 10, 2001, p. 29.
[34] Lippo Group is owned by the Riady family. Its current CEO is James Riady. Lippo is one of Indonesia's largest conglomerates and survived the economic crisis of 1997.

at 76.5 percent held by Cemex and 23.5 percent held by the public.[35] The minister had hoped this move would meet the aspirations of separating Semen Padang from Semen Gresik, yet the scheme would still honor its commitment to Cemex by allowing it to increase its holdings in Semen Gresik to 76.5 percent. Under the proposed deal, the government would sell its 51 percent stake in Semen Gresik to Cemex, but at the same time, it would acquire a majority stake in Semen Gresik's Padang and Tonasa units. However, the Gresik unit still owned 49 percent of the Padang unit (and the Tonasa unit), with the 51 percent majority held by the government. Laksamana came up with a net income of US$200 million after the whole deal was completed. His calculation was simple: the government would exercise a put option amounting to 51 percent of Semen Gresik shares to Cemex worth US$529 million. The government would then buy 51 percent each of Semen Padang and Semen Tonasa for a combined worth of US$554 million. Then the government needed to give out 51 percent of this US$554 million— that is, US$282.54 million—to Cemex. As a result, the government would receive US$246.46 million.

Laksamana's proposal could not be implemented because Titik Nazif Lubuk demanded a bigger share in Semen Padang for the government. She asked for 75 percent instead of 49 percent, arguing that only with a majority can the government control Semen Padang.[36]

Governor Zainal Bakar[37] defended the management team of Semen Padang when in January 2002, Laksamana planned to replace Ikhdan Nizar and Saafroedin Bahar in Semen Padang.[38] Zainal's political career had been deeply embedded within the provincial bureaucracy since his graduation from the Faculty of Law of Andalas University in 1968.[39] Zainal was appointed governor in 1998. His support for Ikhdan Nizar

---

[35] "Pemerintah buyback SP dan ST dari Cemex", *Bisnis Indonesia*, 1 Dec. 2001.

[36] "Pemerintah diminta Mayoritas Lagi di SP", *Bisnis Indonesia*, 29 Jan. 2002.

[37] Zainal Bakar was born in Pariaman on 16 Aug. 1940. He received his primary education in Pariaman (1955); junior-high education in Padang (1958); and senior high school in Pariaman (1961). He graduated from the Law Faculty of Andalas University in Padang (1967). Most of his career was spent serving the bureaucracy in the Ministry of Home Affairs.

[38] "Kaji ulang pergantian direksi Semen Padang", *Bisnis Indonesia*, 5 June 2002.

[39] Zainal Bakar's first post was in Agam where he served as chief section in the district chief's office. Then in 1981 he was promoted to the governor's office in the section for public relations. In 1993 he served as the provincial secretary, the one who dealt with the daily operations of the province.

was an outcome of a political process on the regional level. Golkar supported Zainal for his post with the hope that he would guard the interests of the party in the province; therefore, he had to listen to the provincial branch of the party. He was accountable to the provincial parliament in accordance with the regulation on regional autonomy. He declared that the central government had to talk to him or the provincial government before such a replacement could take place. Initially, Titik Nazif Lubuk rejected Laksamana's plan because Ikhdan and Saafroedin were her allies.[40]

Due to strong resistance by Titik Lubuk and Zainal Bakar, Laksamana had to consider his moves carefully. He adopted three political measures to ensure that he could appoint a new CEO for Semen Gresik, replace the management and board commissioners of Semen Padang, and persuade Zainal Bakar to become his ally.

Laksamana appointed Satriyo as the new CEO of Semen Gresik. Satriyo, a Javanese who joined the company in 1984, later served as its finance director (2000–01). To keep his position, Satriyo had little choice but to implement the order from the SOE minister. Laksamana intended to use Satriyo as his proxy for dealing with Ikhdan Nizar. After his installment as CEO of Semen Gresik, Satriyo called for an annual meeting of shareholders with the agenda of replacing the management team and the board of commissioners of Semen Padang in 2002. In March 2002, Laksamana wrote a letter to Satriyo with instructions to replace the management team of Semen Padang.[41] The letter mentioned that the replacement was due to an internal restructuring process, which was being undertaken to push the performance of Semen Padang. Satriyo responded by writing a letter to the company's board of directors.[42] It indicated that as a shareholder of Semen Padang, Semen Gresik was asking for an annual meeting of shareholders. One month later, Ikhdan replied with a request to explain the replacements.[43] Satriyo answered that the replacements were

---

[40] "Sumbar Tolak Pergantian Manajemen SP", *Bisnis Indonesia*, 3 Jan. 2002.

[41] Letter from Minister of SOE to the Board of Directors of Semen Gresik, No. SR-294/M-BUMN/2002, dated 28 Mar. 2002. See Serikat Pekerja Semen Padang, *PT Semen Gresik Biang Kerok Kemelut di PT Semen Padang* (Padang: Serikat Pekerja Semen, 2003), p. 61.

[42] Letter of Director Semen Gresik to the Board Director of Semen Padang, No. 2853/KS.00.01/1001/04.002, dated 30 Apr. 2002. See Serikat Pekerja Semen Padang 2003, p. 61.

[43] Letter of Director Semen Padang, No. 701/KRE/Dirut/05.02, dated 2 May 2002. See Serikat Pekerja Semen Padang 2003, p. 61.

needed in order to improve the performance of Semen Padang. Ikhdan responded with two letters expressing his disappointment with Satriyo's explanation.[44] Ikhdan appealed: he wanted specific reasons as to why he and other members of the management team of Semen Padang should be replaced, and he wanted time to prepare an adequate defense.

Although Satriyo never disclosed his intention for calling a general shareholders' meeting in his letter, Ikhdan guessed that he meant to topple him as the top manager of Semen Padang. After receiving Ikhdan's letter, Satriyo wrote an appeal to the court of Padang to seek an opinion on the legality of the meeting. Satriyo's appeal centered on three objectives: to get permission for a general shareholders meeting; to get permission to invite the entire body of shareholders to attend such a meeting; and to be allowed to hold the meeting in Jakarta. The court of Padang issued a verdict refusing Satriyo's appeal.[45]

After having recognized that Semen Gresik could not rely on the verdict issued by the court of Padang, Satriyo wrote a letter to Semen Padang's management demanding an extraordinary general meeting of shareholders. In this letter, Satriyo still insisted on his main reason for replacing the management of Semen Padang: the decreasing rate of profit before tax; the decreasing cash flow that could potentially cause a major cash deficit by the end of 2002; a failed cost-reduction program; and a failed program to increase market share.[46] Ikhdan resisted by citing the court of Padang.[47] Satriyo wrote another appeal to the court of Padang requesting an extraordinary meeting, but the court again refused.[48] In October, Satriyo wrote an appeal to the Supreme Court asking to re-evaluate the verdict issued by the court of Padang.

In mid-March 2003, the Supreme Court issued a verdict revoking the decision issued by the court of Padang.[49] With this decision, Satriyo

---

[44] Letter of Director Semen Padang, No. 806/KRE/Dirut/05.02, dated 22 May 2002, and letter No. 883/KRE/Dirut/05.02, dated 29 May 2002. See Serikat Pekerja Semen Padang 2003, p. 62.

[45] Determination No. 93/PDT/P/2002/PN.PDG, dated 12 June 2002.

[46] Letter of Director Semen Gresik No. 4810/KS.00.01/1001/07.2002, dated 10 July 2002. See Serikat Pekerja Semen Padang 2003, p. 63.

[47] Letter of Director Semen Padang No. 122/KRE/DIRUT/07.02, dated 30 July 2002. See Serikat Pekerja Semen Padang 2003, p. 64.

[48] Determination of the Court of Padang No. 124/PDT/P/2002/PN.PDG, dated 7 Sept. 2002.

[49] Supreme Court Verdict No. 3252/Pdt/2002.

then conducted an extraordinary shareholders' meeting with the agenda of replacing the management team of Semen Padang and its commissioners. He demanded that the management of Semen Padang be required to finish its financial audit, as they must be responsible for the operations of the company in 2002. Such an audit was demanded by Satriyo as the CEO of Semen Gresik in order to meet a requirement of companies listed on the Jakarta Stock Exchange. The initial response from Ikhdan was to question the grounds of the Supreme Court verdict sustaining Satriyo's request.[50]

In early May 2003, Satriyo demanded that Ikhdan prepare all the necessary documentation for the extraordinary meeting.[51] In response, Ikhdan Nizar refused to cooperate with the plan for an extraordinary meeting. At the Hotel Dharmawangsa in Jakarta, a position was formulated vis-à-vis Ikhdan and his allies and their refusal to attend the shareholders' meeting.[52] The president commissioner of Semen Padang, Saafroedin Bahar, rejected the meeting because it was based only on the decision of the Supreme Court. He strongly recommended that Semen Gresik postpone the extraordinary shareholders meeting.[53]

Although the management of Semen Padang under Ikhdan rebelled, Satriyo, on 12 May 2003, presided over the extraordinary shareholders' meeting. The previous director of research and development at Semen Padang, Dwi Soetjipto, a Javanese, was appointed president director.[54] Laksamana's move to place a Javanese as the top manager of Semen Padang was a brave decision, because only a Minangkabau such as Ikhdan Nizar and Azwar Anas had previously occupied the position. Ismed Yuzairi, the former chief of command in Bukit Barisan responsible for Sumatra, and opposed to Ikhdan Nizar, was appointed as president commissioner to replace Saafroedin Bahar. He was appointed in response to the political tension that faced Laksamana and the management of Semen Padang under Dwi Sutjipto. Laksamana appointed Ismed with the clear intention of protecting his decision to appoint the management of Semen Padang under Dwi Sutjipto. Considering the political processes related

---

[50] "Supreme Court Sustains Semen Gresik Appeal", *Bisnis Indonesia*, 20 Apr. 2002.

[51] Letter of Semen Gresik No. 03432/HK.02/4010/05.03, dated 1 May 2003.

[52] "Menyingkirkan Orang Lama", *Gatra*, 17 May 2003, p. 41.

[53] Saafroedin Bahar, in Serikat Pekerja Semen, Padang 2003, pp. 9–10.

[54] Dwi Soetjipto was born in Surabaya in 1955. He graduated from the Surabaya Institute of Technology in chemical engineering, and he served as the director for research and development at Semen Padang since 1995.

to the privatization of Semen Padang, Laksamana's choice of placing Ismed was a good strategy because of his background as the former chief of command in the West Sumatra region. Since Ismed belongs to the Minangkabau ethnic community, the other politicians in the region would easily accept him.

The so-called old management and commissioners of Semen Padang, led by Ikhdan and Saafroedin, declared the meeting of 12 May 2003 illegal; therefore, they retained their posts for some time.[55] Ikhdan and Saafroedin alleged that they had been replaced by new figures who were not supportive of Semen Padang's separation from Semen Gresik. Their resistance to Satriyo led to a chaotic situation because of the existence of two management teams. The conflict had apparently been mitigated as Satriyo pushed harder to isolate Ikhdan and Saafroedin by instructing banks to block their access to Semen Padang accounts. In late June, the new management team under Dwi Sutjipto began to carry out their daily duties.

With the above political development, Azwar's role became less influential, and therefore he was unable to offer any political protection to Ikhdan Nizar and Titik Nazif Lubuk. Azwar was no longer occupying his position in the DPA. Habibie, his political patron, was no longer president of the country, and Megawati now ran the government. More-over, Azwar realized that it was almost impossible to block Laksamana's move to topple Ikhdan Nizar from Semen Padang, because it was under the authority of the minister. More importantly, Golkar was no longer in power; PDI-P was. Azwar saw no opportunity to get involved directly except for offering opinions that had no political importance.

Laksamana persuaded Zainal Bakar to side with him. This oppor-tunity appeared when Zainal approached Laksamana and sought political support for his effort to appease Titik Lubuk and other members of the provincial assembly for a separation of Semen Padang. The relations between the governor of West Sumatra, Zainal Bakar, and the elites in the provincial assembly started to deteriorate due to decreasing trust. Titik Nazif Lubuk had begun to put pressure on Zainal regarding his commitment to achieve the separation of Semen Padang from Semen

---

[55] Report of the background of conflict between Semen Padang and Semen Gresik by the board of commissioner of Semen Padang, signed by Saafroedin Bahar and dated 8 June 2003, reprinted in *PT Semen Gresik biang kerok kemelut di PT Semen Padang* (Padang: Serikat Pekerja Semen, 2003), p. 83.

Gresik after a year.[56] It was clear that up until November 2002, the future of Semen Padang's independence was not very bright, as Minister Laksamana had never issued any formal agreement. As the holder of the maklumat, Governor Zainal mentioned that the decision to separate Semen Padang was not within his authority but instead rested under the authority of the central government. In addition, the governor made clear that the separation of Semen Gresik was never approved by the central government.

Five months later, the regional assembly began to pressure Zainal. This was possible because in the middle of April 2003 Zainal had to report to the provincial assembly. His political future depended on his ability to convince the assembly, of which Titik Nazif Lubuk was the deputy, that he had done enough to separate Semen Padang from Semen Gresik. Facing this problem, Zainal lobbied the minister of social welfare, Jusuf Kalla,[57] a member of Golkar, who responded promptly and was ready to offer a solution. Jusuf received informal permission from Laksamana offering a solution acceptable to both Zainal Bakar and Laksamana.[58] This process of appointment was unusual because the privatization of Semen Gresik was not under the authority of Minister Jusuf, as he was responsible for social affairs. His readiness and willingness to accept this difficult task was important to Laksamana's decision to let Jusuf deal with the issue. Laksamana carefully calculated that Jusuf was from Golkar, one of its chairpersons on the national level, and such a position was crucial because he would deal with fellows from Golkar. While Laksamana did not openly challenge regional elites, Jusuf had the confidence to take action.

Zainal held the mandate to separate Semen Padang from Semen Gresik, so he prepared to deliver the annual accountability report to the provincial assembly. The councilors would have neglected Zainal's report if he could not separate Semen Padang, and therefore his post as governor

---

[56] "Gubernur menolak di-deadline", *Padang Ekspress*, 4 Nov. 2002.

[57] Jusuf Kalla was born in Watampone on 15 May 1942. He graduated from the Faculty of Economic of Hasanuddin University, Makassar. He was involved in the establishment of Golkar since its beginning in the mid-1960s. He was also a successful businessperson. Through Golkar, he served as the coordinating minister for social affairs (2001–04) under the Megawati government, and minister for trade and industry (1999–2001) under the Abdurahman Wahid government.

[58] Interview with Minister Jusuf Kalla, "Ongkosnya jauh lebih murah", *Tempo*, 4 May 2003, p. 130.

would be in jeopardy. Zainal could only continue in his job if the councilors accepted his annual report. According to the new regulation on decentralization, the governor was accountable to the provincial assembly. Jusuf's main task was to offer a solution that would be accepted by Laksamana and Titik Nazif Lubuk and her friends who were councilors. Jusuf offered a solution called a "split off", that is, the redistribution of shares in which Semen Padang would be owned by the central government (51 percent), Cemex (25 percent) and the public (24 percent).[59] The share composition for Semen Gresik was similar. With this scheme, the central government did not need to spend any money; it simply had to distribute the shares. Laksamana and Governor Zainal both accepted Jusuf's proposal. Laksamana wrote a letter reflecting his readiness to agree to splitting Semen Padang from Semen Gresik[60] as stipulated in Jusuf's proposal. As a consequence of this agreement, Zainal had no choice but to allow Laksamana to embark on his plan to weaken the power of the provincial elites by replacing Ikhdan Nizar and Saafroedin Bahar.

Cemex's Response and the Outcome

After several rounds of bidding, the Mexican company Cemex was appointed a partner in Semen Gresik, and in October 1998 it purchased 14 percent of Semen Gresik's shares for US$122.1 million. While the Ministry of SOE was allowing Cemex to purchase 14 percent of Semen Gresik's shares, it also offered Cemex a put option, which could be executed within three years of September 2001 as agreed in the conditional sales and purchase agreement (CSPA). In February 1999 Cemex continued to purchase shares of Semen Gresik on the Jakarta Stock Exchange until it had accumulated 24 percent of the company's shares.

The strength of Cemex lies in the mobility of its capital (Winters 1996). This investment defined the involvement of Cemex in the dispute over the separation of Semen Padang from Semen Gresik. Cemex dealt with Laksamana. In the initial stage of the dispute over the separation of Semen Padang, Cemex never threatened Laksamana for his inability to arrange the transfer of Semen Gresik shares to Cemex. On many occasions, Cemex expressed its understanding of the difficulties Laksamana

---

[59] The term *split off* differs from *spin off*. *Spin off* is a term that was used by Ikhdan to separate Semen Padang from Gresik and make Semen Padang a state-owned enterprise without the shares of Cemex.
[60] Letter of Minister SOE No. S-14/M-MBU/2003, dated 16 Apr. 2003, signed by Laksamana Sukardi.

Conflict over the Privatization of Semen Padang 137

faced. This attitude changed in 2000, when Laksamana failed to make a decision over the purchase of additional shares of Semen Gresik by Cemex. In December 2000, for the first time, the CEO of Cemex in Indonesia, Francisco Noriega, threatened to withdraw from Indonesia.[61] When the situation was deteriorating, as indicated by Laksamana's inability to adopt necessary measures to stop the illegal takeover of Semen Padang, Cemex started to express frustration.

In August 2003, Cemex began to send strong signals to Laksamana. Cemex wrote a letter to Laksamana urging him to settle the dispute between Ikhdan and Laksamana.[62] If Laksamana could not play such a role, Cemex threatened to bring the case to an international arbitrage body. Later on, Cemex viewed the new management of Semen Padang under Dwi Sutjipto as having failed to run the company well due to the failure to finish the financial report and to change mid-level management.[63] For Cemex, Dwi failed to finish the audited financial report because he was unable to settle IDR50 billion (US$5 million) from the Ikhdan Nizar management team's 2002 expenditures.[64] Cemex set a deadline for the central government to complete the consolidated financial statement of Semen Gresik.[65]

Finally, in November 2003, Cemex took its initial step to withdraw by bringing the case to an international arbitrage body. It considered that its step was in accord with the CSPA it signed with the central government, which stated that Cemex could bring the central government to an international arbitrage body if it failed to show good will. Cemex now refused new negotiations with the SOE minister,[66] demanding the cancellation of its agreement signed in 1998 to acquire Semen Gresik.[67] Cemex asked the central government to return its entire investment of approximately US$290 million for a 25-percent stake in Semen Gresik. Cemex would not discuss other things in the arbitrage outside of how to pressure Laksamana to return Cemex's investment. In February 2004, the International Center for Settlement of Investment Disputes (ICSID)

---

[61] "Sulit kuasai Semen Padang, Cemex ancam hengkang dari RI", *Bisnis Indonesia*, 11 Dec. 2001.

[62] "Cemex Considers Bringing SP to Arbitrage", *Bisnis Indonesia*, 14 Aug. 2003.

[63] "Cemex Brings SG's Case to International Arbitrage", *Bisnis Indonesia*, 21 Nov. 2003.

[64] "Yang menyesakkan napas Satriyo", *Tempo*, 13 Apr. 2003; see also *Jakarta Post*, 7 Apr. 2003.

[65] "Cemex janjikan neraca selesai oktober", *Bisnis Indonesia*, 12 Oct. 2003.

[66] "Cemex Refuses Making Peace with RI", *Bisnis Indonesia*, 12 Dec. 2003.

[67] "Indonesia's Dispute with Cemex Intensifies", *The Wall Street Journal*, 11 Dec. 2003.

in Washington, DC, registered the case after a request from Cemex regarding its dispute with the central government of Indonesia.[68]

Conclusion

What relevance does this case study have for the broader argument of this book? To answer that question, one should look at the main elements of the story. By the late 1990s, at the beginning of this story, there was already a long-standing dispute over Semen Padang, which started when the Habibie government had to control the fiscal deficit. The newly established government body, the Ministry of State Owned Enterprises, had to implement an order from the IMF to restructure the economy by privatizing some of the state-owned enterprises, among which was Semen Padang. While it was quite easy for Suharto to pressure the provincial elites of West Sumatra to accept his rule of making Semen Padang a part of Semen Gresik in 1995, it was very difficult for the governments after him—including those under Habibie, Abdurahman Wahid and Megawati—to convince these politicians to accept the rules of the central government. The difficulty was related to the changes in the institutions governing the country and in the networks of politicians.

As with Kaltim Prima Coal in East Kalimantan, it can easily be shown that political networks worked in the case of Semen Padang. While Suwarna's political networks in East Kalimantan were hardly based on political parties, a political party—Golkar, which had been ruling the region since the beginning of the New Order in 1966—heavily mediated the networks at work in West Sumatra. These political networks were created by personal connections, mutual trust and Minangkabau ethnicity. Compare this with two other cases in which ethnic ties are clearly visible in the conflict over Semen Padang. It was through Golkar that these politicians encountered each other and strengthened their relations. An exception may apply to the ties between Azwar Anas and Ikhdan Nizar, who encountered each other in Semen Padang. However, it was through Golkar that they found the capability to strengthen themselves to face challenges from the central government. Golkar provided them a better means with which to challenge Laksamana, the minister of SOE, since he undoubtedly was supported by PDI-P. In short, these political networks highlighted the fact that Indonesian political and economic conditions were far from

---

[68] ICSID is affiliated with the World Bank and is tasked with settling disputes between governments and private investors.

immutable. During the New Order regime, political alliances were focused on Suharto, but after his departure it seems that networks of people and political parties replaced him.

These local politicians were able to establish political networks because they were in full control of the raw materials for production. The abundance of limestone for the operation of the cement factory turned out to be another source of power for local politicians because of its immobility. Compared to mobile sources of power such as capital, extractive resources are immobile. This immobility is associated with the fact that the resources are attached to the land, or more precisely that the raw material is physically *in* the land. This raw material thus became the power that the local elites (Moran 1974) used to bargain with the central government.

While the networks of politicians remained intact, the rules of the game governing the country changed through democratization and regional autonomy regulations. The old regulation that governed the relationship between the center and the region embodied in Law No. 5/1974 was replaced with a new one, Law No. 22/1999. The institution that governed political parties was also replaced with a new one in 1999 allowing more parties to compete in the election. The outcome of the changes, mainly in the political sphere, was a weaker central government, as compared to the central government under Suharto's New Order. The weakness of the central government was associated with two facts, that more political parties competed for power resulting in a coalition government, and that the central government was forced to accommodate regional demands.

As far as the case of Semen Padang concerned, the Indonesian political economy after the fall of Suharto was characterized by a deep and long political battle for controlling the economic resources between the central and local governments. The case highlights the weaknesses of the central government in adopting necessary action when the local elites in Padang took over the Semen Padang plant. Instead of considering the use of existing institutions, the central government embarked on various political measures. In response, the local elites reacted by employing political means to defend their interests. Such political fights indicate that the government was weak and unable to establish a solid institution for protecting its economic policy. The logical consequence of the absence of solid mechanisms for dispute resolution—namely institutions—was that the foreign investor felt insecure and even threatened. Logically, the foreign investor threatened to withdraw from the country, especially after investing capital.

CHAPTER 6

Resources Conflict in Riau:
An Oil Block's Tale

Introduction

This chapter presents a case study centering on the resources conflict over the Coastal Pekanbaru Plain (CPP) oil block located in Siak district, Riau. The central government came into conflict with the provincial government in 1999 two years before the expiration of the contract for the oil block with Caltex Pacific Indonesia (CPI)—a company that belongs to the US multinational corporations Texaco and Chevron.[1] The conflict stemmed from the request by the provincial government, which had developed its own political capability, for a fair distribution of income from Riau's oil. The dispute erupted when the central government strongly downplayed the provincial government's request.

At the center of this case study, in a way reminiscent of similar situations in East Kalimantan and West Sumatra, was the behavior of provincial politicians vis-à-vis the central government. These behaviors were located in a broader context of institutional change in 1998. However, Saleh Djasit, the governor of Riau between 1998 and 2004, proved less successful in taking advantage of the dramatic changes in the political landscape that occurred during his time in office—in contrast with figures like Suwarna and Ikhdan Nizar. In particular, he failed to find benefit from the collapse of the centralized form of central-local relations structured under the Suharto government; to construct political networks at both the national and provincial levels; and, at the national level, to forge relations of trust and mutuality with national political figures from Riau like Syarwan Hamid, former minister of home affairs under the Habibie

---

[1] In 2005 Chevron bought Caltex. CPI changed to Chevron Pacific Indonesia.

140

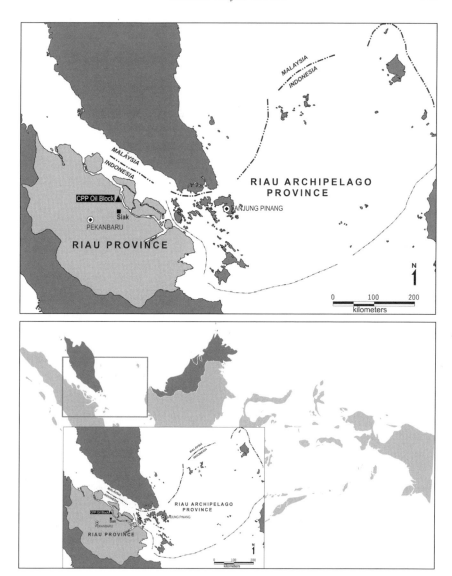

Map 3. Riau Province and Riau Archipelago Province

government, who influenced the policies of decentralization by creating the team that formulated the rules. Even though he had a personal relationship with Syarwan, he was unable to convince the former minister to side with him in his dispute over the Coastal Plain of Pekanbaru (CPP). At the provincial level, Saleh had to confront Tabrani Rab, one of the advocates of the Riau Freedom Movement (Riau Merdeka, RM). This political rift forced Saleh and Tabrani to compete for the support of the Malay ethnic group in Riau. In short, Saleh was unable to benefit from the processes of democratization and decentralization of Indonesia.

Saleh Djasit's failure emphasizes the relevance of a political network. At the same time, it is necessary to scrutinize the political behavior of Purnomo Yusgiantoro, the minister of energy and mineral resources under Megawati, to secure the central government's interest by winning a majority 92.5 percent of CPP shares (the rest of 7.5 percent went to Siak district). The case presented material for debate about the nature of Indonesia's post-Suharto politics and economy as well as the changing nature of center-province relations.

Riau Politics Under Suharto

Riau was an outcome of the Riau People's Congress (Kongres Rakyat Riau, KRR) held on 2 February 1956, in which the Riau people demanded a separate province. The KRR successfully convinced the central government under the Sukarno government's Djuanda cabinet to establish Riau as a distinct province independent of Central Sumatra province. Among the reasons stated at that time, Riau's elites argued that Central Sumatra was too large, and therefore could not adequately provide services to Riau's people (Mardjani 1959: 16). The territory of Riau province was proposed to include the districts of Kampar, Bengkalis, Inderagiri and the Riau Archipelago. Then, in 1957, the creation of Riau province was enacted into law. One year later, in 1958, the Riau province was formed.

In 1972 Suharto allowed only three political parties to compete for election: PPP (the United Development Party), Golkar (the government's dominant party); and PDI (the Democratic Party of Indonesia). From 1971 to 1997, Golkar always won the elections in Riau with 70 to 85 percent of the votes cast. In 1971 Golkar won 75.68 percent of votes cast; in 1977, 58 percent; in 1982, 75 percent; in 1987, 80 percent; and in 1992, 83.67 percent—the highest.[2]

Under Colonel Arifin Achmad, the first governor of the province, Golkar began to influence local politics. Achmad was appointed on 15 November 1966. He was of Riau origin and was made assistant III of the

---

[2] Data from the Election Committee (LPU and KPU) for various years, quoted in *Kompas*, 4 Feb. 2004.

Sumatra military command. His support derived mainly from the student movement that opposed the Sukarno government in the late 1960s. Nevertheless, Suharto and the military provided approval for Arifin. Arifin served for almost ten years as Riau's governor. Under Arifin's rule, Golkar began to prove its dominance. He did this by controlling the votes of the Riau people through the local leaders.

Suharto dismissed Arifin in 1978 due to the decreased votes for Golkar in the 1977 elections. That year, Golkar's share of the vote dropped to only 58 percent, much lower than the 75.68 percent share received in 1971. Moreover, Arifin demanded 1 percent of the total oil produced in the province for Riau. Suharto refused Arifin, who voiced the interest of Riau's local elites (Rab 2002b: 458). Due to his experience, Suharto never again appointed a governor with a Malay background in Riau.

Since that time, Riau experienced a relatively similar fate as other regions in the country, particularly East Kalimantan. There were two sources of grievance against the Suharto government in Riau: political, in that the governor's post that had never been occupied by Riau elite; and economic, in that Riau had not received fair income from the revenues earned from extracting oil from Riau's soil.

Riau experienced pressure from Suharto, who intentionally appointed governors with a military background and Javanese blood. The affair of 2 September 1985 revealed clearly how Suharto put his rule into practice. It was the election of Riau governor for 1985–90. At the time, the provincial parliament was split. Most of the provincial assembly members at the time supported Ismail Suko with 19 votes.[3] The regional councilors elected him because he was a local Riau elite with Malay blood. Ismail was the most viable candidate among the Riau elites to be endorsed as governor. His political career was impressive, having served as provincial secretary from 1968 to 1975 and chair of the provincial parliament from 1975 to 1985. In this election, Ismail was sidelined when he had to only accompany the main candidate supported by Suharto. Not daring to oppose Suharto's wish, Ismail voluntarily withdrew his candidacy for governor of Riau.[4]

---

[3] Ismail Suko was born in Kampar in 1932. He received his primary school education in Kampar, his junior high school education in Pekanbaru and Padang Panjang and his senior high school education in Jakarta. He received his bachelor's degree from the Economics University of Indonesia, then his doctorate from the Administrative School (LAN) in 1966. In 1968 he returned to Riau to work in the provincial bureaucracy.

[4] See his interview in "Saya kan hanya pelengkap penderita", *Tempo*, 14 Sept. 1985.

Imam Munandar, the candidate supported by Suharto, was a military man and a Javanese, supported by only 17 votes in the provincial assembly.[5] Iman's career was mainly within the military, where he rose from low rank to the high rank of commander-in-chief for Irian Jaya (now Papua) territory in 1975. Since 1980, he served as the governor of Riau. Even though he lost the elections in the provincial assembly, Suharto supported him. The political institution of Law No. 5/1974 offered Suharto the power to ignore the voice of the province's local elites. He had the privilege to choose the governor based on his own political calculation and economic interest.

Between 1980 and 1990, Imam successfully maintained Golkar's influence in the province with an average of 80 percent of the vote in two elections. To achieve that goal, he had adopted measures to control the civil service in Riau through the corps of Indonesian civil servants (the Korpri). In 1980 only 17,000 Korpri members registered, however, in 1985 that number increased to 52,070 members.[6] Open civil-service employment in 1985 had 27,000 employees; also, he imposed on employees of private companies to join Korpri. Having successfully controlled Korpri, he urged its members to recruit their families, relatives and friends to vote for Golkar in 1982. Consequently, the voters for Golkar increased from 900,000 in 1977 to about 1.1 million in 1982.

Another political measure adopted by Imam was approaching the Riau people by implementing a policy of reviving Malay culture. He set up a cultural center called Balai Adat in Pekanbaru in 1984. He recruited local ethnic leaders for village-level government. Calculating that these leaders must play an important role among their followers, he recruited them with the hope that they would persuade their followers to vote for Golkar. In this way, Imam succeeded in controlling the vote for Golkar in the elections of 1982 and 1987 in Riau.

For the period 1988–1993, Suharto appointed another Javanese military person, Soeripto, to serve as governor of Riau.[7] Soeripto's career

---

[5] Imam Munandar was born in Blitar on 15 June 1927. His education developed as follows: HIS (1940); junior high school (1943); senior high school (1951); Voluntarily Defense/Peta (1944); Army School of Staff/Seskoad (1967); National Defense School/ Lemhanas (1973); and Lemhanas (1975).

[6] Provincial Riau Government, *Riau Makmur: Memori pelaksanaan tugas kepala Tingkat I Riau Oktober 1980–Oktober 1985, H. Imam Munandar* (Pekanbaru: Provincial Riau Government, 1985).

[7] Soeripto was born in Madiun on 18 Nov. 1934. He graduated from the Military Academy (1960), the Army School of Staff/Seskoad (1972), and Seskogab (1975).

track within the military ran mainly through the intelligence service. He served as an assistant for intelligence in both the Cendrawasih territory of Irian Jaya and also Siliwangi in West Java. He received the high rank of commander-in-chief for Sumatra in 1982, and served as the chief of the Strategic Reserve Command in 1986. Due to Suharto's heavy hand in Riau, most of the provincial assembly members chose Soeripto for governor. Out of 45 members of parliament, 35 chose Soeripto for governor (Rab 2002a: 95). Perhaps the local councilors had learned that it was impossible to oppose Suharto's wish. In the next election, Soeripto was appointed, and he served another term from 1993 to 1998. Eventually, Soeripto preferred to work in the interest of Suharto instead of Riau's population. With the appointment of his political ally as governor, Suharto established a firm grip of economic policy, which was mainly intended for political consolidation. Equally important was Suharto's interest in controlling the abundant oil and vast forest reserves available in Riau.

Oil Under Suharto: Pertamina and Caltex Pacific Indonesia

In the early 1970s, Suharto merged two oil companies established by the Sukarno government: Pertamin and Permina. Even though such a merger already took place in the late 1960s, it was in 1971 that the Suharto government structured the company, called Pertamina, as a solely state-owned enterprise to be responsible for managing the country's oil business. With the issuance of Law No. 8/1971, Suharto granted Pertamina the right to deal with the foreign investors who were interested in Indonesia's oil industry. The establishment of Pertamina was part of Suharto's efforts to create economic rent, mainly via contracts for his political and business allies, from the operation of the company (Aden 1992: 93). Such goals were achieved by installing his political ally, Ibnu Sutowo, to serve as Pertamina's CEO. Sutowo was a military man with a background in medicine.

In addition to the establishment of Pertamina, Suharto achieved two other goals: First, through Ibnu Sutowo's hand, he forced foreign investors to agree to contract production sharing or CPS (Bartlett III 1972). A CPS differs very much from the previous form of agreement, a contract of work (CoW). In a CoW, Pertamina received profits based on the sale of oil; in the CPS scheme, in contrast, Pertamina would have management control, and contracts would be based on production sharing rather than profit sharing (Bartlett III 1972: 285).

Second, Suharto was able to silence local elites who wanted to have a share of the revenue from an oil contract with foreign investors. In Riau, as mentioned earlier, Suharto depended on the governors of his choice to secure the central government's interests in extracting oil.

The company known as Caltex Pacific Indonesia (CPI) started operations in Riau in 1924 when a geologist from Standard Oil Company of California, a US company, reported oil reserves in central Sumatra. Based on this report, Standard Oil of California established NV Nederlansche Pacific Petroleum Maatshapij. After it received an exploration permit from Sultan Siak in 1935, the company initiated serious surveys. It first discovered oil in Duri in 1940. In the late 1940s, the company started to operate again, and in 1949 it drilled Minas field. Yet it was in the late 1950s that CPI began to invest heavily, amounting to US$50 million nationally. The most striking change occurred in the early 1960s, when the Suharto government reached an agreement for a CoW with CPI for the first time. Another development happened again in the early 1970s, when the Suharto government, through the president's right-hand man Ibnu Sutowo, imposed a CPS on CPI.

Under such circumstances, Suharto was able to control the oil of Riau. The oil contract between the Suharto government and CPI called for a split in revenues only between Pertamina and CPI with a 15:85 ratio. Fifteen percent of total oil revenue went to CPI and 85 percent went to Jakarta (which in 1998 amounted to US$2 billion). Nothing remained in Riau itself (Colombijn 2000).

These contracts with CPI were made entirely under the provision of the CPS in which Pertamina received 85 percent of oil production and the contractor received the rest. The contract between Pertamina and CPI on the Coastal Pekanbaru Plains (CPP) block was no exception. The contract began in 1971, when CPI signed a CPS for 21,975 square kilometers. The first oil field, Kasikan, was found in the CPP block in 1972 and started production in 1975. The entire CPP block holds 27 oil fields with approximately 621 oil wells.

Riau Politics after Suharto

When Suharto departed from the political scene in 1998, the introduction of regional autonomy and political parties brought about new arrangements in the province. The privilege of the president to appoint governors was dissolved, and a new rule on political parties allowed political parties other than Golkar to operate. The results of the 1999 election revealed how the political situation had changed. Five political parties now dominated the political scene at both regional and national levels: PDI-P (Indonesian Democratic Party-Struggle), Golkar, PPP, PKB (National Awakening Party), and PAN (National Mandate Party). In addition to these changes, the country's parliament and political parties were gaining strength relative to the executive.

In Riau, the power of Golkar diminished, even if the party still dominated the political scene with 30.1 percent of the votes cast in the 1999 elections. Compared to the 1997 election results, in which Golkar received 83.56 percent, 30 percent was bad for the party. Megawati's PDI-P received 25.4 percent of the votes.[8]

Judging from the votes garnered by Indonesia's main political parties, the distribution of power at the provincial level in Riau was quite balanced. The combination of Islamic-based political parties could possibly block the interest of Golkar, while Golkar could also receive serious challenges from PDI-P. Under such political balance, Governor Saleh Djasit was less successful in consolidating various political powers at the provincial level in order to defend the interests of Riau against the central government.[9]

Compared to the case of Semen Padang in West Sumatra where the political party structured the interest of local elites, the role of political parties in Riau was less visible in the economy, as it was in the dispute over the CPP oil block. In the case of Semen Padang, Titik Nazif Lubuk significantly depended upon Golkar's network to defend the interests of her friends. Other than that, she and her colleagues in Padang were able to consolidate power at the provincial level before they challenged the central government. The situation in Riau differed in two ways: first, Saleh Djasit was less successful in his effort to consolidate political power at the provincial level; second, he was less able to rely on networks of political parties such as Golkar and PDI-P. Saleh did not find an individual of Riau origin who occupied a position in those parties and

---

[8] Data obtained from the Election Committee; quoted in *Kompas*, 4 Feb. 2004.

[9] Saleh Djasit was born in Pujut, Riau on 13 Nov. 1943. He finished his primary school and secondary education in Riau before joining the military (Sekolah Calon Perwira) in 1967. In 1984 he graduated from the military law college PTHM. Saleh spent most of his military career in the law section (Badan Pembinaan Hukum). Then, during the Suharto years, he served as district chief of Kampar (1986–96), after which he served as a member of the national parliament (1997–98) and governor of Riau (1998–2004).

who could have been his anchor in national politics. The only possible link that connected Saleh with national political power must have been Syarwan Hamid (mentioned above). However, when Syarwan lost his battle to defend the option of a federal Riau, he was quite reluctant to support the local elites who advocated the option of Riau's freedom in bargaining with the central government over the CPP oil block. Furthermore, Syarwan had no direct interest in the CPP oil block, and he was never involved in its management or operation. This behavior indicates his interest in politics at the local level. His involvement in the Riau People's Congress II, which drew him to Riau, is best viewed within the wider perspective of Syarwan's efforts to defend the interests of the central government. With the absence of political support at the national level, Saleh was on his own.

Because of the centrality of Saleh Djasit's role within the dispute, it is necessary therefore to understand his relationship with the central government after the introduction of the decentralization policy in 1999.

After the central government's introduction of its decentralization policy, the governor became responsible to the provincial house of representatives (DPRD) and the president. Yet, in the world of politics, the governor grew more responsive to the DPRD, the highest provincial body in the province, which appointed him. Moreover, the previous hierarchy that existed under the Suharto system of governance had been cut off. Saleh Djasit had to listen the wishes of the provincial councilors while simultaneously trying to appease the president.

Saleh Djasit was embedded within a web created in Riau by Suharto, in which the interests of Jakarta-based conglomerates and foreign investors, most of all CPI, were treated as top priorities. The local population perceived Saleh as a member of Suharto's government, given his position as district chief of Kampar. Saleh, in the eyes of the local population in Kampar, intentionally downplayed the existence of customary land rights to allow Riau Andalan Pulp and Paper to expropriate it.[10] Under the tight control of Suharto, Saleh preferred to side with the central government over Kampar's population; in any case, Saleh lacked the power to challenge the president. Saleh's attitude is reflected clearly in the fact that

---

[10] Regarding this allegation, see "Setumpuk urusan buat Gubernur Baru", *Forum Keadilan*, 16 Nov. 1998.

he was the product of the system of governance created by Suharto. As a result, his relations with the business interests of the Jakarta-based conglomerates were persistent. These relations resurfaced in 2001, when Saleh established a provincial air carrier. The conglomerates contributed the capital.[11]

Saleh's victory as governor of Riau in 1998 was also tainted with strong allegations of money politics. He was allegedly bribing some of the local councilors.[12] At that time, the provincial councilors already enjoyed the freedom to appoint the governor without political intervention from the president. Such an allegation was difficult to deny, since he had connections with conglomerates that no doubt wanted to protect their business interests in Riau. Saleh must have been their candidate, because he showed a willingness to defend those interests. Saleh and the conglomerates had already established a mutual trust rooted in the New Order era. He needed the Jakarta-based conglomerates because they had the necessary skills, capability and access to international capital. This mutual relationship to some extent also defined Saleh's political behavior. Saleh considered the operation of CPI within this framework, in which Riau provided the raw materials, and CPI offered the technology, skill, capital and access to the international market.

In addition, Saleh's long service within the military provided him with an advantage. He was portrayed as capable of protecting business. With his military background, Saleh enjoyed a reputation as someone unwilling to secede from the unitary state of Indonesia. Saleh's long service in the military made him believe that the unitary state had been final for the country, and therefore there was no need for freedom movements. Saleh's willingness to side with the central government or military was manifested in his readiness to fund the purchase of a patrol ship for the navy.[13] As for the purchase of a patrol ship using regional funds, Saleh Djasit argued that such expenditure was necessary and appropriate because of the navy's limited operational capabilities. He added that such

---

[11] "Gagal rebut ladang minyak, terjuni bisnis penerbangan", *Jawa Pos*, 25 May 2001.
[12] Setumpuk Urusan buat Gubernur, *Forum Keadilan*, 16 Nov. 1998.
[13] "Provinsi Riau Membeli Kapal Patroli Cepat untuk TNI AL", *Tempo*, 20 Oct. 2003, available at https://nasional.tempo.co/read/25777/provinsi-riau-membeli-kapal-patroli-cepat-untuk-tni-al [accessed 4 Feb. 2018].

a ship was important to maintaining the security of the coast of Riau Province from the threat of illegal fishing.[14]

The Ill-Fated Riau Freedom Movement: Political Rifts

This section pinpoints the ill-fated Riau Freedom Movement, which triggered a political rift in the province because of the governor's lack of support; and even though the central government did not consider the movement as a real threat, it sent a signal to the central government that the local elite in Riau was already thinking about seceding from the unitary state.

Saleh Djasit experienced his first political defeat in the province when he proved unsuccessful in defending the option of a federal Riau in the event of the Riau People's Congress II, which was to be held in the early 2000. This led to a political fracture at the provincial level. Although Saleh defended at any price the unitary state of Indonesia, he initially allowed the congress to take place with a high hope that the participants would vote for a federal Riau instead of freedom. In the congress, two polemical factions were at work. In one, Syarwan Hamid campaigned for a federal Riau,[15] which Saleh supported. Both Saleh and Syarwan wanted to protect the integrity of Indonesia's territory, and they were willing to stop any movement that wanted to undermine it. In the other, social movement leaders such as Tabrani Rab and Al Azhar (mentioned below) advocated an independent Riau.

These diametrically opposed positions on Riau stemmed from the different backgrounds of the players and their political objectives. Even though Saleh Djasit, Syarwan Hamid, Tabrani Rab and Al Azhar were the products of the New Order government, they originated from different political backgrounds.

Syarwan's decision to offer a federal Riau could be predicted from his political track record. He occupied various important posts in the military, ranging from assistant to the chief of political and social affairs to chief between 1995 and 1996. Syarwan served as a deputy in the

---

[14] For detailed information on this matter, see *Impartial Critical Analysis of Defense Policy, Regional Budget for TNI: A Threat for Civilian Control over the Military*, vol. 1, Mar. 2004, p. 2.

[15] Syarwan Hamid was born in Siak on 10 Nov. 1943. He graduated from the Military Academy in 1966, and then served in the military.

DPR and MPR until 1997. Under the Habibie government, he served as minister of home affairs.

For Syarwan, the most viable option for advancing the interests of Riau was a federal structure (Albintani 2001: 22). In Syarwan's own words, "to be realistic, relations between the central (government) and regions must be improved. Federalism has been successful in promoting people's welfare while still retaining unity. We are not thinking of asking for independence. Federalism is enough, because it is still in the context of unity".[16] Clearly, Syarwan believed that only through a federal Riau could the interests of its people in general be achieved. Judging from Syarwan's previous position in the Habibie government advocating regional autonomy, his latest position on federalism was a big leap.[17] It seems that he now had to deal with the latest political development in Riau, where the choice of independence was on the horizon. In such a political situation, Syarwan could not offer his suggestion of a more autonomous Riau. His calculation was probably only to stop Riau from becoming independent, while at the same time the interest of its political elites could be channeled. Therefore, for Syarwan, a federal Riau was the best possible solution to the problem of choosing between an independent Riau and an autonomous one.

Even though Syarwan was respected, his previous involvement in the Suharto and Habibie governments tarnished his political credibility at the Riau congress. As such, his proposal was also deemed as the central government's agenda for maintaining the unitary state of Indonesia instead of defending the interests of Riau. Tabrani, a proponent of an independent Riau, blamed Syarwan for serving the interests of Jakarta.[18] It was no surprise, then, when congress participants chose freedom for Riau (Rab 2000a: 206–64).

Tabrani Rab and Al Azhar rose to prominence because of their silent resistance to the New Order state and its development strategy. The structure of the political economy in Riau under the New Order regime was designed to benefit Suharto and his political and business allies. While the operation of CPI mainly benefited his development strategy through the control of contracts in Pertamina, the other major business

---

[16] "Scholar Renews Independence for Riau", 19 Nov. 1999.
[17] The regional autonomy laws were drafted under the Habibie government in the office of Ministry of Home Affairs where Syarwan Hamid was minister.
[18] *Jakarta Post*, 16 Nov. 1999.

activities in Riau, mainly forest-based, also served Suharto's interest. It started when Suharto saw the country's vast timber resources as a way not only to jump-start the economy but also to consolidate his political power through economic patronage (Barr 1998; Peluso 1995). The timber industry in Riau, as in elsewhere in the country, began to develop when Suharto passed the Law on Forestry.[19] A vast area that included more than 75 percent (143 million hectares) of Indonesia's total land area—much of it still under traditional claim—was classified as "state forest".[20] The law addressed logging or "conversion" to plantation (i.e., clear-cutting and replanting with monocultural pulp or other estate crops).

Along with Suharto's effort to choose only loyal allies for the bureaucracy, he appointed loyal businesspersons and those who were willing to work under his control to exploit the Riau forest. Suharto employed this strategy because in the mid-1980s he saw that income from oil was on the decline. Business figures in this industry were predominantly close allies of Suharto like Mohammad "Bob" Hasan and the state-owned enterprise Perhutani (Barr 1998). Some conglomerates were instrumental to Suharto's endeavor to develop the timber industry and create rents from it. Under the president, the central government granted them large concessions in Riau. Each of them was given an area as a concession. These concessions were related to Suharto's effort to develop a sustainable source of fiber for the nation's rapidly growing pulp industry. With it, the conglomerates secured the political support of Suharto. Under the political protection of Suharto, these conglomerates unlawfully seized land from indigenous Sakai and Malay communities in Riau.[21]

In addition, the HTI (Industrial Forest Scheme) also secured a channel of funding to conglomerates from the Suharto government; the Department of Forestry subsidized the project by providing 14 percent of the project's total cost in the form of equity capital and 32.5 percent in the form of a no-interest loans with a repayment period of ten years

---

[19] Law on Forestry No. 5/1967.

[20] The term *state forest* indicates the intention of the Suharto government to control land. The law mentions that a state forest comprises land, with or without forest; see article 1, section 4.

[21] Human Rights Watch, *Without Remedy: Human Right Abuse and Indonesia's Pulp and Paper Industry* (Washington, 2003), p. 33.

(Barr 2001: 23). Such massive and cheap funds were very crucial to the initial stages of development for the conglomerates.

Tabrani and Al Azhar initially emerged as the cultural leaders rather than politicians under the Suharto government, because it was the only role that had less intervention from Suharto. Both of them used this limited space to maneuver the political scene. For both of them, Suharto's attitude towards Riau was insolent. Under Suharto's tight control, Tabrani and Al Azhar cleverly hid their resistance by using the economic backwardness of the Riau Malays as cover. They learned that under Suharto, the Malays of Riau were not granted an equitable portion of the benefits of their own economic resources such as oil. As mentioned earlier, some economic resources were given to foreign investors, CPI, in the oil industry; and the large portions of forests were granted to the Jakarta-based conglomerates. The matter grew worse for Tabrani and Al Azhar when the Riau Malays not only became the spectators of economic growth in the Suharto years, but they also were "forced out to leave the soil they have tilled for generations" (Derks 1997: 701). Under the tight control of Suharto, reports on the ways in which this expropriation was executed were scarce, but the little evidence—often orally transmitted—suggests methods that were appalling: "officially sanctioned systematic taunting, harassment and intimidation of those who are not satisfied with the incredibly low *sagu hati* or 'consolation allowance' offered to them in lieu of their land" (Derks 1997: 701). An observer reported a situation in 1997 in which many of the abuses were hidden. After 1998 such abuses were reported publicly.[22]

It is no surprise that Tabrani and Al Azhar both strongly believed that Suharto exploited the wealth of Riau and channeled all of it to Jakarta. They responded to this unfair redistribution. The interest of the local population to survive within state-sponsored development was their first concern. Tabrani and Al Azhar's form of resistance had never been expressed directly because they were aware that such an action was dangerous and politically impossible. They skillfully hid their resistance in the form of a campaign for economic injustice centering on the Malays of Riau. In doing so, the two leaders "attempted to construct new identity" for them (Escobar 1995: 216). The effectiveness of their movement to resist the Suharto government was far from clear. However, both of them were able to circulate the message that the local population should

---

[22] Those who are interested can refer to Human Rights Watch, *Without Remedy*.

be the first to benefit from Riau's resources. Furthermore, Tabrani put this discourse into action by defending the rights of the Sakai people to their ancestral land.

After the fall of Suharto, Tabrani and Al Azhar began putting their vision into action. On many occasions, both of them defended the right of local people against multinationals and Jakarta-based conglomerates. By defending the rights of the local people, Tabrani and Al Azhar gained credibility; people believed that their economic vision would benefit the people of Riau. Their movement then peaked in the form of the Riau freedom movement. The whole idea of Riau's freedom stemmed from the economic injustices experienced by Riau. As such, this movement could be judged as a search for an alternative to Suharto in development strategy.

Saleh Djasit, in contrast, considered Tabrani as an opportunist and an enemy who did not represent the interests of Riau (Abdurrahman 2003: 301). Even in public spaces, Saleh Djasit labeled Tabrani's initiative for an independent Riau as "a political joke".[23] This opinion expressed the governor's trepidation over the political future of Riau, especially in the eyes of the central government. Even though this movement did not have real political strength, it sent an initial warning to the central government to watch this oil-rich province carefully. Saleh understood this because he was a part of the government and had been deeply involved with the military.

The proposal for an independent Riau gave impetus for serious political fractures at the provincial level. Since Saleh Djasit could not defend the choice for a federal Riau, Tabrani and Al Azhar briefly set the agenda for the fight to increase Riau's revenue share from oil production. At this stage, they demanded that the central government give 10 percent of total oil production to Riau. At the initial stage of this dispute, the voices of Al Azhar and Tabrani were highly credible to the Riau population. However, the central government under Abdurahman Wahid did not take this demand into account seriously. Abdurahman considered this movement to be politically irrelevant, because he had learned that Saleh Djasit did not back it. On the contrary, Saleh labeled this movement as being far from the existing rules with which he referred to the decentralization law. Saleh mentioned that "in my province we respect all contracts, but it is true there are many interpretations of autonomy. [Therefore] we have no rules ... There may be demands but there is no

---

[23] "Geliat provinsi minyak", *Gamma*, 21 Mar. 1999, p. 62.

mechanism for enforcement."[24] So Saleh considered the request from Tabrani and Al Azhar for controlling the CPP oil block as demands without enforcement possibilities. Saleh recognized that Tabrani and Al Azhar had moved outside the provincial government's authority.

In the end, Tabrani recognized that the Riau Freedom Movement (Riau Merdeka, RM) did not provide enough political pressure to compel the central government to negotiate revenue sharing. It is true that the RM did not receive warm acceptance from a portion of the Riau people, since some of them did not feel that they were being represented by the participants who attended the congress. The credibility of RM, if they had any, was lost when Tabrani accepted Abdurahman Wahid's offer to join the Council of Regional Autonomy Advisory, a central governmental body under the Ministry of Home Affairs. Tabrani's move to join the central government was considered by those who voted for an independent Riau as betrayal. It was uncommon for a proponent of a separatist movement to join the central government.

Al Azhar took over RM, however, he inherited a movement that had already lost its momentum and credibility. He could not gain renewed momentum to increase the movement's size. Saleh Djasit learned that RM was unable to put pressure on him, and so he quickly took this opportunity to seize the initiative in the fight for revenue sharing. As for the CPP oil block, Saleh was willing to adopt the demand for 100-percent ownership simply because it would boost his political stature in Riau. This time, Saleh had to adopt this stance or he would lose another chance to restore his credibility in the eyes of Riau's people. However, under the decentralization policy Saleh had to seriously take into consideration the provincial councilors who put pressure on him to fight the central government over the CPP oil block. Saleh had to submit an annual accountability report to them; therefore, he did not have any option except to follow.

Intervention by the Central Government

A "Weak Governor"

Even though Saleh had already manifested his loyalty to the central government, he was also the governor who was watched closely by the Minister of Home Affairs Hari Sabarno. Saleh's inability to stop the

---

[24] Saleh Djasit, interview with USINDO in Washington, DC, 18 Sept. 2001.

Congress of Riau People II in early 2000 raised political suspicions at the national level. In the eyes of Hari, Saleh was accommodative to the demand for Riau's independence. Even though Saleh had expressed his trepidation about the outcome of the congress, Hari perceived that Saleh did not perform his duty to stop such an event. After that, Hari seems to have distrusted Saleh, because Hari believed that allowing an independent movement in Riau would be a dangerous game for the future of Indonesia's unitary state. Other than his political calculation, Hari learned that most of the country's oil reserves are located in Riau. The timber industry was also important to the country's economy.

Given the aforementioned background, it is clear that by purchasing a patrol ship for the navy, Saleh was loyal to the central government. Nonetheless, he damaged his reputation for loyalty by his inability to stop the Riau independence movement. It was far from a surprise when Saleh refrained from supporting Tabrani's proposal for a greater share of revenue from oil or the movement for a free Riau. Initially, Saleh expressed his reluctance to support Tabrani's idea for more revenue from CPI. Tabrani entertained the idea of getting 10 percent of CPI's total production. In order to block Tabrani's idea of freedom for Riau, in March 1999 Saleh demanded more revenue sharing. He put forward a demand that Riau receive 10 percent of oil production (Blackburn 1999: 24). His belated involvement cost Saleh much of his credibility as someone who could fight for the interests of Riau. Instead of siding with the movement for greater revenue sharing, or even the movement for Riau's freedom, Saleh apparently sided with the central government.

Saleh tried hard to restore his credibility among the Riau people by endorsing the movement for more revenue sharing. Even though Saleh endorsed the revenue-sharing idea, he distanced himself from the independent movement.[25] He cleverly demanded 100 percent shares initially, reducing his request to a mere 70-percent share of the CPP oil block when the central government rejected it.

Saleh restored his credibility when he advanced Riau's interests in the central government. When Tabrani joined the central government as a member of the Advisory Council for Regional Autonomy, Saleh quickly strengthened his credibility by filling in the space he left behind. This did not mean that Saleh had no place in the struggle when Tabrani

---

[25] Interview with Azlaini Agus, a lieutenant of Al Azhar, in Pekanbaru, Riau, 14 Aug. 2003.

began voicing demands, only that Saleh preferred to deal with the issue cautiously. He tried not to block Tabrani, but at the same time the province criticized Tabrani as a man without credibility to represent Riau's interest. In dealing with the central government, Saleh was diplomatic.

Saleh Djasit quickly took up the opportunity to consolidate Riau's interest. He wanted to ensure that only the province represented Riau. Saleh maintained the target of 100 percent of ownership for Riau, or at least 70 percent. However, he never achieved this, thanks to the opposition of the central government. Facing opposition from Minister Purnomo, Saleh Djasit proposed a reduction of ownership to a 60 percent share, but again the central government turned it down and offered instead only 10 percent.[26] The central government might refer to the production sharing contract between CPI and the Indonesian government represented by Pertamina, which stated that CPI must divest its 10 percent to an Indonesian partner.[27]

The negotiation between Saleh and Purnomo ended with a deadlock because both of them did not reach any agreement regarding the composition of shares in the CPP. Saleh rejected Purnomo's proposal that Riau receive only 10 percent of oil revenues in the CPP.

The Central Government Steps In

There were two central government interventions related to the CPP oil block dispute: allowing for the establishment of Riau Archipelago province; and creating a political network with Azaly Djohan. Minister of Home Affairs Hari Sabarno adopted the first political measure, allowing the formation of the Riau Archipelago province without any recommendation from Governor Saleh Djasit.[28] Hari's political behavior reflected his training and long involvement with the military from the start of his career. After serving as the assistant for social and political affairs in military headquarters during 1994 and 1995, he moved to the parliament representing the interests of the military through the military/police faction. As Minister Hari's main duty was to maintain the integrity of

---

[26] "Riau Province to Jointly Own CPP's Oil Block", *Jakarta Post*, 25 July 2001.

[27] "Pemda Riau ngotot ninta 70% saham CPP", *Bisnis Indonesia*, 20 Nov. 2000.

[28] Hari Sabarno was born in Solo, Central Java, on 12 Aug. 1944. He graduated from the Military Academy in 1967. He served as a member of DPR representing the military/police faction (1999–2001), chairing the faction.

the unitary state, especially after having lost East Timor and endured the constant tensions in Aceh and Papua. According to the decentralization regulation, a new province could only be created if there was a grant of legal permission by the governor of the province in which the new province was previously situated. Hari had a political interest in the proposed Riau Archipelago province. He treated it as important leverage for bargaining with Saleh Djasit (Albintani 2001: 165). From Hari's perspective, granting Riau Archipelago provincial status was a lesser evil than allowing a breakaway Riau state. This political measure, moreover, split the Riau independence movement and undermined the viability of their objective, since it is questionable whether the Sumatran part of Riau Province could ever be sustainable as a state (Wee 2002: 512). In November 2002, with political support from Minister Hari and without a recommendation from Governor Saleh Djasit, the province of Riau Archipelago was established.[29] It meant that Hari had bypassed Saleh Djasit.

Saleh Djasit rejected the establishment of Riau Archipelago Province on economic grounds. According to him, Riau Archipelago was economically unviable as a province because most of its income derived from Riau province's mainland on Sumatra. He maintained that the separation between the mainland and the archipelago would give the latter a net income of only IDR68 billion. This was the amount it would earn from local taxes. According to Saleh Djasit, as a province the archipelago would lose its right to revenue sharing from oil and gas, from which it earned IDR600 billion.

Apart from the fact that the initiators of independence were Riau elites who resided in the mainland part of the Riau Province (on Sumatra), Hari carefully calculated the archipelago's political economy. He learned from this that, in the current setup, the archipelago contributed substantially more to the revenue of the old province than mainland Riau did. There were more resources flowing from insular Riau to mainland Riau than vice-versa (Wee 2002: 511). This meant that, because of its economic resources, Riau Archipelago province was actually economically viable.

Although Riau Archipelago consists of five main islands—Batam, Natuna, Bintan, Karimun and Lingga—Batam has been its economic showcase. The story of the transformation of Batam is important to understanding the viability of Riau Archipelago as a province. Batam started as a support base for a state oil company in 1969, but it became

---

[29] "Provinsi Kepri belum dioperasionalkan", *Sijori Pos*, 4 Nov. 2002.

a bonded zone in 1978. Indonesia, Singapore and Malaysia inaugurated this free-trade zone in 1990 after their leaders agreed to enhance regional economic cooperation. They called it "Sijori", an abbreviated form for Singapore, Malaysia's Johor and Indonesia's Riau.

Due to its geographic proximity to Singapore, the Riau Archipelago could make itself attractive economically. Specifically, it can link to the infrastructure, capital and expertise of Singapore (Yue 1997: 33). This placed Batam to become the major investment site in Riau. Investments from Singapore (including foreign MNCs based in Singapore) became a major source of the island's foreign investment (Yue 1996: 181). Such huge investments are associated with the creation of Batam Industrial Park, the largest industrial park in Batam, with 57 companies operating there in 1995, representing a total investment of over US$200 million (Royle 1997: 94).

Other than Batam, the Riau Archipelago offers economic potential for both fisheries and bonded economic zones. Fisheries industries, due to the nature of the province, have been important. In 2001, total fish production reached 358,000 tons, valued at IDR212 billion. In addition, Bintan Island could also operate as a bonded economic zone like Batam. It has two industrial zones, one in Lagoi aimed at attracting income from the tourism industry, and another in Lobam serving as an industrial zone. There are 93 foreign companies operating on Bintan, which have helped the island to absorb around US$2.3 million in investments.

In addition, Hari Sabarno calculated that some of the political leaders who advocated greater revenue sharing resided on the Riau mainland. Such geographical nuances motivated Hari to embark on his plan to grant provincial status to the archipelago. By doing so, he could manipulate the complex emotional bond between leaders on the mainland and those on the archipelago. Therefore, Hari's endorsement of the new province was welcomed by leaders on the Riau Archipelago, and afterwards he never received any opposition from them.

Minister of Energy and Mineral Resources Purnomo Yusgiantoro[30] adopted the second political measure by establishing an alliance with Azaly Djohan from Siak.[31] Purnomo is an energy economist by training.

---

[30] Born in Semarang on 16 June 1951, Purnomo Yusgiantoro graduated from ITB (1974), the University of Colorado (1988) and the Colorado School of Mines (1986) before earning his PhD from the Colorado School of Mines (1988).

[31] Azaly Djohan was born in Siak on 16 May 1939. He served as Bengkalis district chief in 1989–94, Kampar district chief 1995–98, and assistant secretary for the Riau provincial government in 1998.

Between 1998 and 2000, before he served as the energy and mineral resources minister under both Abdurahman Wahid and Megawati, Purnomo served as the deputy governor of the National Resilience Agency (Lemhanas), the state think tank for defense issues. From 1993 to 1998 he was an advisor to the minister of energy and mineral resources. Azaly's political career was embedded within the structure established by Suharto. In the late 1980s, he was the district chief of Bengkalis, then in the early 1990s he served as the district chief of Kampar, after which he moved to the province to serve as the assistant secretary of the provincial government. When Purnomo approached Azaly, he was the representative of Riau in the Council of People's Assembly. In this position, Azaly resided in Jakarta representing the interest of Riau in the assembly. This indicated that he could deal with politics at the national level. Since he was representing Riau's interests, he had access to the politics of both Jakarta and Riau.

Purnomo's calculation was simple: the political power of Siak was weak in comparison to the provincial government. With it, Purnomo could secure the central government's interest in controlling the CPP through its majority shares. Purnomo undoubtedly could impose his terms on Azaly. On 11 September 2001, Purnomo Yusgiantoro wrote a letter to Saleh Djasit mentioning a condition in which a district government of Siak would be included as part of a team set up by the governor.[32] With his plan to involve Azaly in the provincial team, Purnomo started to cultivate his preference in dealing with the CPP. There were two benefits that Purnomo would receive: a reduction of the potential for conflict at the local level; and the weakening of Saleh Djasit's influence. As for reducing future conflicts at the local level, Purnomo concluded that Siak's involvement in the provincial team would be his best solution. Purnomo perceived that the exclusion of Siak would aggravate potential damage because the CPP oil field is situated in Siak. Such potential damage could be in the form of sabotage or a mass riot that would jeopardize all CPP and CPI operations. If such an event had taken place, Purnomo's interest to tap revenue from the operation of the CPP would be diminished. Here, Purnomo still viewed the CPP as a source of income, regardless of who operated the oil field.

---

[32] Letter from Minister of Energy and Mineral Resources Purnomo Yusgiantoro to Saleh Djasit, no. 3274/30/MEM.M/2001, dated 11 Sept. 2001.

Purnomo's plan to include Siak also served another end, that of mitigating the power of Saleh Djasit in the province. At the time, it was quite clear that Saleh intended to control the negotiations with the central government over the CPP, so Purnomo might have had a plan to weaken Saleh's influence; however, with the call for Riau's freedom the previous year, Purnomo shared the grievances of his colleagues in the central government, such as Hari Sabarno, viewing Saleh as unable to protect the interests of the government in terms of protecting foreign investors in the province, including CPI. Purnomo looked suspiciously at Saleh Djasit's political reluctance to adopt stiff measures against local elites such as Tabrani Rab and Al Azhar. Through this lens, Purnomo might perceive that Saleh would not apply pressure to stop them from disputing the CPP. Purnomo perceived that Saleh's behavior would put his position in jeopardy if he failed to secure his interest in protecting foreign investors.

Azaly Djohan was appointed directly by the Siak district chief, who issued district-level regulations.[33] Supplied with a weapon in the form of Purnomo's approval, Azaly quickly saw an opportunity to advance his interest over that of the CPP. Subsequently, Azaly established a Siak team designed to acquire the oil field. Azaly abolished the word "province" for the team he established, and instead he employed "Riau". Azaly intentionally wanted to exclude Saleh from having access to the CPP.

After receiving pressure from both Purnomo and Azaly, Saleh had no choice except to endorse Azaly's proposal to represent Riau in the negotiations for the CPP. Azaly wrote a letter to Saleh demanding a formal approval from the governor stipulating that Azaly's team would represent the interests of Riau.[34] Saleh had no choice but to agree, and so he gave formal approval that Azaly would represent the interest of Riau.[35]

To strengthen his political interest, Azaly put capital into the company that would control CPP operations. In addition, the location of the

---

[33] See his interview in *Bahana Mahasiswa*, a student newspaper published by Riau University: "CPP punya Siak, itu keliru", *Bahana Mahasiswa*, Jan. 2002. Azaly Djohan was the district chief of Bengkalis in 1989–94 and represented Riau in the MPR. He was born in Siak on 16 May 1939, and served as assistant III of Riau province. He ran for governor in 1998 but was defeated by Saleh Djasit.

[34] Letter of the team of CPP Riau to Governor Saleh Djasit, No. 06/T.CPP.KS/X/SS-2001, dated 11 Oct. 2001, signed by Azaly Djohan.

[35] Letter from Governor of Riau to Minister of Energy and Mineral Resources, No. 500/Ekbang/2470, dated 12 Oct. 2001, and signed by Saleh Djasit.

CPP oil block in Siak benefited Azaly, because he could translate it into political power. These two elements explain Azaly's behavior in the fight for majority ownership of the oil field. Azaly had the intention to own 70 percent of shares in Bumi Siak Pusako (BSP), a local government-owned enterprise intended as a business vehicle to run the CPP oil field. His argument was based on the fact that most of the CPP oil wells, which account for at least 80 percent of production, are located in Siak district. The Siak government was also ready to provide a big portion of BSP's working capital,[36] which amounted to IDR210 billion.[37]

In January 2002 BSP entered into an agreement with the central government with Pertamina as the representative.[38] By December 2001, a month before, they had begun to come together on the terms of the contract. They agreed on the establishment of a joint body that would run the CPP oil field and on the creation of joint operations but had yet to decide the distribution of shares.[39] In August 2002, when CPI should have released its contract, Azaly entered into another agreement on behalf of BSP with the Upstream Oil and Gas Management Agency (Badan Pengelola Kegiatan Hulu Migas, also called Balaks), a new agency set up to supervise the entire downstream oil industry in the country based on Law No. 22/2001. In the new agreement, Purnomo, through the Balaks, gained majority ownership through a split that accorded them 85 percent, thus securing its interest over the revenue from the oil field. The remaining 15 percent did not entirely go to Siak, because it had to divide this share with Pertamina based on an agreement signed in January 2002. At 15 percent, both Pertamina and Siak would therefore each receive 7.5 percent.[40] The new contract sharing production structured CPP's ownership percentages accordingly. With the conclusion of this joint-management contract, Purnomo secured the central government's objective to control the CPP block.

The transfer of the CPP block from CPI to that of the joint operation body—BSP and Pertamina—took place on 9 August 2002. Even

---

[36] Interview with president director of BSP, Azaly Djohan, *Bisnis Indonesia*, 8 Aug. 2002.

[37] "Bumi Siak Pusako terlahir untuk minyak", *Bisnis Indonesia*, 7 Aug. 2002.

[38] *Bulletin Warta Pertamina*, 3 Jan. 2002.

[39] For details of these agreements, see Memorandum of Understanding between Pertamina and PT Bumi Siak Pusako, no. 46/TCB/Riau/XII/2001, dated 29 Dec. 2001, signed by Azaly Djohan of BSP and Eteng Salam of Pertamina.

[40] "Balaks Teken kontrak perdana bagi hasil Blok CPP", *Bisnis Indonesia*, 6 Aug. 2002.

though there was a problem regarding BSP's share ownership scheme, Azaly Djohan nonetheless emphasized that Siak would receive the company's majority ownership.[41]

Compared with the proposals of either Tabrani Rab, in which 10 percent of total CPI income went to Siak, or Al Azhar who sought 100 percent of the CPP block, the resulting 7.5 percent for Siak through Azaly is very small. The overwhelming majority of shares went to the central government—85 percent through Balaks and 7.5 percent through Pertamina. Judging from the initial intention of Riau political elites to gain the majority ownership of the CPP, Azaly's performance seems far from successful. Perhaps Azaly had few choices, because he was aware that BSP's management lacked the technological capability in the field to pump oil—although he could have exploited Siak's position as the site of the oil field. Additionally, the management of BSP had no experience in operating even a small oil field. Therefore, Azaly had to rely on Pertamina for both technology and expertise. Such dependency weakened his political position. Moreover, Azaly's letter to Saleh Djasit indicates that he relied too much on Purnomo for political support. This dependency limited Azaly's choices.

After Azaly was able to secure Siak's interest, he was rewarded with a managerial position at BSP. Azaly served as the company's CEO even though he had no experience in operating an oil company. That said, his expertise did not pose a big problem for either Purnomo or the government of Siak. As for Purnomo, Azaly was instrumental in his effort to block Saleh Djasit's move, and therefore the minister was able to manage the central government's interest. Azaly also advanced the Siak government's interests because of his connections with politicians in Jakarta in his capacity as Riau province's representative in the Council of People's Assembly.

Response of CPI

As early as June 1997, CPI expressed its intention to extend the contract for the CPP oil field. CPI management submitted a request for an extension to the year of 2021. At the same time, Pertamina proposed that it solely operate the CPP. The bargaining position of Pertamina grew

---

[41] "Kami siap operasikan Blok CPP (interview)", *Bisnis Indonesia*, 8 Aug. 2002.

stronger after it received approval from Suharto.[42] However, the Habibie government had never taken approval seriously. As a consequence, Pertamina never received endorsement from the central government. On the contrary, the central government through the Ministry of Energy and Mineral Resources opened the possibility that the CPP oil field would undergo a bidding process.[43] Kuntoro Mangkusubroto, the minister of energy and mineral resources, explained that he was unwilling to embark on this policy because the Suharto government had decided to offer Pertamina the right to operate. In order to prevent open conflict between Pertamina and CPI, Kuntoro thought that a fair bidding process would provide the best possible solution. With it, CPI would virtually lose its privilege as the sole party in the CPP, even though it already had worked the oil field for almost three decades.

Seeking to preventing the loss of the CPP, CPI offered Pertamina a revenue-sharing deal in which CPI would receive 90 percent and Pertamina 10 percent.[44] Pertamina would receive its 10-percent share for free because CPI would pay for it instead as the participating interest for contract extension. Later on, CPI offered a 50:50 split in which both CPI and Pertamina would each receive 50 percent of shares. Pertamina refused CPI's proposal; then the state-owned enterprise demanded a bigger share in a scheme calling for a 35:65 split in its favor. CPI refused, defending its plan for a 50:50 split.[45] If CPI accepted Pertamina's proposal, both Chevron and Texaco, CPI's shareholders, would receive only 17.5 percent each. Humayunbosha, the CEO of CPI and an Indonesian professional with a long career in CPI, argued that if given the smaller shares of only 17.5 percent, Chevron and Texaco would not fully support the CPP with their technology and capital.[46]

The political constellation altered, however, when Saleh Djasit expressed Riau's interest in the venture.[47] With the involvement of Riau, there were now three parties competing to control the CPP oil field. Such a development added a new problem for CPI, one that posed a growing concern for foreign investors, and so they would have to carefully consider

---

[42] "Pertamina and Caltex akan Operasikan Blok CPP di Riau", *Kompas*, 21 Jan. 1999.

[43] "Ladang CPP Mungkin dilelang", *Bisnis Indonesia*, 11 Aug. 1998.

[44] "Caltex tawarkan split 10:90", *Bisnis Indonesia*, 16 Sept. 1998.

[45] "Caltex tolak Pertamina soal porsi bagi hasil CPP", *Bisnis Indonesia*, 31 Jan. 2000.

[46] "Negosiasi saham CPP dibatasi hingga Februari", *Bisnis Indonesia*, 2 Feb. 2000.

[47] "Pemda Riau tolak Caltex garap CPP", *Bisnis Indonesia*, 24 Feb. 2000.

Riau's demands. It would change the attitude of CPI from one of maintaining good relations with the central government to one of seriously paying attention to the growing interest at the local level.

In March 2001 CPI finally gave up on its dream of controlling the CPP with majority shares or a 50:50 scheme because Minister Susilo Bambang Yudhoyono, a military person, and minister of energy and mineral resources at the time, put pressure on foreign investors to accept minority shares. Humayunbosha, the CEO of CPI, persisted in defending the company's interest by proposing a 51:49 split in the central government's favor; in addition, the company offered a revenue sharing scheme of 85:15,[48] in which the central government would get 85 percent from total revenue pumped from the CPP, which was in line with the existing scheme. Even though the local elites in Riau wanted shares in the CPP, as early as March 2001 Humayunbosha paid little attention to them.

With the growing interest of Riau elites such as Tabrani Rab and Saleh Djasit, CPI realized that the prospect of its control over the CPP oil field had become less viable. In April, Saleh Djasit indicated that Riau sought to own all CPP shares. The governor advanced the argument that the CPP oil field must return to the government after CPI's contract expired. Even though Minister Susilo carefully considered Saleh's demand, he did not allow Riau to own a majority of shares. The CEO of Pertamina at the time, Baihaki Hakim, himself a former CEO of CPI, allowed Riau involvement in the negotiation process but retained Pertamina's interest in maintaining majority ownership. At this time, Humayunbosha offered Riau 10 percent of the shares owned by CPI.[50]

However, CPI received a new shock when the new minister of energy and mineral resources for the Abdurahman government, Purnomo Yusgiantoro, excluded them from any negotiation regarding the CPP oil field. The chance for CPI to own even a minority share now became slim. The central government under Abdurahman Wahid obviously wanted to tap more revenue from the CPP while seeking to please Saleh Djasit's interest in capturing shares in the oil field for Riau.

---

[48] "Caltex bersikeras ingin miliki 49 percent saham CPP", *Bisnis Indonesia*, 17 Mar. 2000.
[49] "Pemda Riau minta 100 percent saham CPP", *Bisnis Indonesia*, 3 Apr. 2000.
[50] "Soal Saham CPP picu ketidakpastian hukum", *Bisnis Indonesia*, 23 Nov. 2000.

CPI's strategy for dealing with the CPP oil field changed significantly, especially after Humayunbosha learned that Purnomo had intentionally excluded the foreign company. In the middle of December 2000, CPI flew a white flag and left the central government to make the decision on the CPP. The window of opportunity for CPI to own the CPP had closed by January 2001. Humayunbosha saw a possibility for extending the contract only as a means of generating more profits from the oil field. He proposed a two-year extension of the contract. While maintaining the interest of the corporation in retaining profits from the oil field, Humayunbosha argued that the additional two years simply constituted a transition from CPI to a new operator, adding that the new operator might learn from CPI.[51]

Purnomo listened to CPI's demands for a two-year extension of the contract but he nonetheless refused them. Instead, he allowed an extension of only one year. Purnomo had a reason to extend CPI's operations in the CPP: he had not resolved the proportion of shares for the local elites of Riau and hoped that CPI would increase its production in the CPP.[52] Production in the CPP had decreased from that of 70,000 barrels per day to 50,000 barrels. By allowing CPI an extension, Purnomo hoped that production would increase.

CPI did not have any choice except to accept Purnomo's offer and allow Riau some portion of the CPP oil block. Production in the CPP oil field constituted only one-tenth of entire production. But 680,000 barrels/day was worth protecting. This was a political gesture by CPI to both the central government and the Riau provincial government. CPI wanted to send a clear message that it understood the situation by allowing Riau to have the CPP, but it also wanted the central government to protect CPI's operations in Riau. At this point, CPI tried to protect its entire operations. Even though CPI was aware that the income of the central government had partially depended on CPI's revenue sharing—during the last three years, from 2000 to 2003, CPI contributed around US$3 billion to the central government[53]—Humayunbosha did not want to push the matter any harder. CPI could not pull out from Indonesia due to the nature of its investment, that is, an extractive industry.

---

[51] "Nasib CPP tunggu keputusan politis", *Bisnis Indonesia*, 2 May 2001.

[52] "Caltex perpanjang kontrak CPP 1 tahun", *Bisnis Indonesia*, 13 June 2001.

[53] "Caltex menambah investasi US$400 juta tahun depan", *Koran Tempo*, 15 Dec. 2003.

Conclusion

The conflict in Riau reveals Saleh Djasit's failure to create benefits out of the political changes that occurred during a time of transition. This case also illuminates his weakness in constructing networks with politicians in Jakarta and the province. Why was Saleh unable to secure political support? Two factors stand out. First and foremost, Saleh proved incapable of creating trustful connections with important figures at the national level such as Syarwan Hamid, who is of Riau origin. At the provincial level, Saleh confronted difficulty in establishing a solid network with other politicians because some of them wanted an independent Riau. Instead of consolidating power at the provincial level, Saleh had to admit that he had to compete with other politicians for power and influence. Even when he was finally able to consolidate his influence at the provincial level, he had already lost momentum as the dispute moved in a direction that he could not control. Saleh had to fight for the provincial interest on his own.

Saleh's failure emphasizes the relevance of political networks, the main argument of this book. Saleh case stands contrary to the other two cases discussed here—that of Suwarna and Ikhdan Nizar and that of Titik Nazif Lubuk—in which political ability was successfully developed by means of constructing networks. Even if Saleh were fully aware of the need to construct a political network in order to strengthen his political muscle, it would not have been easy for him. Perhaps Saleh's main career and the broader context of politics in Riau together explain his failure to create a political network. Saleh's career was spent mainly in the province. Contrary to West Sumatra, which was able to produce politicians with influence that extended to the national level, Riau could produce only one person: Syarwan Hamid. Therefore, Saleh's chance of making personal connections was rather slim. When the governor faced a dispute with Purnomo Yusgiantoro, Syarwan did not help him. In contrast, Syarwan Hamid spent his career in national-level politics, and he did not have any close relations with those involved in the disputed oil block. Syarwan's attitude reflects a preference to side with the central government's position.

The behavior of the multinational company (MNC) is also of interest. At the commencement stage of the conflict, it hardly tried to defend its interest. In the process, the MNC was even ready to sacrifice its interest by allowing the central government to become the majority shareholder. However, when the conflict between the central and provincial governments intensified, CPI distanced itself from the problem. CPI already understood that it could do little to protect the interest of the CPP oil block. Equally important, CPI preferred to protect its bigger interest, CPI operations in Riau as a whole, since the CPP oil block accounted for only 10 percent of its total operations there. Of course, such a measure was a political gesture made in order to protect CPI's interest. Lacking the political protection it once received from Suharto, CPI had to adjust to the new environment, in which the power of the central government was mitigated, and the provincial government had become a new force. While no political party or powerful politician offered protection, CPI had to give away the CPP oil block in order to make a clear signal that it was willing to cooperate. Due to the weakness of the central state, CPI had to adopt a political decision.

CONCLUSION

Political Networks and Political Economy

The three cases exhibited in this book demonstrate that political networks matter. Political networks are built from the interpersonal relations of many actors. They move beyond a coincidence of interests because their constitution includes mutual trust and shared goals. The Indonesian experience exhibits that personal ties could structure and restructure political economy. In the past, political networks had involved few members and were used by the central government to manage local politics. After the fall of an authoritarian regime, the central government was challenged by local political actors able to forge their own political networks.

Institutions also matter. Political actors create them through a series of negotiations. They also offer incentives to various political actors so that they can derive benefits from them. The introduction of new institutions is no exception. New institutions serve as the basis for various social, economic and political activities. In Indonesia, it seems that local actors have taken advantage of new institutions.

This study sheds light on the ability of political actors in Indonesia's regions to establish political networks. It also stresses the significance of these political linkages to alter structure in a political economy. Through these political networks, local political actors established connections based on friendship and mutual trust, as well as shared goals with those wielding power in Jakarta. The political networks became significant factors for local actors seeking to go up against the central government over its policies vis-à-vis revenue sharing and the management of mining resources. The disputes that erupted over these issues in turn provided the impetus behind the development of a new pattern of political economy in Indonesia. By comparison, past political networks seem to have possessed a centralizing force that focused on Suharto and to some extent those close to him. In contrast, political networks that existed after the breakup of the New Order exhibited a decentralizing tendency that empowered

169

regional actors. In other words, the hubs of Indonesia's political networks dispersed to the localities.

This book has examined the development of Indonesian political economy between 1998 to 2004 through three case studies: the divestment of shares in Kaltim Prima Coal in East Kalimantan; the privatization of Semen Padang in West Sumatra; and the dispute over the Coastal Pekanbaru Plain oil block in Riau. Although these three studies ostensibly reveal stories about conflicts over revenue-sharing and management of mining resources ending in fights over property rights and natural resources, on a deeper level they really expose the contest for power among various political actors rooted in the central government and/or the provincial government. Their conflicts erupted whenever the boundaries of power and institutions blurred, as powerful figures at the provincial level of government began to question those boundaries.

Aside from the central government's actors, a number of the government officials at the lower levels of government presented in this study were looking for space in which to get involved in the work of shaping institutions. Particularly notable in these cases were the powerful figures who played a role at the provincial level, which included governors and managers of the state-owned companies operating in the provinces. These powerful figures received support from provincial parliamentarians.

While this study focuses on the relevance of political networks established by political actors in the provinces, it does admit the significant role of these political actors and their hold on power. Thus, this study suggests that political networks are important to understanding the political economy of Indonesia after the fall of Suharto. The cases studied in this book make clear that some of the power held by political actors was dependent upon their political positions. However, these politicians did, in fact, also seek political support from powerful politicians in Jakarta. This created or recreated political networks that offered supplementary power to political actors in the province.

However, whether powerful figures at the provincial level of government won battles against the central government and foreign investors is less important than how those figures looked for ways to determine the outcome of their disputes; how they promoted the interests of their respective provinces; and how able they were to oppose national policies. In this respect, although differences existed among politicians at the provincial level, all three cases in this book point in the same direction: provincial-level politicians in a decentralized Indonesia organized themselves in a collective fashion, pursued the interests of their provinces—

Conclusion   171

and to some extent their own interests—and linked with powerful politicians in Jakarta. Other than the decentralization process, these political networks might have developed because of the nature of coalition governments, in which different actors from various political parties occupy high positions in government. Sometimes the interests of the various supporters of coalitions diverge, making it necessary for provincial politicians to find allies among politicians at the national level.

There is a consensus among scholars who study Indonesian political economy that influence over policy during the New Order was very largely limited to Suharto in his position as president (Liddle 1992; McIntyre 2001; McIntyre 2003; Kartasasmita and Stern 2015). Scholars who study the Indonesian political economy of the post-Suharto era agree that influence over policy was limited to the oligarchy nurtured under the New Order (Robison and Hadiz 2004; Hadiz and Robison 2013; Winters 2011, 2013). Robison and Hadiz argue that politico-bureaucrats, businessmen and criminal figures dominated during the New Order. They also suggest, as do other scholars, that rather than disappear, "significant sections of the New Order oligarchy could continue to survive on the basis of new alliances and money politics and thus reconstitute within a new, more open, and decentralized political format" (2004: 225). Hadiz maintains that "old oligarchic and predatory interests were not overcome by *reformasi* but managed to reinvent themselves as democrats and reformers and then preside over newly constructed institutions of governance" (2010: 42–3). And on the decentralization process in East Kalimantan, Hadiz and Robison argue: "tremendous opportunities present themselves by independently replicating at the local level the old centralized relationships between the state and capital" (2003: 13). In a similar vein, some scholars argue that decentralization has in many cases contributed to the rise of local-boss rule (Tornquist et al. 2004: 2–3; Hidayat 2007; Okamoto and Hamid 2008). Choi argues that local elections have allowed entrenched local elites, many of whom gained status under Suharto, to maintain their power (2011: 102). Other scholars argue that in post-Suharto Indonesia, bureaucrats have remained a powerful force in Indonesian politics. Rosser, Roesad and Edwin state: "Notwithstanding the general shift in power away from the bureaucracy to the parliament as a result of democratization, the bureaucracy continues to play a major role in formulating (as well as implementing) government policy" (2005: 63).

The conclusions of these scholars studying Indonesian politics yield important insights: oligarchs are able to reorganize in the new political structure of decentralization; the predatory political and economic regime continues; the rise of local-strongman rule has replaced one-man rule; and regional political economy is simply a replication of what happens in the center. But the narratives these studies offer are far from complete. These scholars overlook the political dynamics in individual regions, or they look only at national-level political dynamics when trying to understand policymaking, overlooking local dynamics; therefore, they tend to treat these two different political entities separately. First, they apparently assume that provincial elites can stand alone when seeking to develop the political power to oppose the central government. Second, they assume that the political process in the province can be insulated from political dynamics in the center. Third, they imply through the logic of their argument that provincial politicians are able to control the economic resources of their regions without political support from powerful politicians in Jakarta.

What is relevant is the fact that politicians at the provincial level came to develop their political capabilities by building linkages with those wielding power in Jakarta, and in turn, these political networks defined their political strengths in confronting the central government. It is also a fact that political networks from Samarinda, the capital of East Kalimantan, and Padang, the capital of West Sumatra, are qualitatively different phenomena. The behavior of politicians at the provincial level was not chiefly of a clientelistic nature; in pursuing their targets, these politicians were not dependent on a personal benefactor within the central government. The ability of provincial politicians to create political networks depends on their ability to create a mutually beneficial connection with those wielding power in Jakarta. In this regard, what is salient is the way in which provincial politicians, mainly from West Sumatra, and to a lesser extent, East Kalimantan, operated quite independently from central government control. In fact, they were able to link up with national-level politicians who strongly opposed the central government. Provincial politicians were aware that the natural resources in their provinces placed them in a strong political position. Provincial politicians made use of political parties on the regional level. In East Kalimantan, PDI-P was interested in cooperating with the military; therefore, it not only supported incumbent candidates for governorship but also backed them up in their pursuit to control PT Kaltim Prima Coal. In West Sumatra, a similar story can be told. Golkar also had interests in the province because local politicians opposed to the central government came mainly from their

Conclusion   173

ranks, as did the one of the commissioner of Semen Padang and a provincial politician from Golkar. The political networks of Golkar politicians were apparent in the case of Semen Padang, and most of them fully supported the interest of Semen Padang's CEO in separating Semen Padang from Semen Gresik. Politicians on the provincial level were not controlled or managed by those in Jakarta, not in any real sense. Politicians in the provinces did not limit or exclude the demands of their large populations; however, they did manipulate their constituents in order to gain strong bargaining positions.

In all cases, political networks established by local actors proved essential, and each case presented here exhibits a different type of link with a varying degree of influence. The links in these networks are both personal and communal in character. Political actors form these individual links at both national and local levels based on friendship, mutual trust and a certain degree of intimacy. Communal bonds form, too, defined by ethnicity, religion or place of origin. These linkages can also operate beyond personal and communal modes, as in the case of membership in political parties. Even though these political linkages ostensibly strengthen one another and facilitate a boost in changes to the structure of a political economy, a closer look reveals only certain linkages at work. Therefore, this study demonstrates that political networks established by political actors in West Sumatra were the strongest because they possessed all these different kinds of links. Political networks forged by local actors in East Kalimantan were strong but much weaker than those in West Sumatra because the political networks created by local actors there lacked ties along ethnic lines. In Riau, political networks apparently were undergoing a slower transition.

This book emphasizes political networks created under new institutional arrangements. However, this study shows that political networks established in Indonesia exhibit different qualifications and different methods of voicing. These differences are apparent in forms of friendship and the ability to mobilize local populations based on ethnicity, religion, economic interests and the existence of national-security threats. The three cases of East Kalimantan, West Sumatra and Riau highlight different trajectories. The Riau case, for example, exhibits a weak political network. Political actors in the province could not develop a solid political network on an individual, communal or structural level because they held different opinions about the political future of Riau province. Taking advantage of this political situation, the central government intervened by establishing political networks with local actors who disagreed Riau Merdeka's proposal to impede the secession threat.

Changes in Indonesian Political Economy

The first area of change lay in the institutional shift from a centralized government to a decentralized one. This started in 1999 when the Habibie government introduced Law No. 22/1999 on Regional Autonomy and Law No. 25/1999 on Intergovernmental Fiscal Balance. At this time, the regulations on sharing revenue earned from natural resources were also introduced. In general, Law No. 22/1999 and Law No. 25/1999 both stated that the regional governments, which included both the regencies/municipalities and the provinces, received a much bigger share of income derived from local resources compared with their share under Suharto. For example, in the forestry sector, the provincial share became 16 percent, and the regency's share 32 percent while the central government's share was reduced to only 20 percent. Under Suharto, the central government's share totaled 55 percent while the regions (without a precise classification of either the province or regency) received 45 percent. With mining-sector commodities such as gas, the regency received 12 percent of all revenue and the province received 6 percent. From oil and gas, the biggest share went to central government—85 percent for oil and 70 percent for gas.

Many politicians at the provincial level changed their political behavior after they realized that the central government was now less competent at protecting property rights and distributing income from natural resources than it was under Suharto. The central government no longer was the sole dominant force determining the distribution of natural resource income. This change led to the rise of aggressive behavior by provincial governments that began pushing their interests. As the three cases here discuss, the governors and powerful figures in the provinces had been unhappy with the regulations on revenue sharing in the extractive sector. Following the introduction of the country's decentralization policy with Law No. 22/1999 and the regulation on intergovernmental fiscal balance with Law No. 25/1999, the discussion of revenue distribution became a hot-button issue, particularly for resource-rich provinces such as Riau and East Kalimantan. The governor of Riau even proposed rewriting the existing regulations on basic mining and greater sharing of revenue from oil. While certainly not a decisive victory for the governors and other provincial-level politicians, these developments reflect the growing strength and determination of provincial actors to realize better

Conclusion 175

income from the extractive sector. They certainly indicate the growing power of provincial politicians.

A second important area of change is apparent in the conflicts that erupted between the provincial and national governments, which led to ambiguity with respect to institutions and existing rules on the distribution of income from natural resources. In the three cases under investigation, provincial politicians tried to blur the well-defined boundaries regarding the rules over natural resources. This ambiguity in property rights over natural resources is a logical outcome of political tussles. Having engaged in disputes with the central government, provincial politicians needed to mobilize all political resources at their disposal, including political networks, against those wielding power in Jakarta. The battles waged by politicians in the provinces created serious rifts inside the government because they were situated in different positions. As explained in this study, such a dispute indeed took place in the divestment case of Kaltim Prima Coal in East Kalimantan. However, what arose was in fact more than mere friction within the central government. The friction also affected provincial governments that disobeyed central government policies.

This friction was associated with the capability of powerful figures at the provincial level of government—mainly the governor, managers of state-owned enterprises and the chairperson of the parliament—to mobilize the political support necessary to fight the central government, which is one of the main reasons to organize political networks. These networks were initiated from the provinces; by using them, provincial politicians began to challenge the central government. In the process of increasing power on the part of powerful figures from the provinces, many exciting developments were taking place at the local level in Indonesia. This paved the way for the governor—and also other politicians in the provinces—to create more space to maneuver and to emerge as an important player in his region. At first, according to Law No. 25/1999 on Decentralization, provincial parliamentarians elected the governor, and in return the governor was accountable to the provincial parliament, though the governor still had to report to the president. This new institution opened a space for both the governor and the provincial parliamentarian to organize or even challenge the central government. With the elimination of the hierarchical links that existed under the New Order government, governors and provincial politicians no longer had an obligation to serve the interests of the central government. In other words, they now had to respond to the wishes of their constituents instead of the central government.

Future Prospects: Institutions in Decentralizing Indonesia

The future of Indonesia is likely to depend on the ability of various actors to establish stable institutions. As mentioned in the beginning of this chapter, political actors create institutions. They establish political networks in order to negotiate what kind of institutions they want. Evaluation of the three cases presented in this book demonstrates that local actors forged political networks before they attempted to dispute revenue sharing or management of natural resources, which led to a contest of power with central government. In the end, these disputes created uncertainty because the existing regulations were constantly being questioned.

This study has argued: with the fall of Suharto, decentralization and democratization have (1) removed key obstacles to politicians on the provincial level, making it easier for them to organize support by forging political networks to pursue their own interests; (2) provided an incentive for provincial-level politicians to manipulate politics in the provinces; (3) increased the political space for politicians on the provincial level to wage disputes with the central government; and (4) created ambiguity for institutions that led to battles over power. At a time when provincial politicians were mustering their strength, the central government made no coherent policy, and provincial governments acted contrary to its directives. Part of this political environment is associated with the nature of the coalition governments that started with Abdurahman Wahid's government and continued under Megawati.

What are the prospects for Indonesia's future? What are the implications of these political fights for the evolution of institutions in Indonesia? This study emphasizes that the changes that occurred between 1998 and 2004 served as the basic foundation for the ensuing transformation that took place on both economic and political fronts. Decentralization policies were put in place in 1999–2000 and revised in 2004 and 2014 to address new political dynamics. Despite the revisions, the basic tenets of these policies remain the same in the sense that local actors have more room to maneuver. The key difference is that democratic processes have been pushed to the local level through direct elections, which were introduced in 2005.

From this vantage point, such questions might be answered by looking at the ability of local politicians to pose challenges to the central government regarding rights to natural resources and the central government's response to those challenges. The newly established institutions offered provincial politicians a way to create political space to manage their regions. However, in a decentralized Indonesia, the central government still controls natural resources. In order to protect its rights, the central government has preferred to wage political battles with various politicians in the provinces. Since the central government has more resources at its disposal than the provincial governments—the institutions it has created, its access to funds, and its support from foreign investors —it is able to defeat provincial politicians.

The rising importance of provincial politicians can also be seen in the various political measures the central government implemented in order to secure its revenue from the extractive sectors. The central government was under pressure because revenue from extractive resources was shrinking. For example, in 2001, state revenue from non-tax income, which includes income from extractive resources, totaled 7.9 percent of GDP; in 2002, it decreased to 5.6 percent; and in 2003, it shrank even further to 4.2 percent (Ministry of Finance of Republic of Indonesia 2004: 30–1). This reduced revenue was a result of the decreasing income from extractive resources. This meant that the central government had to continue to secure revenue in this sector even though it had to battle provincial governments. At the time this book was written, the Indonesian government seemed very much dependent upon extractive commodities for its income, even though the international prices for these commodities are volatile.

The future of Indonesian politics and its economy are to be seen in the ability of various political actors to establish solid institutions that they will honor. In fact, Law No. 22/2001 on Oil and Gas did not offer regional governments participation in the process. Such a law ignited disputes over income distribution or claims to property rights. In order to establish solid institutions, the central government must adequately address its internal weakness. Indonesia's central government had anticipated another round of conflicts over natural resources between 1998 and 2004. It had issued regulations intentionally accommodating the interests of regions through Minister of Energy and Mineral Resources (MEMR) Regulation No. 35/2004. It was renewed by MEMR Regulation No. 37/2016, which ruled that the region where a natural resource is located has a participating interest right of 10 percent. The central government already took the necessary political step of accommodating any new demand by the regions for a fair distribution of income proportional to their rising power. It even created solid institutions to accommodate the demands or interests of provincial governments and their politicians. However, as this study indicates, there is no guarantee that the conflicts over ownership, management and rent distribution of natural resources will stop. The decentralization policy made this step possible because the local government already had greater authority. What is important here for the future should be the question: How could the various levels of governments reach agreements on collective action to create institutions that would reduce disagreements and maximize benefits for both parties?

There are two examples worth studying to compare with the three cases under investigation in this book. It seems that political actors in the central government understand the rising power of local actors and their ability to establish political networks and engage in disputes. With respect to oil exploration in Cepu, for example, the central government quickly recognized that the interests of provincial and local politicians are important and acted accordingly to allocate shares to them. As a result, the provincial and local government together received 10 percent of the shares in the oil enterprise, while the central government represented by Pertamina and the US multinational Exxon Mobil each received 45 percent. To some extent, it is safe to argue that the central government set up political networks in coordination with local actors. However, it created institutions in line with local political actors.

In another example, which involves the case of shares in a mining company located in Nusa Tenggara, Newmont Nusa Tenggara, things were no different. It appears that the central government carefully studied the disputes at the heart of the three cases in East Kalimantan, West Sumatra and Riau examined in this book. To do so, it had to take seriously the rising power of provincial politicians. Newmont Nusa Tenggara is a multinational company owned by US and Japanese companies. The company had to comply with the rule to allocate its shares to an Indonesian party by way of sales of shares. From the beginning, the central government hesitated in purchasing shares. It had to do so because its officials perceived the possible rejection by provincial and local politicians if it attempted to buy all the shares. In fact, the central government was not the only party aware of this latest political development. National companies that wanted to purchase the shares also understood the situation. It is no surprise that a national coal company owned by the powerful politician Aburizal Bakrie initially pursued a coalition with provincial as well as local governments. They formed a company to purchase the shares, which they named Daerah Maju Bersama. In the end, this company successfully purchased 24 percent of Newmont's shares. The example of this mining company points to an important issue:

Multicapital, a company controlled by the Aburizal family, had to form networks with provincial politicians from West Nusa Tenggara and the local government of Sumbawa because the shares were offered to them. Only by coming to a mutual agreement were Aburizal and provincial and local government able to purchase the shares. The provincial and local governments offered an important resource: the shares offered by the central government. However, they had no funds. Fortunately for them, Aburizal did.[1] Soon, a marriage of interests formed as follows: Aburizal provided the funds to purchase the shares, while the provincial and local governments received golden shares. The issue was "resolved with the central government, demonstrating that it was ready to compromise with local political players" (Kennedy School of Government 2013: 120).

Concluding Remarks

Political networks are links that involve many actors and cut across boundaries of ethnicity, geography, political party and interests. One typically imagines a political network expanding outward from its center to the regions, situating the central power as the primary hub. The reality of political networks grows much more complex whenever it involves a series of mutual negotiations among actors seeking agreement on certain issues and goals. Political networks in Indonesia, at least according to this study, are mostly created and sustained by local actors seeking to foster political ties to both national and local politicians. Thus, local political actors constitute their own hubs. From this perspective, political networks are also motivated by negotiation with power holders, access to natural resources and political recognition.

This study explains that there can be little doubt that Indonesia has been undergoing an important change since the late 1990s. If the central government has grown somewhat weaker, it may enjoy greater power relative to the provincial government if compared to Suharto's New Order government, even though it must also tolerate increasing local power. Overall, post-Suharto governments have had weak relations with local governments and been less able to maintain the institutions that have governed both politics and the economy.

---

[1] In November 2016, Newmont Nusa Tenggara changed ownership when Amman Mineral International bought an 82-percent share.

All the cases under investigation thus institutionally embody three different concerns: the capability of local actors to construct political networks; the contest for power between center and province; and the urgency of creating new institutions capable of accommodating the new power arising from the provinces. It is true that the central government has rights to natural resources. However, given the ability of provincial politicians to develop political networks that link to those wielding power in Jakarta while they manipulate politics on the provincial level, the central government faces the difficult task of maintaining and protecting its rights to regional natural resources. In other words, with the introduction of the central government's decentralization policy, politicians in the provinces began to seek loopholes in existing rules in order to reconcile them with the politicians' new power.

The conflicts described here, between the center and the provinces, obviously created institutional uncertainties due to weak enforcement. Nevertheless, stable institutions are key functions in facilitating overarching enforcement mechanisms. This study suggests that stable institutions are likely to emerge as long as political actors in the center and the provinces are able to agree on their construction. Considering the facts of the three cases investigated, this study concludes that unstable institutions are the outcomes of political processes that encourage change in incentives. Since political processes are important to the manipulation of incentives (North 1995b: 9, as quoted in Ahrens 2002: 73), they need to be considered.[2] Instead of viewing the creation of rules as an enterprise free from politics, it would make a better theoretical stance to view institutional choices as a process of negotiated settlement among the actors involved. Since negotiated settlement among various actors is a key element in establishing stable institutions, it requires preconditions as follows: (a) a redefinition of rights; (b) joint arrangements; and (c) an accommodation of interests.

In the context of broader changes, Indonesia's central and provincial governments need to redefine their rights regarding natural resources.

---

[2] This point is a modification of an argument developed by Douglass C. North, as quoted by Joachim Ahrens: "If the highest rate of return in an economy comes from piracy we can expect that the organization will invest in skills and knowledge that will make them better pirates. Similarly, if there are high return to productive activities we will expect organizations to devote resources to investing in skill and knowledge that will increase productivity".

Conclusion   181

Redefining rights can be thought of as a first step toward stable institutions. Because politicians in the provinces tend to blur and/or question rights to natural resources, everyone's rights remain uncertain; that is, none of the parties involved know what their rights are. Without redefining rights over resources, the central government faces constant challenges from politicians in the provinces. Assigning all rights to the central government will not work. The redefinition should delineate rights that belong to the center and the provinces. The next possible step is a joint arrangement between the central and provincial governments. This joint arrangement could take the form of cooperation in order to reach a common ground where disputing parties can discuss their differences. In situations where conflicts arise, the involved parties have two choices: cooperate or not. As long as the parties are aware that conflicts are costly, they may consider cooperation. Theoretically, cooperation offers maximum benefits to conflicting parties (Ostrom 1990), because through a cooperative action they can reach a mutual agreement and at the same time negotiate for their interests. The last requirement is the accommodation of interests among involved parties. Though politicians in the center are in a better position than those in the provinces, their power is not as strong as it was under Suharto. A weaker central government may need to tolerate the increasing power of politicians in the provinces. This middle ground is necessary in order to mitigate friction and furthermore provide a way to tailor rules to accommodate the parties involved. Such a step is necessary because the political actors who directly interact with one another and with the changing political context can modify rules over time in order to better harmonize them with the specific political environment of their setting.

However, even though central and local actors agree to accommodate each other, no one knows Indonesia's future. The history of this country proves that the structure of a political economy changes with political transformations. Such transformations usually involve fighting among political actors. This study illustrates that changes in political networks, from the centralistic tendency of the past to the decentralized government of today, altered the structure of a country's political economy. Looking at the long horizon, we see that Indonesia may experience different types of political transformations, which may also provide an impetus for the development of new political networks that in turn alter the structure of its political economy. The linkages that connect between the center of political power and the regions are very dynamic because the negotiation process between the central and local governments is far from complete. In 2004 the central government tried to take back its authority from local governments, which was partially a success. There is no guarantee that the central or local governments are satisfied with this latest institutional arrangement. The linkages involve actors from many tiers of government—central, provincial and local. As this study points out, political actors at the national and local levels were deeply engaged in heated conflicts over the management and revenue sharing of strategic natural resources located in the regions, however, they managed to achieve settlements.

APPENDICES

Appendix 1

No.	Contractor	Project	Expiry Date
1	Chevron Pacific Indonesia (CPI)	Siak	2013
2	JOB Pertamina-Costa	Gebang	2015
3	Total EP Indonesie	Mahakam	2017
4	Pertamina Hulu Energi	Offshore North West Java (ONWJ)	2017
5	Inpex Corp	Attaka	2017
6	Medco EP Indonesia	Lematang	2017
7	(JOB) Pertamina-Petrochina	Tuban	2018
8	JOB Pertamina-Talisman	Ogan Komering	2018
9	ExxonMobil	North Sumatra Offshore B	2018
10	CNOOC	Southeast Sumatra	2018
11	Total	Tengah	2018
12	ExxonMobil	NSO Extention	2018
13	Vico Indonesia	Sanga-Sanga	2018
14	Chevron Indonesia Company	West Pasir and Attaka	2018
15	Kalrez Petroleum	Bula	2019
16	Citic	Seram Non Bula	2019
17	Pertamina-Golden Spike	Pendopo and Raja	2019
18	JOB Pertamina-Hess	Jambi Merang	2019
19	ConocoPhillips	South Jambi B	2020
20	Kondur Petroleum	Malacca Strait	2020
21	Lapindo	Brantas	2020
22	JOB Pertamina-Petrochina	Salawati	2020
23	Petrochina	Kepala Burung Blok A	2020
24	Energy Equity	Sengkang	2020
25	Chevron Indonesia Company	Makassar Strait Offshore Area A	2020
26	CPI	Rokan	2021
27	Kalila	Bentu Segat	2021
28	Petronas	Muriah	2021
29	Petroselat	Selat Panjang	2021
30	Medco E&P Tarakan	Tarakan Block East Kalimantan	2022
31	Pertamina	Coastal Plains and Pekanbaru	2022
32	Pearl Oil (Tungkai) Ltd	Tungkai Block	2022
33	Energy Equity Epic	Sengkang Block	2022

Source: *Forum Keadilan* (2012) and *Detik*.

Appendix 2

No.	Contractor	Owner
1	PT Karya Bumi Baratama	Circlone Korea (85%), Indonesia (15%)
2	PT Barasentosa Lestari	GMR Group (India)
3	PT Nusantara Termal Coal	Permata Energy Resources
4	PT Kalimantan Energi Lestari	Sumber Mitra Jaya
5	PT Ratah Coal	Adaro Energy
6	PT Juloi Coal	Adaro Energy
7	PT Lahai Coal	Adaro Energy
8	PT Pari Coal	Adaro Energy
9	PT Sumber Barito Coal	Adaro Energy
10	PT Kalteng Coal	Adaro Energy
11	PT Maruwai Coal	Adaro Energy

Source: *Bisnis Indonesia* (2015).

Appendix 3

No.	Block Name	Contractor	Location
1	Offshore North-West Java	Pertamina Hulu Energi ONWJ	West Java
2	Mahakam	Pertamina Hulu Mahakam	East Kalimantan
3	West Madura Offshore	Pertamina Hulu Energi WMO	East Java
4	Ketapang	Petronas Carigali Ketapang	East Java
5	Kangean	Kangean Energy Indonesia	East Java
6	Rapak	Chevron Rapak	East Kalimantan
7	Ganal	Chevron Ganal	East Kalimantan
8	Muriah	Petronas Carigali Muriah	Central Java
9	Merangin II	Sele Raya Merangin II	South Sumatra
10	Simenggaris	JOB Pertamina Medco Simenggaris	East Kalimantan

Source: *Bisnis Indonesia* (2017).

BIBLIOGRAPHY

Materials Cited

Newspapers

Bisnis Indonesia
Jakarta Post
Kaltim Pos (Samarinda)
Kompas
Koran Tempo
Media Indonesia
Times (London)

Journals

Economist (London)
Gatra (Jakarta)
Inside Indonesia: Bulletin of the Indonesia Resources and Information Programme (IRIP)
Tempo (Jakarta)

Unpublished Materials

Coal Contract Agreement between PT Kaltim Prima Coal and Indonesian Government
Framework Agreement between PT Kaltim Prima Coal and Indonesian Government
Law No. 22/1999
Law No. 25/1999

References

Abinales, Patricio. 2000. *Making Mindanao*. Manila: Ateneo de Manila University Press.
Abdurahman, Sukri. 2003, "Hubungan pemerintah pusat dan daerah: kasus Riau", in *Krisis masa kini dan Orde Baru*, ed. Muhamad Hisyam. Jakarta: Yayasan Obor Indonesia.

Bibliography

Acemoglu, Daron and James Robinson. 2012. *Why Nations Fail: The Origins of Power, Prosperity and Poverty*. New York: Crown Publishing.

Aden, Jean. 1992. "Entrepreneurship and Protection in the Indonesian Oil Service Industry", in *Southeast Asian Capitalists*, ed. Ruth McVey. Ithaca: SEAP Cornell University Press.

Ahrens, Joachim. 2002. *Governance and Economic Development: A Comparative Institutional Approach*. Cheltenham: Edward Elgar Publishing.

Albintani, Muchid. 2001. *Dari Riau merdeka sampai otonomi nol*. Pekanbaru: Unri Press.

Anderson, Benedict. 2009. "Afterword", in *Populism in Asia*, ed. Kosuke Mizuno and Pasuk Pongpaichit. Singapore and Kyoto: NUS Press and Kyoto University Press.

Aoki, Masahisa, 2001. *Toward a Comparative Institutional Analysis*. Cambridge, MA: MIT Press.

Arrow, K. 1963. "Uncertainty and the Welfare Economics of Medical Care", *American Economic Review* 55: 941–73.

Aspinall, Edward. 2013. "A Nation in Fragments: Patronage and Neoliberalism in Contemporary Indonesia", *Critical Asian Studies* 45, 1: 27–54.

Aspinall, Edward and Greg Fealy, eds. 2003. *Local Power and Politics in Indonesia: Decentralisation and Democratisation*. Singapore: ISEAS.

Aspinall, Edward and Gerry van Klinken, eds. 2011. *The State and Illegality in Indonesia*. Leiden: KITLV Press.

Barabási, Albert-Laszlo. 2002. *Linked: How Everything Is Connected to Everything and What It Means for Business, Science, and Everyday Life*. New York: Plume.

————. 2016. *Network Science*. Cambridge: Cambridge University Press.

Barr, Christopher, 1998. "Bob Hasan: The Rise of Apkindo and the Shifting Dynamics of Control in Indonesia's Timber Sector", *Indonesia* 65 (April): 1–36.

————. 2001. "Profit on Paper: The Political Economy of Fiber and Finance in Indonesia's Pulp and Paper Industries", in *Banking on Sustainability: Structural Adjustment and Forestry Reform in Post-Suharto Indonesia*. Bogor, Indonesia: CIFOR.

Bartlett, Anderson III. 1972. *Pertamina: Indonesian National Oil*. Jakarta and Tulsa: Amerasian.

Baswedan, Anies Rasyid. 2007. "Regional Autonomy and Patterns of Democracy in Indonesia". PhD dissertation, Northern Illinois University.

Bates, Robert. 1995. "Social Dilemmas and Rational Individuals: An Assessment of the New Institutionalism", in *The New Institutional Economics and Third World Development*, ed. John Harriss, Janet Hunter and Colin M. Lewis. London: Routledge.

Bertrand, Jacques. 2004. *Nationalism and Ethnic Conflict in Indonesia*. Cambridge: Cambridge University Press.

Bhakti, Ikrar Nusa, Sri Yanuarti and M. Nurhasim. 2009. "Military Politics, Ethnicity, and Conflict in Indonesia". CRISE Working Paper No. 62, Centre for Research on Inequality, Human Security and Ethnicity, Oxford.

Blackburn, Susan. 1999. "Riau", in *Perspective from the Periphery: ACFOA Election Monitors' Report*. ACFOA Development Report. Deakin, Australia: ACFOA.

Booth, Anne. 1989. "Central Government Funding of Local Government Development Expenditure", in *Financing Local Government in Indonesia*, ed. Nick Devas. Athens, OH: Ohio University Press.

———. 2014. "Before the 'Big-Bang': Decentralization Debates and Practice in Indonesia, 1949–99", in *Regional Dynamics in a Decentralized Indonesia*, ed. Hal Hill. Singapore: ISEAS.

Buehler, Michael and Paige Tan. 2007. "Party Candidate Relationships in Indonesian Local Politics: A Case Study of the 2005 Regional Election in Gowa, South Sulawesi Province", *Indonesia* 84: 41–69.

Bünte, Marco. 2009. "Indonesia's Protracted Decentralization: Contested Reform and Their Unintended Consequences", in *Democratization in Post Suharto Indonesia*, ed. Marco Bünte and Andreas Ufen. London: Routledge.

Carpenter, D.P., K.M. Esterling and D.M. Lazer. 2004. "Friends, Brokers, and Transitivity: Who Informs Whom in Washington Politics", *Journal of Politics* 66: 224–46.

Chauvel, Richard. 2010. "Electoral Politics and Democratic Freedom in Papua", in *Problems of Democratisation in Indonesia: Elections, Institutions and Society*, ed. Edward Aspinall and Marcus Meitzner. Singapore: ISEAS.

Choi, Nankyung. 2009. "Democracy and Patrimonial Politics in Local Indonesia", *Indonesia* 88: 131–64.

———. 2011. *Local Politics in Indonesia: Pathway to Power*. Oxon: Routledge.

Colombijn, Freek. 2000. "A Peaceful Road to Freedom", in *Inside Indonesia* 60 (Oct.–Dec.). Available at http://www.insideindonesia.org/a-peaceful-road-to-freedom.

Crouch, Harold. 1978. *The Army and Politics in Indonesia*. Ithaca: Cornell University Press.

———. 2010. *Political Reform in Indonesia after Soeharto*. Singapore: ISEAS.

Davidson, Jamie S. 2005. "Decentralization and Regional Violence in the Post-Suharto State", in *Regionalism in Post-Suharto Indonesia*, ed. Maribeth Erb, Priyambudi Sulistiyanto and Carole Faucher. London: RoutledgeCurzon.

———. 2015. *Indonesia's Changing Political Economy: Governing the Road*. Cambridge: Cambridge University Press.

Derks, Will. 1997. "Malay Identity Work", *Bijdragen tot de Taal-, Land- en Volkenkunde* 153: 699–716.

Devas, Nick. 1989. "Local Government Finance in Indonesia", in *Financing Local Government in Indonesia*, ed. Nick Devas. Athens, OH: Ohio University Press.

Djohermansyah Djohan. 2003. *Kebijakan otonomi daerah 1999.* Jakarta: Yarsif Watampone.

Dolinschek, S. 1990. "The Development of a Coal Mine in Indonesia", in *Mineral Development: Asia and Pacific: Proceedings of the 2nd Asia-Pacific Mining Conference,* ed. M. Simatupang and James F. McDivitt. Manila: ASEAN Mining Federation.

Duncan, Christopher R. 2007. "Mixed Outcomes: The Impact of Regional Autonomy and Decentralization on Indigenous Ethnic Minorities in Indonesia", *Development and Change* 38, 4: 711–33.

East Kalimantan Statistical Bureau. 2001. *Population Census.* Samarinda: East Kalimantan Statistical Bureau.

Emmerson, Donald K. 1976. *Indonesia's Elite: Political Culture and Cultural Politics.* Ithaca: Cornell University Press.

Erb, Maribeth and Priyambudi Sulistiyanto. 2009. *Deepening Democracy in Indonesia?: Direct Elections for Local Leaders (Pilkada).* Singapore: ISEAS.

Erman, Erwiza. 2007. "Deregulation of the Tin Trade and Creation of a Local Shadow State: A Bangka Case Study", in *Renegotiating Boundaries: Local Politics in Post-Suharto Indonesia,* ed. Henk Schulte Nordholt and Gerry van Klinken. Leiden: KITLV Press.

Escobar, Arturo. 1995. *Encountering Development: The Making and Unmaking of the Third World.* Princeton: Princeton University Press.

Fitrani, Fitria, Bert Hofman and Kai Kaiser. 2005. "Unity in Diversity? The Creation of New Local Governments in a Decentralising Indonesia", *Bulletin of Indonesian Economic Studies* 41, 1: 57–79.

Fowler, J.H. 2006. "Legislative Cosponsorship Networks in the U.S. House and Senate", *Social Networks* 28, 4: 454–65.

Fowler, James et al. 2011. "Causality in Political Networks", *American Political Research* 39, 2: 437–80.

Friedman, Milton. 1982. *Capitalism and Freedom.* Chicago: Chicago University Press.

Granovetter, Mark. 1973. "The Strength of Weak Ties", *The American Journal of Sociology* 78, 6: 1360–80.

———. 1992. "Economic Action and Social Structure: The Problem of Embeddedness", in *The Sociology of Economic Life,* ed. M. Granovetter and R. Swedberg. Boulder: Westview Press.

Greif, Avner. 1992. "Institutions and International Trade: Lessons from the Commercial Revolution", *American Economic Review* 82, 2: 128–33.

Grossman, M. and C.B.K. Dominguez. 2009. "Party Coalitions and Interest Group Networks", *American Politics Research* 37, 5: 767–800.

Gunaratna, Rohan. 2002. *Inside Al Qaeda: Global Network of Terror.* New York: Columbia University Press.

Hadiz, Vedi. 2010. *Localising Power in Post-Authoritarian Indonesia: A Southeast Asia Perspective.* Stanford: Stanford University Press.

———. 2016. *Islamic Populism in Indonesia and the Middle East*. Cambridge: Cambridge University Press.

Hadiz, Vedi and Richard Robison. 2003. "Neo-Liberal Reforms and Illiberal Consolidations: The Indonesian Paradox", Southeast Asia Research Centre Working Paper Series, City University of Hong Kong.

———. 2013. "The Political Economy of Oligarchy and the Reorganization of Power in Indonesia", *Indonesia* 96: 35–57.

Haggard, Stephan. 2000. *The Political Economy of the Asian Financial Crisis*. Washington, DC: Institute for International Economics.

Halberstam, Y. and Brian Knight. 2016. "Homophily, Group Size, and the Diffusion of Political Information in Social Networks: Evidence from Twitter", *Journal of Public Economics* 143: 73–88.

Haris, Syamsuddin et al. 1998. *Menggugat pemilihan umum Orde Baru*. Jakarta: Obor.

Harvard Kennedy School. 2013. *The Sum Is Greater than the Parts: Doubling Shared Prosperity in Indonesia through Local and Global Integration*. Jakarta: Gramedia.

Heaney, M.T. and F. Rojas. 2007. "Partisans, Nonpartisans, and the Antiwar Movement in the United States", *American Politics Research* 35, 4: 431–64.

———. 2008. "Coalition Dissolution, Mobilization, and Network Dynamics in the U.S. Antiwar Movement", *Research in Social Movements, Conflicts and Change* 28: 39–82.

Heinz, J.P., E.O. Laumann, R.L. Nelson and R.H. Salisbury. 1993. *The Hollow Core: Private Interests in National Policy Making*. Cambridge, MA: Harvard University Press.

Herzig, Pascale. 2010. "Communal Networks and Gender: Placing Identities among South Asians in Kenya", *South Asian Diaspora* 2, 2: 165–84.

Hidayat, Syarif. 2007. "Shadow State?", in *Renegotiating Boundaries: Local Politics in Post-Suharto Indonesia*, ed. Henk Schulte Nordholt and Gerry van Klinken. Leiden: KITLV Press.

Hill, Hal. 1996. *The Indonesian Economy since 1966: Southeast Asia's Emerging Giant*. Cambridge: Cambridge University Press.

Hofman, Bert and Kai Kaiser. 2004. "The Making of the 'Big Bang' and Its Aftermath: a Political Economy Perspective", in *Reforming Intergovernmental Fiscal Relations and the Rebuilding of Indonesia*, ed. James Alm, Jorge Martinez-Vasquez and Sri Mulyani Indrawati. Cheltenham: Edward Elgar Publishing.

Huckfeldt, R. and J. Sprague. 1987. "Networks in Context: The Social Flow of Political Information", *American Political Science Review* 81, 4: 1197–216.

———. 1993. "Citizens, Contexts and Politics", in *The State of the Discipline II*, ed. Ada W. Finifter. Washington, DC: American Political Science Association, pp. 281–303.

———. 1995. *Citizens, Politics, and Social Communication: Information and Influence in an Election Campaign*. Cambridge: Cambridge University Press.

Human Rights Watch. 2003. *Without Remedy: Human Rights Abuses and Indo-nesia's Pulp and Paper Industry.* Washington, DC: Human Rights Watch.

Hutchcroft, Paul D. 1998. *Booty Capitalism: The Politics of Banking in the Philip-pines.* Ithaca: Cornell University Press.

Jackson, Karl D. "Bureaucratic Polity: A Theoretical Framework for the Analysis of Power and Communication in Indonesia", in *Political Power and Com-munication in Indonesia*, ed. Karl D. Jackson and Lucian Pye. Berkeley: University of California Press.

Kahin, Audrey. 1999. *Rebellion to Integration: West Sumatra and the Indonesian Polity.* Amsterdam: Amsterdam University Press.

Kahler, Miles. 2009. *Networked Politics: Agency, Power and Governance.* Ithaca, NY: Cornell University Press.

Kartasasmita, Ginandjar. 2013. *Managing Indonesia's Transformation.* Singapore: World Scientific.

Kartasasmita, Ginandjar and Joseph J. Stern. 2015. *Reinventing Indonesia.* Singa-pore: World Scientific.

Khan, Mushtaq. 1995. "State Failure in Weak States: A Critique of New Institu-tionalist Explanations", in *The New Institutional Economics and Third World Development*, ed. John Harris, Janet Hunter and Colin M. Lewis. London: Routledge.

Kimura, Ehito. 2007. "Marginality and Opportunity in the Periphery: The Emergence of Gorontalo Province, North Sulawesi", *Indonesia* 84: 71–95.

———. 2013. *Political Change and Territoriality in Indonesia.* London: Routledge.

King, Dwight Y. 2003. *Half-Hearted Reform: Electoral Institutions and the Struggle for Democracy in Indonesia.* Westport: Praeger.

Kingsbury, Damien and Harry Aveling, eds. 2003. *Autonomy and Disintegration.* London: RoutledgeCurzon.

Knoke, David. 1990. *Political Networks: The Structural Perspective.* Cambridge: Cambridge University Press.

Koger, G., S. Masket and H. Noel. 2010. "Cooperative Party Factions in Ameri-can Politics", *American Politics Research* 38: 33–53.

Kotler-Berkowitz, Laurence. 2005. "Friends and Politics: Linking Diverse Friend-ship Networks to Political Participation", in *The Social Logic of Politics: Personal Networks as Context for Political Behavior*, ed. Alan Zuckerman. Philadelphia: Temple University Press.

Kuntjoro, Mudradjat. 1995. "Desentralisasi fiskal di Indonesia: dilema otonomi dan ketergantungan", *Prisma* 24, 4: 3–17.

Kurtz, C.F. 2009. "Collective Network Analysis", unpublished paper. Available at http://www.cfkurtz.com [accessed 4 February 2018].

Laumann, E.O. and D. Knoke. 1987. *The Organizational State: Social Choice in National Policy Domains.* Madison: University of Wisconsin Press.

Lazer, David. 2011. "Networks in Political Science: Back to the Future", *PS: Political Science & Politics* 44, 1: 61–8.

Leith, Denise. 2003. *The Politics of Power: Freeport in Suharto's Indonesia*. Honolulu: University of Hawai'i Press.

Lembaga Penyelidikan Ekonomi dan Masyarakat Universitas Indonesia. 2002. *Analisis Dampak Ekonomi PT Kaltim Prima Coal*. Jakarta: LPEM UI.

Liddle, William R. 1992. "The Politics of Development Policy", *World Development* 20, 6: 739–807.

Lubis, Bersihar. 2001. *Who's Who Cemex (Suntingan Dosa-Dosa Cemex)*. Jakarta: Yayasan Swadaya Mandiri.

Lukes, Steven. 2005. *Power: A Radical View*. 2nd ed. New York: Palgrave Macmillan.

MacIntyre, Andrew. 1990. *Business and Politics in Indonesia*. Sydney: Allen and Unwin.

———. 2001. "Institutions and Investors: The Politics of the Economic Crisis in Southeast Asia", *International Organization* 55, 1: 81–122.

———. 2003. *The Power of Institutions: Political Architecture and Governance*. Ithaca: Cornell University Press.

Mackie, Jamie. 1980. "Integrating and Centrifugal Factors in Indonesian Politics since 1945", in *Indonesia: The Making of a Nation*, ed. J.A.C. Mackie. Canberra: Research School of Pacific Studies, Australian National University.

Mackie, Jamie and Andrew MacIntyre. 1994. "Politics", in *Indonesia's New Order: The Dynamics of Socio-Economic Transfromation*, ed. Hal Hill. Honolulu: University of Hawai'i Press.

Magenda, Burhan. 1991. *East Kalimantan: The Decline of a Commercial Aristocracy*. Ithaca: Cornell University Press.

Malley, Michael S. 2003. "New Rules, Old Structures and the Limits of Democratic Decentralisation", in *Local Power and Politics in Indonesia: Decentralisation and Democratisation*, ed. Edward Aspinall and Greg Fealy. Singapore: ISEAS.

———. 2009. "Decentralization and Democratic Transition in Indonesia", in *Democratic Deficits: Addressing Challenges to Sustainability and Consolidation around the World*, ed. Gary Bland and Cynthia J. Arnson. Washington, DC: Woodrow Wilson International Center for Scholars.

Mardjani, Ma'rifat. 1959. *Realisasi propinsi Riau-Djambi*. Jakarta: Pustaka Njiur Melambai.

McCargo, Duncan. 2005. "Network Monarchy and Legitimacy Crisis in Thailand", *The Pacific Review* 18, 4: 499–519.

McCarthy, John F. 2007. "Sold Down the River: Renegotiating Public Power over Nature in Central Kalimantan", in *Renegotiating Boundaries: Local Politics in Post-Suharto Indonesia*, ed. Henk Schulte Nordholt and Gerry van Klinken. Leiden: KITLV Press.

McClurg, S.D. 2006. "The Electoral Relevance of Political Talk: Examining Disagreement and Expertise Effects in Social Networks on Political Participation", *American Journal of Political Science* 50, 3: 737–54.

Menard, Claude and Mary M. Shirley. 2005. "Introduction", in *Handbook of New Institutional Economics*, ed. Claude Menard and Mary M. Shirley. Dordrecht: Springer.

Mietzner, Marcus. 2007. "Party Financing in Post-Suharto Indonesia: between the State Subsidies and Political Corruption", *Contemporary Southeast Asia* 29, 2: 238–63.

———. 2014. "Indonesia's Decentralization: The Rise of Local Identities and the Survival of the Nation-State", in *Regional Dynamics in a Decentralized Indonesia*, ed. Hal Hill. Singapore: ISEAS.

Migdal, Joel. 1987. "Strong States, Weak States: Power and Accommodation", in *Understanding Political Development*, ed. Myron Weiner and Samuel P. Huntington. Illinois: Waveland Press.

———. 1988. *Strong Societies and Weak States: State-Society Relation in the Third World*. Princeton: Princeton University Press.

Milgrom, P., D. North and B. Weingast. 1990. "The Role of Institutions in the Revival of Trade: The Law Merchant, Private Judges, and the Champagne Fairs", *Economics and Politics* 2, 1: 1–23.

Ministry of Finance of Republic of Indonesia. 2004. *Financial Note and Draft of State Budget 2004*. Jakarta: Ministry of Finance.

Moran, Theodore H. 1974. *Multinationals and the Politics of Dependence: Copper in Chile*. Princeton: Princeton University Press.

Morishita, Akiko. 2005. "Today's Local Politics in Indonesia 1998–2004: Who Controls the Political and Economic Interests in Kalimantan?", unpublished paper for the 4th International Conference of Jurnal Antropologi Indonesia, Jakarta.

———. 2008. "Contesting Power in Indonesia's Resource-Rich Regions in the Era of Decentralization: New Strategy for Central Control over Regions", *Indonesia* 86: 81–108.

Mutz, D. 2006. *Hearing the Other Side: Deliberative versus Participatory Democracy*. New York: Cambridge University Press.

Nanang, Martinus. 1998. "Grassroot Political Participation: A Case of Desa Mencong, East Kalimantan", *Jurnal Sosial-Politika* 1: 1–10.

Newman, Mark, Albert Lazlo Barábasi and Duncan Watts. 2006. *The Structure and Dynamics of Networks*. Princeton: Princeton University Press.

Nickerson, D.W. 2008. "Is Voting Contagious? Evidence from Two Field Experiments", *American Political Science Review* 102, 1: 49–57.

Nishihara, Masashi. 1971. *Golkar and the Indonesian Elections of 1971*. Ithaca, NY: Modern Indonesia Project, Cornell University.

North, Douglass. 1990. *Institutions, Institutional Changes and Economic Performance*. Cambridge: Cambridge University Press.

———. 1994. "Economic Performance Through Time", *The American Economic Review* 84, 3: 359–68.

———. 1995. "The New Institutional Economics and Third World Development", in *The New Institutional Economic and Third World Development*, ed. John Harris, Janet Hunter and Colin M Lewis. London: Routledge.

North, Douglass and Robert Paul Thomas. 1973. *The Rise of the Western World: A New Economic History*. New York: Cambridge University Press.

Okamoto, Masaaki and Abdul Hamid. 2008. "Jawara in Power: 1999–2007", *Indonesia* 86: 109–38.

Ostrom, Elinor. 1990. *Governing the Commons*. Cambridge: Cambridge University Press.

———. 2005. "Doing Institutional Analysis", in *Handbook of New Institutional Economics*, ed. Claude Menard and Mary M. Shirley. Dordrecht: Springer.

Pabottingi, Mochtar. 1995. "Historicizing the New Order's Legitimacy Dilemma", in *Political Legitimacy in Southeast Asia: The Quest for Moral Authority*, ed. Muthiah Alagappa. Stanford, CA: Stanford University Press.

Padang Press Club. 2001. *Kembalikan Semen Padang ke pangkuan negara*. Padang: Padang Press Club.

Peluso, Nancy. 1995. *Rich Forest, Poor People: Resource Control and Resistance in Java*. Berkeley: University of California Press.

Pemerintah Daerah Riau. 1985. *Riau Makmur: Pelaksanaan Tugas Gubernur Kepala Tingkat I Riau H. Imam Munandar: Oktober 1980–Oktober 1985*. Pekanbaru: Pemerintah Daerah Riau.

Pepinsky, Thomas B. 2009. *Economic Crisis and the Breakdown of Authoritarian Regimes: Indonesia and Malaysia in Comparative Perspective*. Cambridge: Cambridge University Press.

———. 2013. "Pluralism and Political Conflict in Indonesia", *Indonesia* 96: 81–100.

Podolny, Joel M. and Karen L. Page. 1998. "Network Forms of Organization", *Annual Review of Sociology* 24: 57–77.

Prasetyawan, Wahyu. 2017. "Indonesia's Mining Industry: An Institutional Approach", in *Southeast Asia Beyond Crises and Traps*, ed. Khoo Boo Teik et al. Basingstoke, UK: Palgrave Macmillan.

Prijono, Achmad. 1990. "The Decade of the Eighties: The Start of Large-Scale Coal Development in Indonesia", in *Mineral Development in Asia and Pacific: Proceedings of the 2nd Asia-Pacific Mining Conference*, ed. M. Simatupang and James F McDivitt. Manila: ASEAN Mining Federation.

Rab, Tabrani. 2002a. *Tempias: Kilas balik kritik Prof. Dr. H. Tabrani Rab 1998–2001*. Bandung: Alumni.

———. 2002b. *Menuju Riau berdaulat*. Pekanbaru: Riau Cultural Institute.

Ramage, Douglas. 1995. *Politics in Indonesia: Democracy, Islam and the Ideology of Tolerance*. London: Routledge.

Ray, D. and G. Goodpaster. 2003. "Indonesian Decentralization: Local Autonomy, Trade Barriers and Discrimination", in *Autonomy and Disintegration in Indonesia*, ed. D. Kingsbury and H. Aveling. London: RoutledgeCurzon.

Robison, Richard. 1986. *Indonesia: The Rise of Capital*. Sydney: Allen and Unwin.

————. 1992. "Industrialization and the Economic and Political Development of Capital", in *Southeast Asian Capitalists*, ed. Ruth McVey. Ithaca: Cornell Southeast Asia Program.

Robison, Richard and Vedi Hadiz. 2004. *Reorganising Power in Indonesia: The Politics of Oligarchy in an Age of Markets*. London: RoutledgeCurzon.

Rosenau, James N. 2008. *People Count! Networked Individuals in Global Politics*. Paradigm Publishers.

Rosser, Andrew, Kurnya Roesad and Donni Edwin. 2005. "Indonesia: The Politics of Inclusion", *Journal of Contemporary Asia* 35, 1: 53–77.

Royle, Stephen A. 1997. "Industrialisation in Indonesia: The Example of Batam Island", *Singapore Journal of Tropical Geography* 18, 1: 89–98.

Ryaas, Rasyid Muhammad. 1994. "State Formation, Party System, and the Prospect for Democracy in Indonesia: The Case of Golongan Karya (1967–1993)", PhD dissertation, University of Hawai'i.

Sadli. M. 1993. "Recollections of My Career", *Bulletin of Indonesian Economics Studies* 29, 1: 35–51.

Said, Salim. 2001. *Militer Indonesia dan Politik: Dulu, Kini dan Kelak*. Jakarta: Pustaka Sinar Harapan.

Sakai, Minako. 2003. "The Privatisation of Padang Cement: Regional Identity and Economic Hegemony in the New Era of Decentralisation", in *Local Power and Politics in Indonesia: Decentralisation and Democratisation*, ed. Edward Aspinall and Greg Fealy. Singapore: ISEAS.

Schulte Nordholt, Henk and van Klinken, G. 2007. *Renegotiating Boundaries: Local Politics in Post-Suharto Indonesia*. Leiden: KITLV Press.

Schwarz, Adam. 2000. *A Nation in Waiting*. Boulder, CO: Westview Press.

Serikat Pekerja Semen Padang. 2003. *PT Semen Gresik Biang Kerok Kemelut di PT Semen Padang*. Padang: Serikat Pekerja Semen.

Shiraishi. Takashi. 1999. "The Indonesian Military in Politics", in *The Politics of Post-Suharto Indonesia*, ed. Adam Schwarz and Jonathan Paris. New York: Council of Foreign Relations Press.

————. 2002. "Hegemony, Technocracy, and Networks", in *Hegemony, Technocracy, Networks*, ed. Takashi Shiraishi and Takeshi Hamashita. Kyoto: Kyoto University, Center for Southeast Asian Studies.

Sidel, John T. 1999. *Capital, Coercion and Crime: Bossism in the Philippines*. Stanford, CA: Stanford University Press.

————. 2007. *Riots, Pogroms, Jihad: Religious Violence in Indonesia*. Singapore: NUS Press.

Smith, Benjamin. 2008. "The Origins of Regional Autonomy in Indonesia: Experts and the Marketing of Political Interests", *Journal of East Asian Studies* 8, 2: 211–34.

Slaughter, A.M. 2004. *A New World Order*. Princeton: Princeton University Press.

Swedberg, R. and M. Granovetter. 1992. "Introduction", in *The Sociology of Economic Life*, ed. M. Granovetter and R. Swedberg. Boulder, CO: Westview Press.

Tadjoeddin, Zulfan Muhammad, Widjajanti Suharyo and Satish Mishra. 2001. "Regional Disparity and Centre-Regional Conflicts in Indonesia", working paper for the United Nations Support Facility for Indonesian Recovery. Jakarta: United Nations.

Tans, Ryan. 2012. *Mobilizing Resources, Building Coalitions: Local Power in Indonesia*. Honolulu, HI: East-West Center.

Tim Spin Off PT Semen Padang. 2001. *PT Semen Padang: Dari spin off menuju perusahaan kelas dunia*. Padang: Tim Spin Off PT Semen Padang.

Tomsa, Dirk. 2008. *Party Politics and Democratization in Indonesia: Golkar in the Post-Suharto Era*. London: Routledge.

———. 2015. "Local Politics and Corruption in Indonesia's Outer Islands", *Bijdragen tot de Taal-, Land- en Volkenkunde* 171: 196–219.

Tornquist, Olle et al. 2004. "First Round Study of the Problem of Options of Indonesian Democratisation", unpublished paper. http://www.sum.uio.no/publications/pdffulltek/torquist.pdf (site no longer available).

Turner, Mark and Owen Podger. 2003. *Decentralisation in Indonesia: Redesigning the State*. Canberra: Asia-Pacific Press.

Tyson, Adam. 2010. *Decentralization and Adat Revivalism in Indonesia: The Politics of Becoming Indigenous*. London: Routledge.

Vatikiotis, Michael R.J. 1993. *Indonesian Politics under Suharto: The Rise and Fall of the New Order*. London: Routledge.

van Klinken, Gerry. 2007a. *Communal Violence and Democratization in Indonesia: Small Town Wars*. London: Routledge.

———. 2007b. "Return of the Sultans: Communitarian Turn", in *Local Politics in the Revival of Tradition in Indonesian Politics: Deployment of Adat from Colonialism to Indigenism*, ed. Jamie S. Davidson and Favid Henley. London: Routledge.

———. 2009. "Patronage Democracy in Indonesia", in *Rethinking Popular Representation*, ed. Olle Törnquist, Neil Webster and Kristian Stokke. New York: Palgrave Macmillan.

von Lübke, Christian. 2012. "Striking the Right Balance: Economic Concentration and Local Government Performance in Indonesia and the Philippines", *European Journal of East Asian Studies* 11, 1: 17–44.

Vu, Tuong. 2010. *Paths to Development in Asia: South Korea, Vietnam, China, and Indonesia*. Cambridge: Cambridge University Press.

Watts, Duncan J. 2001. *Small Worlds*. Princeton: Princeton University Press.

Wee, Vivienne. 2002. "Ethno-Nationalism in Process: Ethnicity, Atavism and Indigenism in Riau, Indonesia", *The Pacific Review* 15, 4: 497–516.

Winters, Jeffrey. 2011. *Oligarchy*. Cambridge: Cambridge University Press.

———. 2013. "Oligarchy and Democracy in Indonesia", *Indonesia* 96: 11–33.

World Bank. 2003. *Decentralizing Indonesia: A Regional Public Expenditure Review Overview Report*. Washington: World Bank.

Yue, Chia Siow. 1996. "The Sijori Growth Triangle: Challenges, Opportunities and Strategic Response", in *Growth Triangle in Southeast Asia*, ed. Imran Lim. Kuala Lumpur: ISIS Malaysia.

————. 1997. "Singapore: Advanced Production Base and Smart Hub of the Electronics Industry", in *Multinationals and East Asian Integration*, ed. Wendy Dobson and Chia Siow Yue. Singapore: ISEAS.

INDEX

Abinales, Patricio, 84
Abeng, Tanri, 123, 124
Acemoglu, Daron, 7, 25
Achmad, Arifin, 142
Advisory Council for Regional
   Autonomy, 156
Anas, Azwar, 113, 117, 118, 119,
   120, 121, 122, 123, 124, 125,
   133, 134, 138
Anderson, Benedict, 1
Andojo, Adi, 72
Al Azhar, 150, 153, 154, 155, 161,
   163
Al Qaeda, 27
Aneka Tambang, 18
Aoki, Masahisa, 25
Arrow, Kenneth, 23
Aryawijaya, Roes, 104
Awaludin, Hamid, 31

Badan Pengelola Kegiatan Hulu
   Migas, 162
Bahar, Saafroedin, 116, 122, 124,
   130, 133, 134, 136
Baharuddin Dt. Rangkayo Baso, 116,
   118
Bank Duta, 49, 50
Banten, 43
BAKIN, 90
Bakar, Zainal, 130, 131, 134, 135
Bakrie, Aburizal, 4, 31, 106, 107,
   108, 109, 111, 178

Barabási, Albert-László, 6, 27, 28, 29
Barzel, Yoram, 24
Basri Durin, Hasan, 117, 119, 120
Basuki, Wiwoho, 31
Bates, Robert, 24
Bertrand, J., 44
Booth, Anne, 37, 38, 60
BP International, 86, 94
Bratanata, 64
Brodjonegoro, Sumantri, 64
Budiardjo, Ali, 63
Budiardjo, Miriam, 72
Buehler, Michael, 41, 42
Bünte, Marco, 41

Caltex Pacific Indonesia (CPI), 63,
   64, 140, 145, 146
Cemex of Mexico, 122, 124, 126, 127,
   128, 129, 130, 136, 137, 138
Central Axis, 66
Chevron Pacific Indonesia, 18, 140,
   164
Choi, Nankyung, 41, 42, 84, 171
communal violence, 45
contract of work, xiv, 52, 63, 145
Contract Production Sharing, 63, 73,
   145

Davidson, Jamie, 36, 49
Djasit, Saleh, 140, 142, 147, 148,
   150, 154, 155, 157, 158, 160,
   161, 163, 164, 165, 167

Djohan, Azaly, 157, 159, 161, 162, 163
Djohan, Djohermansyah, 31, 71
Djuanda, 63, 142
dual function, military, 55

economic crisis, 1, 69, 73, 121
Erb, Maribeth, 41
Erman, Erwiza, 45
ethnic violence, 44
    Madurese, 44
    Maluku, 44
    Poso, 44

Fatah, Eep S., 72
Faroek Ishak, Awang, 93, 94, 110
Fealy, G., 42
Freeport, McMoran, xiv, 52, 107
    Indonesia, xiv, 18, 19, 52
    sulphur, 63
floating mass, 14

Gafar, Affan, 71 72
Gorontalo, 43
Guided democracy, 37, 54
Gunaratna, Rohan, 27

Habibie, 14, 38, 39, 40, 65, 66, 67, 68, 69, 70, 71, 72, 73, 76, 77, 120, 122, 123, 124, 134, 138, 140, 151, 164, 174
Hadiz, Vedi, 1, 2, 3, 4, 8, 49, 50, 84, 171
Hakim, Baihaki, 165
Hamid, Abdul, 43, 171
Hamid, Syarwan, 68, 69, 71, 72, 140, 148, 150, 167
Hardikusumo, Hartoto, 31
Hartarto, 67, 68
Hartono, 69

Hasan, Mohammad, 49, 63
Hatta, Mohammad, 37
Herziq, Pascale, 29
Hidayat, Syarif, 43, 171
HTI (Industrial Forest Scheme), 152
Hutchcroft, Paul, 32

ICMI, xi, 68, 123, 124, 128
illegality, 51
IMF, 62, 67, 121, 138
Inalum, xiii
institutions, definition, 7

James, Paul, 41
Jose B. Fernandez, 32

Kaharoeddin Rangkayo Basa, 117
Kahler, Miles, 27
Kalla, Jusuf, 135
Kanter, Nico, 105, 106
Kartasasmita, Ginandjar, xviii, 14, 31, 48, 49, 52, 171
Khan, Musthaq, 24
Kimura, Ehito, 37, 43, 44, 46, 52
Knoke, David, 6, 28, 75
Kumar, Ann, 41
Kusumah, Mulyana W., 72

LKAAM, 116, 118, 119, 120, 124, 125, 128
Lazer, David, 5, 6
Leith, Denise, 17, 52, 63
Liddle, W., 48, 171
Liem Sioe Liong, 49
local strongman, 43, 172

Madjid, Nurcholish, 72
Mahyudin, 109
Mallarangeng, Andi, 30, 71, 72

Malley, Michael, 42, 44
Mangkusubroto, Kuntoro, 164
Masyumi, 115
McCargo, Duncan, 31, 32
McCarthy, John F., 45
McVey, Ruth, 41
Megawati, Sukarnoputri, 52, 65, 66, 67, 77, 92, 108, 120, 129, 134, 138, 147, 160, 176
Melati Bhakti Satya, PD, 90
Melati Intan Bhakti Satya, PT, 90
Menard, Claude, 25
Miguel Cuaderno, 32
Makasar, 47
Morishita, Akiko, 45
Muhammad, Fadel, 31
Muhammadiyah, 66, 115
Munandar, Imam, 144
Mundjiat, Imam, 92
Mutojib, 79, 89, 94, 110

Nasution, Adnan Buyung, 72
Nasution, A.H., 117
Nazif Lubuk, Titik, 113, 115, 124, 126, 127, 128, 130, 131, 134, 135, 136, 167
networks, definition, 6, 26–9
Newmont Nusa Tenggara, xiii, 18, 178
Nitisastro, Widjojo, 30, 48, 56
Nizar, Ikhdan, 112, 113, 115, 124, 126, 127, 130, 133, 134, 136, 138, 140, 167
Noriega, Fransisco, 137
North, Douglass, 7, 22, 23, 24, 180
Nusamba, 50, 63

Okamoto, Masaaki, 43, 171
oligarchy, 8, 50, 171
    definition, 3, 4
Omar Abdalla, 31
Ostrom, Elinor, 24, 25, 181

Pabottingi, Mochtar, xviii, 54
Panigoro, Arifin, 31
Pangestu, Prayogo, 49
Partai Amanat Nasional (PAN), 15, 65, 66, 67, 72, 77, 83, 119, 147
Partai Demokrasi Indonesia (PDI), 14, 15, 59, 60, 65, 83, 129, 142
Partai Demokrasi Indonesia-Perjuangan (PDI-P), 15, 65, 66, 67, 72, 77, 79, 83, 88, 92, 110, 119, 129, 134, 138, 147
Partai Keadilan Sejahtera (PKS), 15
Partai Komunis Indonesia (PKI), 57, 117
Partai Persatuan Pembangunan (PPP), 14, 59, 83, 115, 142
Pepinsky, Thomas, 1, 2, 3
Perhutani, 152
Permina, 64, 145
Pertamin, 64, 145
Perti, 115
Pesantren Al-Mukmin, 31
pluralist, approach, 2, 3
political network, 5–6
Pratama, Rama, 72
PRRI (Revolutionary Government of Indonesian Republic), 115, 116, 117
Prawiranegara, Sjafruddin, 115
Prem Tinsulanond, 31, 32
property right, 10, 22, 23, 24, 35, 170, 174, 175, 177

Rab, Tabrani, 141, 142, 151, 153, 154, 155, 157, 161, 163, 165
Rais, Amien, 66, 67
Rasyid, Ryaas, 30, 68, 70, 71
regional proliferation, 37, 43
Rio Tinto, 86, 94, 104, 105, 106, 107, 108, 111
Robinson, James, 7, 25
Robison, Richard, 2, 3, 4, 47, 50, 84, 121, 171

Sabarno, Hari, 155, 157, 161
Sakai, Minako, 42, 45
Sadli, M., 56, 62, 86
Salim, David, 90, 94
Salim, Emil, 56
Semen Cibinong, 127
Semen Gresik, 10, 112, 121, 122, 123, 124, 126, 127, 128, 129, 130, 131, 132, 133, 134, 135, 136, 137, 138, 173
Seskoad, 56
Shiraishi, Takashi, 30, 55, 58
Shirley, Mary, 25
Shell, 63, 64
Sidel, John, 31
Sinaga, Kastorius, 72
Singedekane, Agnita, 92
Sjahranie, Wahab, 81
Slaughter, A.M., 28
Smith, Benjamin, 8, 30, 39, 40
Sochib, Chasan, 43
Soeripto, 144, 145
Soetjipto, 92
Stanvac, 63, 64
Subianto, B., 42
Sudharmono, 31
Sukardi, Laksamana, 77, 79, 90, 91, 92, 94, 104, 110, 113, 126, 127, 128, 129, 130, 131, 133, 134, 135, 136, 137, 138
Suko, Ismail, 143
Sulistiyanto, Priyambudi, 41
sultanship, 45
Supardjan, Ery, 81
Syafii, Theo, 92
Syaukani, 93, 94, 110
Surbakti, Ramlan, 31, 71
Sutowo, Ibnu, 63, 64, 145, 146
Sutowo, Ponco, 31
SOKSI, 57

Tambang Batubara, Perum, 86
Tangguh, project, 106, 107
Tanjung, Akbar, 66, 125
Tanjungpura, Kodam, 88
Tans, Ryan, 3
Team 7, 40
Tomsa, Dirk, 3, 56
Tyson, Adam, 46

Urbaningrum, Anas, 71, 72

van Klinken, G., 42, 44, 45, 46, 51

Wahid, Abdurahman, 52, 66, 67, 77, 120, 138, 154, 155, 160, 165, 176
Wardhana, Ali, 56
Watts, Duncan, 6, 27, 28
Widarsa, 31
Winters, Jeffrey, 2, 3, 4, 5, 62, 136, 171

Yani, Achmad, 117
Yayasan Dharmais, 50
Yayasan Dhakab, 50
Yudhoyono, Susilo Bambang, 165
Yusgiantoro, Purnomo, 79, 92, 142, 159, 160, 165
Yuzairi, Ismed, 133

Zain, Harun, 117, 118, 119, 120, 123

KYOTO CSEAS SERIES ON ASIAN STUDIES
Center for Southeast Asian Studies, Kyoto University

List of Published Titles

The Economic Transition in Myanmar after 1988: Market Economy versus State Control, edited by Koichi Fujita, Fumiharu Mieno, and Ikuko Okamoto, 2009

Populism in Asia, edited by Kosuke Mizuno and Pasuk Phongpaichit, 2009

Traveling Nation-Makers: Transnational Flows and Movements in the Making of Modern Southeast Asia, edited by Caroline S. Hau and Kasian Tejapira, 2011

China and the Shaping of Indonesia, 1949–1965, by Hong Liu, 2011

Questioning Modernity in Indonesia and Malaysia, edited by Wendy Mee and Joel S. Kahn, 2012

Industrialization with a Weak State: Thailand's Development in Historical Perspective, by Somboon Siriprachai, edited by Kaoru Sugihara, Pasuk Phongpaichit, and Chris Baker, 2012

Popular Culture Co-productions and Collaborations in East and Southeast Asia, edited by Nissim Otmazgin and Eyal Ben-Ari, 2012

Strong Soldiers, Failed Revolution: The State and Military in Burma, 1962–88, by Yoshihiro Nakanishi, 2013

Organising Under the Revolution: Unions and the State in Java, 1945–48, by Jafar Suryomenggolo, 2013

Living with Risk: Precarity & Bangkok's Urban Poor, by Tamaki Endo, 2014

Migration Revolution: Philippine Nationhood and Class Relations in a Globalized Age, by Filomeno V. Aguilar Jr., 2014

The Chinese Question: Ethnicity, Nation, and Region in and Beyond the Philippines, by Caroline S. Hau, 2014

Identity and Pleasure: The Politics of Indonesian Screen Culture, by Ariel Heryanto, 2014

Indonesian Women and Local Politics: Islam, Gender and Networks in Post-Suharto Indonesia, by Kurniawati Hastuti Dewi, 2015

Catastrophe and Regeneration in Indonesia's Peatlands: Ecology, Economy and Society, edited by Kosuke Mizuno, Motoko S. Fujita & Shuichi Kawai, 2016

Marriage Migration in Asia: Emerging Minorities at the Frontiers of Nation-States, edited by Sari K. Ishii, 2016

Central Banking as State Building: Policymakers and Their Nationalism in the Philippines, 1933–1964, by Yusuke Takagi, 2016

Moral Politics in the Philippines: Inequality, Democracy and the Urban Poor, by Wataru Kusaka, 2017

Liberalism and the Postcolony: Thinking the State in 20th-century Philippines, by Lisandro E. Claudio, 2017